D1738728

The Way We Lived Then

The Way We Lived Then

Jean Robin

Ashgate

Aldershot • Brookfield USA • Singapore • Sydney

Published by

Ashgate Publishing Ltd
Gower House, Croft Road,
Aldershot, Hampshire GU11 3HR
England

Ashgate Publishing Company
Old Post Road
Brookfield, Vermont 05036–9704
USA

Ashgate website: http://www.ashgate.com

ISBN 0 7546 0066 1

British Library Cataloguing-in-Publication Data
Robin, Jean
  The Way We Lived Then
  1. Colyton (England)—Social conditions—19th century. 2. Colyton (England)—History—19th century. 3. Colyton (England)—Rural conditions.
  I. Title.
  942.3'5'081

US Library of Congress Cataloging-in-Publication Data
Robin, Jean
  The Way We Lived Then / Jean Robin
      p.   cm.   Includes bibliographical references (p.   ) and index.
  1. Colyton (England)—History. 2. Colyton (England)—Social conditions.
  I. Title.
  DA690.C71 R63 2000   99–089607
  942.3'57–dc21   CIP

This volume is printed on acid-free paper.

Printed and bound by Athenaeum Press, Ltd.,
Gateshead, Tyne & Wear.

Contents

Preface

On an autumn night in 1873, in the east Devonshire market town of Colyton, a crowd gathered in the London Road. The street was lit up by the flames coming from a burning effigy on a cart which was being drawn to and fro past the house of a middle-aged widow. Stones were thrown, and windows smashed, while a young man wearing a long-tailed coat and a box hat moved in and out of the shadows. He was conspicuous enough to be arrested by the police when they arrived at the scene, following a warning given by a naval rating who was home on leave. Further arrests were made, and the stone-throwers were brought before the magistrates and fined.[1]

When I first started my researches on Colyton, I had no idea that I would become concerned with incidents of the kind which has just been described and which is put into context in the last chapter of this book. I was working at the Cambridge Group for the History of Population and Social Structure, an academic institution which specializes in demography, that is to say the study of statistics of births, deaths, marriages and other events which can be related to whole communities rather than to individuals. Little room there, it might be thought, for an account of a single disturbance in Colyton's streets.

My task initially was to build up life histories of families and individuals living in the parish for the forty years ending in 1891, and so to continue the work that had already been completed by other members of the group from as early as 1540 up to 1851. These life histories were not full dossiers in the biographical sense, nor could they be, because before 1841, the year of the first national census to name all individuals in the country, the main source of information lay in the parish records of marriages, baptisms and deaths. The 'life histories' of individuals would therefore be limited to the dates on which they either came into the world or were christened; and the ages at which they married, bore their children, possibly were widowed and remarried, and finally died. Family histories were built up by grouping together this kind of information for individuals who were related to each other, and the whole process was known as family reconstitution.

By 1851, however, I was fortunate in having a whole new source of information to add to the parish registers,[2] in the shape of the national censuses, published in full after a lapse of 100 years at ten-year intervals, and currently available from 1841 to 1891.[3] These censuses allowed new ground to be broken in two respects. First, the naming of everybody living in Colyton on each census day meant that the whole population of the parish could be considered instead of only the two-thirds who used the Church of England for their rites of passage, together with the handful of Nonconformists for whom baptism, marriage and death records have been recovered.   Second, the censuses not only named everyone living in the parish, which was home to just over 2,500 people in 1851, but also listed them by the households in which they lived, giving their exact relationship to the household head. Everyone's age was entered, though not always accurately it must be admitted, and in addition the occupations of those at work were recorded. This last information meant that some form of class structure could be worked out, in order to see how far economic and social differences affected vital statistics.

The occupations listed in the censuses were often ambiguous, however. If a man was simply recorded as 'blacksmith', how could it be known whether he was the owner of the forge, or a paid employee? Was a woman 'supported by her children' from the better-off part of society, or from the working class? Clearly, the data base would be much improved if these kinds of questions could be answered, and for this it would be necessary to find further sources of information.

Fortunately, a comprehensive survey of landholding in Colyton had been undertaken in 1844, with a view to assessing the amount of tithes payable on each property. The document listed all owners of land in the parish and gave the exact size of their holdings, however small;[4] as a result, those who owned real estate could be distinguished from the propertyless. This information, which naturally became less accurate as time passed and land changed hands, was augmented by the electoral rolls, which each year until 1885 named owners and tenants of property of sufficient value to enable them to vote.[5]

When it came to identifying the poor, two more sources proved invaluable. First, the minute books of the Guardians of the Poor in the Axminster Union, to which Colyton belonged, named at fortnightly intervals all those normally able-bodied men and women who fell sick and were unable to support themselves and their families unless they received outdoor relief;[6] and second, the charitable trust of the Feoffees of Colyton gave a Christmas present in cash annually to the heads of all poor households, the names of the recipients being recorded each year in the treasurer's book up to 1873.[7] By using these documents, a more accurate picture of the economic groups in the parish could be obtained.

While I was working through this material, I became increasingly interested in the real people behind the statistics, and in the lives they led. For example, the Feoffees' minutes shed light on who held the administrative power in the parish, and on how that power was used, as well as recording the multifarious charitable activities in which the Feoffees were engaged. Reading the accounts of meeting after meeting, I became fascinated by the workings of the trust's grammar school, and the characters of the sometimes eccentric masters who taught there.[8] The guardians' minutes were a mine of information on how the poor were looked after, whether in sickness, old age or temporary difficulties, as in the case of the farm labourer, necessarily out at work all day, whose wife died, leaving him to care for five children under the age of twelve.[9] The censuses themselves, which allowed individuals to be traced from one decade to the next, showed that the population was constantly changing.

This build-up of information began to show patterns of life in the different social classes from childhood, through the middle years to old age, covering not only those who stood out from the rest of society, but taking the whole population into account. Spreading the net wider, I visited the British Library at Collindale to read the local newspapers of the time[10] which provided a mass of information and anecdote on local activities and quarrels, but also allowed me to acquire a considerable amount of evidence on the kinds of criminal offences committed by Colytonians and the punishments they received on conviction. This was of particular importance as enemy action in the Second World War destroyed the records of Axminster petty sessions, where cases concerning residents of the parish were first heard. Then the Team Rector of Colyton, the Reverend David Gunn-Johnson, generously presented the Cambridge Group with a copy of his MA thesis, *A Country Catholic*, which was invaluable in explaining the religious disagreements, amounting almost to warfare, which raged in the parish in the 1860s and 1870s. Other lesser sources, too numerous to mention here, helped to add flesh to the bare bones provided by statistical analysis.

This book is the result of these researches. It is intended for the general as well as the academic reader, its text contains no statistical tables, and its purpose is to tell the story, as faithfully as possible, of one English rural parish in the second half of the nineteenth century through the lives of its people, and to show how the community dealt with perennial social problems in the context of its own time.

Notes

1. *Devon Weekly Times* (hereafter *D.W.T.*), 3.10.1873.

2. Colyton parish registers held in the Devon Record Office (hereafter D.R.O.). 3483 A/PR3, baptisms 1838–1863; 3483 A/PR15, baptisms 1864–1887; 3483 A/PR8, marriages 1837–1872; 3483 A/PR16, marriages 1872–1919; 3483 A/PR9 burials 1836–1852; 3483 A/PR18, burials 1853–1901.

    Colyton parish register held by the Team Rector of Colyton. Baptisms, 1888–.

    Colyton registers held in the Public Record Office (hereafter P.R.O.). R.G. 4/3559. Independent chapel, baptisms, 1815-1857; R.G. 8/6. George's chapel, baptisms, 1824–1862; burials, 1832–1862.

    Colyton Parish Council: register of public graves, 1859–1878; burial book, 1865–1902.

D.R.O., R 7/8/c. Axminster marriage notice book, 1838–1916.

3. Census returns for Colyton parish. P.R.O. 1841, H.O. 107/214; 1851, H.O. 107/1862; 1861, R.G. 9/1373; 1871, R.G. 10/2035 and R.G. 10/2036; 1881, R.G. 11/2129; 1891, R.G. 12/1669.

   Census returns for Axminster Union House (workhouse). P.R.O. 1851, H.O. 107/1862; 1861, R.G. 9/1371; 1871, R.G. 10/2033; 1881, R.G. 11/2127; 1891, R.G. 12/1667.

4. P.R.O. IR 29/9. Colyton land apportionment, 1844.

5. D.R.O., voters' list A, south division, 1832–1868; east division, 1869–1885; voters' list B, east division, 1869–1885.

6. D.R.O., Axminster Union Minute Books (hereafter A.U.M.B.), vols 7–15.

7. D.R.O., F 17/3, treasurer's book.

8. D.R.O., F 17/2, receipts and payments; F 17/7–9, minutes and order book of Feoffees' meetings; F 17/12–13, garden allotments; F 17/14, grammar school.

9. D.R.O. A.U.M.B., vol. 8, 28.9.1855.

10. D.W.T., 1861–1890. *Honiton and Ottery St Mary Weekly News*, 1878. *Honiton and Ottery Weekly News and General Advertiser*, 1879. *Honiton and Ottery Gazette and East Devon Advertiser*, 1883–1884.

Acknowledgements

I would like to thank the Economic and Social Research Council for the support they have given me through the Cambridge Group for the History of Population and Social Structure, where this book has been written. My debt to all members of the group for their unfailing helpfulness is great. Roger Schofield, Richard Wall and Richard Adair read and commented on various chapters, as did David Thomson while visiting the group, and Jim Oeppen and Rosalind Davies gave welcome advice on statistical and demographic matters. I must particularly mention Peter Laslett, not only for his constructive comments on the book as it progressed, but also for his persistence, without which it would never have been started, while Ann Thompson's practical help and critical support have been unfailing.

I have relied heavily on previous work carried out by group members. The family reconstitution completed by Tony Wrigley from 1538 to 1837, and by Wrigley and Richard Wall from 1837 to 1851, was the solid foundation on which my own reconstitution from 1851 to 1891 was based, while Leigh Shaw-Taylor's analysis of the Colyton land apportionment, 1844, was of great benefit to me. Pamela Sharpe's PhD thesis, *Gender-specific demographic adjustment to changing economic circumstances, 1538 to 1837*, provided the historical background necessary for an understanding of Colyton in the second half of the nineteenth century.

Beyond the group, I would like to thank the Reverend David Gunn-Johnson, Mrs Joan Tomkinson and Mr John Cochrane of the Colyton Parish History Society, and the staff of the Devon Record Office in Exeter for all the help they gave me. The present-day Feoffees of Colyton were unfailingly generous in opening their archives and I owe them a debt of gratitude. Finally, my thanks go to Joan Davis, Elaine Lingham and Jean Low for their comments, and to my husband for interrupting his own work in order to help me with researches in the Devon Record Office.

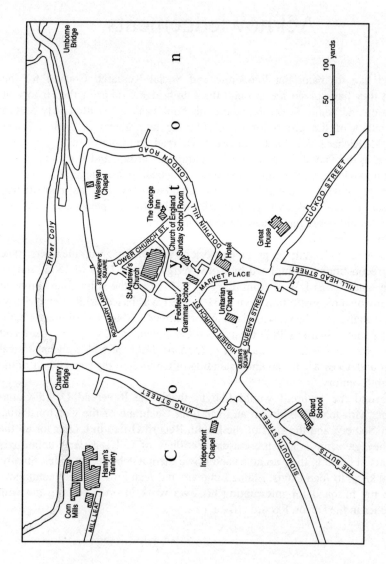

Map 1. The Town of Colyton in the Late Nineteenth Century

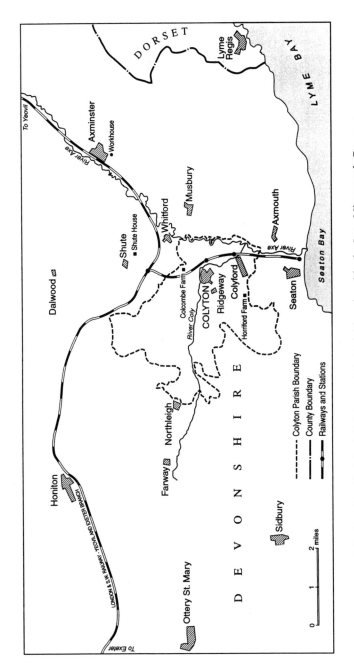

Map 2.   The Parish of Colyton and its Neighbourhood in the Late Nineteenth Century

Chapter 1

Setting the Scene

Samuel Seaward was born in Colyton, a small market town in East Devonshire, in 1846. Some time in the 1930s, when he was a nonagenarian, he recorded his memories of boyhood in the form of a stroll through the town.[1] What he saw describes a way of life quite unfamiliar to present-day Colytonians, even though the street patterns and many of the buildings would be instantly recognisable.

Passing the free grammar school which had been founded in the sixteenth century, Samuel came on the Market House, with a large copper in one corner. Here, a meat soup was made twice weekly in the winter and sold to all comers at the cut price of 2d a gallon. Behind this building lay the 'clink' or lock-up, left unused since the day when an old man incarcerated for being drunk set fire to his straw bed and was burnt to death. Nearby was a shop belonging to a female herbalist and apothecary, the window being decorated with huge glass bottles filled with coloured water. The Great House, where Sir Walter Yonge entertained the Duke of Monmouth in 1680, lay to the south of the town, and to the north-east, between Colyton and Whitford, was the green field above Colcombe Farm where every summer a party known as 'Mr Rapsey's Dance' was held, with tea being served from a tent, and Mr Rapsey himself playing his fiddle for the dancers. At this time, a coaching service to London was still operating, the nearest railway stations being some distance away in Exeter and Taunton, although carriers journeyed to these towns twice weekly, carrying passengers and goods, and changing horses half-way at a posting inn.

To Samuel, however, it was the parish church of St Andrews which was the focus of the town. When he entered it, he found in the middle of the aisle a vast wooden structure surmounted by a golden angel blowing a trumpet and containing a central pulpit flanked by desks with red velvet cushions for the priest and the clerk. One range of high pews faced the pulpit, so that their occupants had their backs to the altar, and another was positioned under the church tower; this was where some of the principal residents of the town held sittings. The other members of the congregation were to be found in long galleries running down each side of the nave, occupied by men on one side and women on the other. The men's gallery was shared with the choir, which was led by an orchestra comprising a violin, cello, double bass, flute and clarinet, while the Sunday-school children were lodged in two upper galleries, known as the 'birdcages'.

This parish church, with its beautiful exterior, was to become central to the deep divisions which split Colyton's community during the 1860s and 1870s. However, just as a knowledge of Victorian history increases our understanding of society today, so it is necessary to go further back into Colyton's past in order to appreciate how this discord came about, and how historical events influenced the character of the nineteenth century parishioners, who have been described as 'independent, stubborn, jealous of their traditions and fiercely loyal'.[2]   A strong sense of the past, and a long-standing support for Protestantism, were fundamental to the nourishment of these characteristics.

Colyton's recorded history was of long standing. It was well established when the Domesday book was compiled in 1086, with a manor held by the king, a mill, a church, and arable land, pasture, meadows and coppice.[3] By the early thirteenth century it was big enough to be given the right to hold a fair,[4] still extant 600 years later, and in 1340 it was granted the status of a borough, to be governed by an annually elected mayor.[5]

It might be thought that the people of Colyton would lead a peaceful life, far from the royal court in the capital, but national upheavals did not pass them by. The Courtenay family, earls of Devon, who had succeeded to the manor of Colyton, were deeply involved in the fifteenth century Wars of the Roses, so deeply indeed that the sixth earl, fighting on the Lancastrian side, was taken prisoner by Yorkists and beheaded at York in 1462. The seventh earl suffered the same fate four years later at Salisbury, while the eighth earl was killed at the battle of Tewkesbury.[6] The family's misfortunes did not end there. Henry Courtenay, Marquis of Exeter and Lord of the Manor of Colyton was arrested on the orders of Henry VIII and found guilty of treason. He too was beheaded in 1539, an event which led to the foundation of the charitable organisation of the Feoffees of Colyton, a body of great importance to the parish, as will be seen in the next chapter.

The seventeenth century saw both the Civil War between the Royalists and Cromwell's Parliamentarians, and the Duke of Monmouth's rebellion against King James the second, and Colytonians were deeply affected by the two events. In the Civil War, their sympathies lay with the Parliamentarians, who had a garrison at Lyme Regis in Dorset, but they were in no position to take sides openly as the Royalists were encamped only four miles away at Axminster. Skirmishes between the two sides involved fighting in the parish, and a number of soldiers' burials were recorded in the parish register for 1644.[7] The people of Colyton learnt what it was to have to endure street-fighting and house searches, but they also suffered from large-scale looting by soldiers from both sides of the conflict. John Hewes, a serge-maker of Colyton, complained that when the town was invaded for a second time by men from the Lyme garrison, the soldiers, pretending to search for men and arms, entered his cock loft and carried off cloth worth £10 which he had hidden there. He had also found it necessary to give a Captain Wood four and a half yards of cloth for a suit, in order to save the rest of his stock from looting. The unfortunate Hewes was similarly robbed by soldiers on several occasions.[8] The damage which the fighting caused to agriculture and the wool trade in the parish was intensified in 1645 by a severe outbreak of bubonic plague which raged for 13 months and is estimated to have killed a fifth of the population.[9]

The Duke of Monmouth's rebellion forty years later also left its mark on Colyton. The parish was already a centre of radical dissent from High Church Anglicanism, and it supported the Protestant side. About eighty-six men, representing a quarter of the total adult male population of Colyton, joined the duke's forces when he landed at Lyme in 1685, fighting and losing the battle of Sedgemoor. Their motives were summed up in the statement made by Joseph Speed, when captured after the battle, that his whole purpose in joining the Duke of Monmouth's forces was 'to fight for the Protestant religion which my own conscience dictated to me'. [10] In addition to those who died in the fighting, five Colytonians were subsequently executed for their part in the rebellion.[11] Once again, the townspeople suffered from looting, this time by the victorious troops who stole lace worth no less than £325 from the store of the lace dealer William Bird.[12]

After the rebellion, peace returned to Colyton, although its economy was affected by the foreign wars in which the country as a whole engaged during the eighteenth century. The pull of Protestantism within the Church of England, and of Nonconformism outside it, was reinforced, with Presbyterians, Baptists and Unitarians all being represented in the parish. In 1715 the Presbyterian church alone had a congregation of 200 people, and although Nonconformism lost some measure of popularity amongst all classes in the second half of the eighteenth century,[13] the Anglicans of the parish remained in the Protestant rather than the High Church tradition. By the nineteenth century Protestantism and Nonconformism had taken very deep root in Colyton, and it is no surprise that the young Samuel Seaward should make the parish church the centrepiece of his description of the town.

Although Samuel's reminiscences give a flavour of life in Colyton in the mid-nineteenth century, the impression they leave is perhaps more cosy than reality warrants. No mention is made of the girls as young as seven learning their trade in the lace schools, nor of the eleven- or twelve-year-old boys who had to leave home in order to earn a living. There is no reference to the numerous heads of families who were unable to make ends meet without receiving relief either through the Poor Law, or from the private charity run by the Feoffees of Colyton; nor to the single mothers and their illegitimate children who were part of the community. The care of the elderly, once their working lives were over, is not described, any more than is the drunkenness and crime met with from time to time in Colyton's streets. All these matters will be dealt with in later chapters, but at this point a brief description of the parish as a whole will provide the background against which Colytonians lived their lives.

In the census year of 1851 the parish contained some 2,500 people.[14]
Roughly two-thirds of them lived in the town itself, while the remaining third
were to be found in the hamlet of Colyford lying a mile or so to the south, and
on the outlying farms with their cottages, which were scattered over the parish.
Colyton ranked second in area and third in the size of population of the
seventeen parishes making up the Axminster Poor Law District to which it
belonged.

The rolling hills and valleys surrounding the town supported a system of
mixed farming, comprising arable land, numerous orchards, and an important
dairy industry. People today who have walked in the lanes of the parish at
around four o'clock in the afternoon will have experienced the Colyton rush-
hour, evidenced not by motor traffic, but by the large herds of cows ambling
home to their yards for milking.

Colyton town itself lies at the mouth of a valley, and was described by a
Nonconformist minister writing in the early nineteenth century as 'most
delightfully situated within three miles of the British Channel, fine views of
which present themselves at very short distances, as also the devious courses of
two beautiful rivers, the little Coly and the larger Axe, which present
innumerable objects to charm the eye and elevate the heart'.[15] The River Coly
was important to the town not only for its looks, but as a source of power for
flour and paper mills, and for providing the water supply to a tannery which is
still in existence today.

Present-day inhabitants of Colyton, or indeed of most other small country
towns of comparable size, would be astonished at the variety and choice
offered by small businesses which were in existence in 1851. The tannery
produced the raw material for the manufacture of leather goods such as harness
and saddlery, boots and shoes, and gloves. A variety of drapers, tailors,
dressmakers and milliners provided clothing, and a widow trading in ladies'
and gentlemen's wardrobes dealt in second-hand garments. In addition to
several butchers and two bakers and confectioners, there were a number of
grocery shops, as well as a fishmonger, while dairies sold milk and butter, and
a maltster and brewer made beer. A tallow chandler provided candles, and beer
and cider houses, inns and an hotel were available for relaxation. The town
boasted two hairdressers, two watchmakers, two druggists and two bookshops,
one of which also sold stationery, while the other engaged in printing as well as
bookselling.

Blacksmiths, an iron founder, a whitesmith and a tinman–brazier engaged
in metalwork, and hardware was sold in an ironmongery. Woodwork
employed wheelwrights, sawyers, joiners and carpenters, who together with
thatchers, plumbers, builders and stonemasons were available for housing
needs, as well as for general maintenance work on farms and other buildings.
In addition to all these services, parishioners who were ill had a choice between
two doctors, and a veterinary surgeon looked after animal well-being.

Finally, the cottage industry of lacemaking made an important contribution to Colyton's economy, carried out as it was by women and girls. Unfortunately, female earning power was a double-edged sword, as it was held that it had a depressing effect on men's wages, 'the farmers and employers giving less in proportion as the wives could earn something on which the family could be supported'.[16] It is certainly true that agricultural labourers in Devon were amongst the lowest paid in the country, their cash wages of 7s to 8s a week being made up to around 12s 6d (or 62p nowadays) when the value of harvest payments, and benefits received in kind such as cider, ale and cottage rent, were added in.[17]

Taking men and women, boys and girls together, Colyton in 1851 had a total work force of over 1,100 people, and as many as two-fifths of them were females. Lacemaking occupied nearly half of these, while just under a third were in some form of domestic work, but women were also to be found among the small business heads, and four widows were tenants of farms, including the largest in the parish. On the male side, just half the working men and boys living in the parish in 1851 were employed in agriculture, and its importance to the prosperity or otherwise of Colyton was very great.

Halfway through the nineteenth century, then, Colyton was a lively small market town, drawing in traffic from outside to the markets held three times a week, and to its monthly cattle sale and two annual fairs. It was not big enough to have developed separate areas inhabited by only one class, equivalent to today's housing estates, and the well-to-do, the middle class and the poor lived in close proximity. As a result, little could go on which was not quickly known throughout the community.

Inevitably, as time went on, changes occurred. Communications were improved in the 1860s by the construction of the South Western Railway main line from Yeovil to Exeter. This passed through the neighbouring village of Shute, where a station was built about a mile and a half from Colyton town, and created a direct link with London. It was augmented in 1868 by a link down to the coast at Seaton which passed close to both Colyton and Colyford. By 1872, there were two branch banks in the town, and its inhabitants no longer had to travel to Axminster in order to deposit their cash.

The 1860s and 1870s also saw major developments in education. The free Church of England Sunday school founded in 1835 was re-established as a day-school in 1861.[18] It was in operation until 1876, the year in which school attendance became compulsory, by which time a school board had been appointed, and new board school buildings erected. The extension of parliamentary suffrage in 1885 to men of twenty-one years of age and over, with the exception of bachelor sons living at home, living-in domestic servants and men of no fixed abode, was a turning point, giving as it did a voice to the poor as well as to the better-off members of society; but the single event of the greatest immediate significance to the majority of parishioners was the severe and prolonged agricultural depression which began to be felt in the mid-1870s. Its effects in Colyton were long lasting, and were still in evidence in 1887, when the committee set up to plan the celebrations for Queen Victoria's Jubilee found itself unable to raise enough funds to meet the cost of a parish dinner. Committee members thought they would have to make do with sports and refreshments, putting the lack of funds down to the fact that many Colytonians were known to be very badly off that year. A benefactor must have intervened, because in the event the men of the parish were given a dinner in a marquee set up in the Colcombe Hotel yard, followed by a tea for the women.[19]

So far the working life of the parish has been touched upon, but nothing has been said about how people used their leisure. This was not easily come by for most of the population in the nineteenth century, but even so, a number of diversions were available to Colytonians.

The town was not large, and had no permanent theatre. In the days before cinema, radio and television, local talent had to provide most of such entertainment as there was, although outside performers would occasionally arrive for a one- or two-night stand. These events were well attended, and nearly 500 people, or a fifth of the total population of the parish, watched Mr M.L. Upright perform, with many more being unable to gain admission. His songs, character acting, quick changes of dress and artistic make-up were loudly applauded, as was the tableau, lit by coloured fire, which ended his performance.[20]

Colytonians themselves were the principal performers in the series of entertainments known as Penny Readings which enlivened the long winter evenings. The programme of one such event has survived and shows that those taking part included a retired glass merchant, a solicitor, the stationmaster, the postmaster's daughter, and the vicar, who had a fine tenor voice and who took part in a duet entitled 'Deserted by the Waning Moon'. Piano-playing, readings and recitations completed the bill, which attracted an audience of 124 people.[21] At another Penny Reading held in the board school, Miss Ackerman's contralto voice was said, rather surprisingly, to have 'literally brought down the house'.[22] Music was also provided by the Colyton Philharmonic Society which gave concerts in the Assembly Rooms, and dinners, balls, and lectures all took place from time to time.

The kinds of entertainment so far described were more suited to the middle and upper classes of Colyton than to the working population, as even one penny would be hard to find for labourers with large families to support. A Working Man's Reading Room was in existence in 1887,[23] but most of the social activities for the working class required their active physical involvement. For example, the Colyton branch of the Devon Volunteer Rifles, equivalent to part of today's Territorial Army, provided a hobby for a number of village men. The rifle range was the venue for regular shooting matches, often for prizes, either between members of the Colyton Company themselves, or between Colyton and volunteers from other parishes. The matches were not without their dangers. On one occasion, Rifleman Smith was shot clean through his arm, 'by mistake', and required the immediate attendance of Mr Snook, the medical officer for the parish.[24] When the Colyton Company marched to Shute House for an inspection in 1887, it comprised sixty-four rank-and-file volunteers, two sergeants, two buglers, two lieutenants and one captain. The ceremony was followed by the provision of bread, cheese and beer before the march back to Colyton.[25]

An annual ploughing competition was held under the auspices of the Colyton District Agricultural Society and its successors, with prizes also going for spar-making, hedging, and turnip-hoeing,[26] while the Cottage Garden Society held its first show in 1864.[27] Other outdoor events included the occasional steeplechase and race meeting, while in 1886, Colyton Football Club was founded. The game played was not soccer, but rugby football, and six months later the Colyton team beat Crewkerne grammar school by 3 goals and 2 tries to 2 goals and 1 try.[28] The twice-yearly fairs were another source of entertainment open to everyone who chose to attend. In the early years of the period, the sale of stock was the principal reason for the fairs, but by the 1880s the depression had resulted in very few animals being brought in, so that the fairs became largely devoted to amusements.[29]

The dinners and balls held after the meetings of the various societies attended by the well-to-do Colytonians were mirrored for the working classes by the festivals of the separate Men's and Women's Mutual and Providential Societies, with the later addition of the Ancient Order of Foresters. These annual proceedings, at which the business of the year was laid before the membership, concluded with dinner and dancing.[30] All these events, however, were occasional, and for the working men of Colyton it was the inns and beer shops that provided the year-round refuge from crowded cottages.

This, then, is the background to daily life in Colyton in the second half of the nineteenth century. It remains to look at the institutions which administered the secular and the religious life of the parish.

Notes

1. 'Old Colyton. What it was like ninety years ago. A stroll through the streets with a Native'. Reminiscences of Mr Samuel Seaward, dictated to his son, Mr Basil Seaward, and kindly made available by the Reverend David Gunn-Johnson, Team Rector of Colyton.

2. D.A. Gunn-Johnson, 'A Country Catholic: a study of the emergence of the Oxford Movement in an East Devon Parish'. Unpublished thesis accepted for the Archbishop of Canterbury's MA degree, December 1994, p. 206.

3. O.J. Reichel, in W. Page, ed., *The Victoria County History of Devonshire*, vol. I, London 1906, pp. 404–5, 411.

4. R. Polwhele, *The History of Devonshire*, vol. I, 1793, reprinted Dorking, 1977, p. 310.

5. G.P.R. Pulman, *The Book of the Axe*, 1875, reprinted Bath, 1969, p. 789.

6. Ibid., p. 799.

7. P. Sharpe, 'Gender-specific demographic adjustment to changing economic circumstances: Colyton 1538–1837', unpublished Ph.D thesis, University of Cambridge, 1988, pp. 74–5.

8. Ibid., pp. 86–8.

9. R.S. Schofield, 'An anatomy of an epidemic: Colyton, November 1645 to November 1646', *The Plague Reconsidered*, Local Population Studies Supplement, Stafford, 1977, pp. 95–126.

10. P. Sharpe, 'Gender-specific demographic adjustment', 1988, pp. 53–4.

11. R.G. White, *The History of the Feoffees of Colyton, 1546–1946*, Bridport, 1951, pp. 12–13.

12. G.P.R. Pulman, *The Book of the Axe*, 1875, p. 808.

13. P. Sharpe, 'Gender-specific demographic adjustment', 1988, pp. 57–8.

14. Information on Colyton parish in 1851 is drawn from the census, ref. Public Record Office H.O. 107/1862, Districts 2a–2e.

15. G.E. Evans, *Colytonia: a chapter in the history of Devon*, Liverpool, 1898, p. 3.

16. *Report of the Commissioners on Children's Employment*, 1863, HC vol. XVIII, p. 251.

17. E.H. Hunt, 'Industrialization and regional inequality. Wages in Britain 1750–1914', *Journal of Economic History*, XLVI (4) 1986, table 6, p. 965; *Parliamentary Papers* L, HMSO, 1861, p. 589.

18. R. Bovett, *Historical notes on Devon schools*, Exeter 1989. I am grateful to Mrs Joan Tompkinson of the Colyton Parish History Society for this reference.

19. *Devon Weekly Times* (hereafter *D.W.T.*), 29.4.1887 and 24.6.1887.

20. Ibid., 7.2.1873.

21. Programme dated 4.11.1880 held in the Devon Record Office.

22. *D.W.T.* 31.12.1886.

23. Ibid., 25.11.1887.

24. Ibid., 14.11.1862.

25. Ibid., 15.7.1887.

26. Ibid., 31.10.1879.

27. Ibid., 24.6.1864.

28. Ibid., 1.10.1886, 4.3.1887.

29. Ibid., 14.10.1887.

30. Ibid., 26.11.1886, 10.6.1887.

Chapter 2

The Holders of Power

In the days before elected parish councils, which were not established until 1894, the major source of power in a rural parish was often to be found in the person of a squire, or large landowner. This was not the case in Colyton, since the two landowners who between them owned two-thirds of the titheable area of the parish in 1851 both lived outside its boundaries.[1]

The larger landowner, Sir John de la Pole, was indeed Lord of the Manor of Colyton, and his family had been associated with the parish since the sixteenth century, but he had his seat in the neighbouring parish of Shute. His standing in Colyton was high, and he fulfilled the type of social obligation generally associated with those in his position. For example, he provided a bullock for roasting and distribution to the poor at Christmas, along with a quantity of bread, and there is a record of his birthday being celebrated in Colyton by a dinner at the Dolphin Hotel for his tenants and others connected with the estate, some 200 people in all. Proceedings started with tea and coffee served at 7 o'clock, followed by dancing, and a supper, the party continuing until three in the morning and ending with rousing cheers.[2] On another occasion, the church bells were rung to celebrate Sir John's birthday, to the annoyance of a parishioner who complained that the vicar, while recognising the Lord of the Manor in this way, had ignored the queen's birthday.[3] The de la Poles' landed possessions in Devon, however, extended well beyond Colyton, and the family also owned an estate in Berkshire.[4] Sir John spent much of his time away from the district, leaving his business in Colyton in the hands of his agent, Captain Dick. The second large landowner, Sir Edward Elton, also lived in a nearby parish, but there is no evidence that he played any part in Colyton's daily affairs.

In the absence of any county gentry or members of the aristocracy living in Colyton, parish matters were left largely in the hands of men drawn not only from the small professional class of surgeons, ministers of religion and retired naval officers, but from the tenant farmers, shopkeepers and master craftsmen. These were the men who controlled the two principal organisations within the parish which were concerned with administration, that is to say the Vestry on the one hand, and the Feoffees of Colyton, assisted by their Twentymen, on the other.

The Vestry was an organisation which had originated in the distant past as a meeting of parishioners to deal with ecclesiastical matters, but in 1601 it became concerned in varying degrees with the administration of the Poor Law, and in the ensuing years it gradually acquired further civil duties concerning the parish. It appointed the parish officers, including the churchwardens of the parish church, and the way-wardens responsible for the upkeep of the roads, and received nominations for the Overseers of the Poor, as well as levying the poor rate and the church rate. Members were elected only by those sufficiently well off to be ratepayers, so that the Vestry could not be considered representative of the parishioners as a whole.[5]

In other parishes, the Vestry carried out a variety of duties of the kind taken over later by the parish councils, but in Colyton many of these functions had long ago been passed to the Feoffees and their Twentymen to perform. As both bodies drew their membership from the same small pool of professional men and the middle classes, there was little friction between them, and indeed, the Feoffees allowed the Vestry committee the use of the grammar school for its meetings 'on account of the inconvenience felt from the cold and damp in the vestry room of the church'.[6]

The Feoffees of Colyton were, and still are, the administrators of a charitable trust which came into being in 1546, seven years after Henry Courtenay, Marquis of Exeter and Lord of the Manor of Colyton, had been tried for high treason on the orders of King Henry VIII. He was duly executed, and his estates were forfeited to the crown. But after his death, a number of public-spirited inhabitants of Colyton raised between them the then very considerable sum of £1,000, and with it were allowed to buy back part of the confiscated manor, with the stipulation that the rents and proceeds should be expended in such good, godly and commendable uses as they should determine. The purchase was confirmed by a deed of enfeoffment, dated 6 January 1546 and signed by the king, which is held in the archives of the Chamber of the Feoffees of Colyton to this day.

King Henry also granted the Feoffees the management of fairs and markets, and from the very start their chamber functioned as a parochial organisation to which the townspeople looked for the administration of parish affairs. The Feoffees were assisted in this work by twenty men of Colyton, originally nominated by their fellow parishioners, but as the years passed the Chamber of Feoffees and the Twentymen became entirely self-electing.

An early task of the Feoffees was to establish a free grammar school in the town, the upkeep and running of which remained of first importance to them over the years. By the middle of the seventeenth century they had also taken on the responsibility for Colyton's water supply, tapping springs above the town and taking water down to a large underground tank which still exists, although two smaller overflow tanks have been lost. A document dated 10 September 1641 records the grant by Sir John Pole and others of the necessary water course. At about the same time the Feoffees formed and equipped Colyton's first fire-fighting brigade.

Towards the end of the seventeenth century, the Feoffees faced an unpalatable task. As was described earlier, a number of Colyton men were involved in the battle of Sedgemoor in 1685, fighting on the rebel Duke of Monmouth's side, and two of them were later tried at Exeter and condemned to execution in Colyton. The Feoffees were ordered to stand at the entrance to the town to meet the two men, John Sprague and William Clegg, as they arrived from Exeter on the way to their deaths, which are believed to have taken place at The Elms, an open space at the foot of Sidmouth Street.[7]

The eighteenth century witnessed a decline in the Feoffees' effectiveness, as they neglected their responsibilities for the upkeep of roads and bridges, public buildings and the water supply, but during the first half of the nineteenth century they became more active, and by 1851 they had been a force to be reckoned with in the administration of the parish for a number of years.[8] At this time, however, both the Feoffees, who were the trustees of the charity, and their helpers the Twentymen, had suffered recent losses, either by death or through other causes, and so in 1852 it was decided to fill the vacancies which had occurred, and at the same time to revise and improve the rules of the trust, subject to the approval of the Charity Commissioners in London, who kept a general watch over the dealings of the chamber. The minutes of various chamber meetings in 1852 and 1853 therefore provide an excellent opportunity to see exactly who was chosen to run the Trust's affairs, and how far the Feoffees and Twentymen were restrained by their Deed of Articles.

At this time, the Feoffees were twelve in number when at full strength. To qualify for election they needed to own property within the parish, but were not required to live there. This provision opened the door for the election of Sir John de la Pole and Sir Edward Elton, as befitted the two principal landowners in Colyton, but neither played any appreciable part in the routine affairs of the chamber. Sir John had the better attendance record, being present at six of the 255 meetings held between 1851 and 1870, the year of his last appearance, but Sir Edward came only once, to add his signature to the new deed.

It was thought desirable that the remaining Feoffees should live in the parish so that they could easily participate in the multifarious activities of the chamber, and ten local men were invited to accept the office but three of them declined, preferring the less responsible role of Twentyman to that of a trustee. Three more absentee landowners were therefore elected as Feoffees, leaving only seven who were Colyton residents. They comprised the vicar, who in fact stayed in the parish for only three months a year as he held another office in Oxford, two owners of small areas of land, one of whom was also a Justice of the Peace, a retired naval captain, a retired veterinary surgeon, and two farmers.

The Twentymen held full voting rights in the chamber and, like the Feoffees, were obliged to own property in the parish, but they also had to be residents, and if they removed from Colyton or omitted to attend meetings for a year, their appointment ceased. These rules were intended to ensure that the Twentymen should be readily available to help in the chamber's affairs, but in practice, only two were of independent means and so had abundant leisure. The other eighteen all had to earn a living, two as farmers and the remainder as heads of businesses, varying from quarrying to bakery, so that their work for the chamber cut into their limited free time. One of their number was appointed bailiff, the equivalent of a present-day executive officer, and in return for his heavy workload he was paid an annual salary of £20,[9] but all the other Twentymen, like the Feoffees, received no attendance allowances or financial return for their efforts, apart from the occasional refund of actual travelling costs when visiting the trust's properties in Honiton and Ottery St Mary. Indeed, in some respects it was positively disadvantageous to be a member of the chamber. In 1882 young William Tucker won a free place to the Feoffees' grammar school, but the chamber ruled that as a Twentyman's son he was not entitled to take up his scholarship, since to do so would contravene the order made in 1826 that 'if any Feoffee or Twentyman shall either directly or indirectly accept any Share or gratuity out of the Funds arising from this Trust, the same shall be immediately considered as incapacitated from holding either of the said Offices ...' To make the matter crystal clear, the Feoffees went on to resolve that in future no son of any member of the chamber should be eligible to be elected as a Free Boy to the school.[10]

The trust deed imposed a number of other restrictions on the members of the chamber. The Feoffees were not allowed to take out a lease on any of the trust's farms or land, although they could rent on a yearly basis if they proved to be the highest bidder. The Twentymen were allowed to lease trust property for a maximum of seven years, again if they were the highest bidder, but any new lease up for tender had to be advertised by printed notices posted at various strategic points throughout the parish, so that bidding was open to all. No lease of any kind could be granted without a conference of the Feoffees and Twentymen, none of whom were allowed to convert any part of the trust's income to any purpose whatsoever without the consent of the majority, and no two members of the same family could serve in the chamber simultaneously.

The chamber was no respecter of persons when defending its integrity. In 1851 Sir John de la Pole asked the Feoffees to consider granting him the shooting rights on the trust's Cownalls estate, which adjoined his own land, but his request was politely refused.[11] He was equally unlucky twenty-three years later when he asked for an exchange of lands at Cownalls.[12] His successor, Sir William de la Pole, who in his turn had been elected a Feoffee, fared no better. The chamber minutes of 11 December 1876 simply state 'The Bailiff was instructed not to pay a demand made by Sir W. Pole for Head Rent'.[13]

The farms, houses and cottages owned by the Feoffees in Colyton, Honiton and Ottery St Mary produced almost all of the trust's income which, averaged out between 1851 and 1890, came to just under £450 a year,[14] a sum sounding modest enough, but representing approximately £18,150 today, when changes in the retail price index have been taken into account.[15] The difference in value is considerably more striking if wages are taken as the basis for comparison, rather than the general cost of living. It has already been shown that a farm worker earned around 12s 6d a week in cash wages and benefits in kind, and the Feoffees' income was sufficient to pay the yearly cost of employing one half-time and thirteen full-time agricultural labourers. Today, a work force of similar size would require an annual expenditure of some £108,838, a figure based on the weekly wage for unspecialized adult farm workers of £155.04, set by the Agricultural Wages Board in 1996. Even so, the trust's income was small compared to the returns from the property of Sir John de la Pole and Sir Edward Elton, who between them owned more than twelve times as much land in Colyton as did the Feoffees.[16] But while the absentee landlords took the bulk of their net income from their properties out of the parish, the Feoffees spent nearly all of theirs in Colyton, and so made a real difference to the local economy, either through the payment of wages to those carrying out work commissioned by them, or through their disbursements to the poor.

The part played by the chamber in the relief of poverty in Colyton will be discussed later, and so will their contribution to the education of the young through their grammar school, but a brief account of their other activities for the benefit of Colytonians will show how much influence they had on the daily life of the parish.

The water supply to the town was a constant preoccupation, and the Feoffees were frequently approached to arrange improvements to the system. As just one example, when a private pump which had been supplying 252 individuals in the town broke down, the Feoffees agreed as a matter of urgency to sink a well in the square and install a cast-iron pump within suitable guard posts.[17] As well as dealing with emergencies and continuing to improve the water supply over the years, the chamber employed a water bailiff at a salary of £6–8 a year to keep the system in good running order.

Again, the Feoffees, with the approval of the Charity Commissioners, took the initiative in providing gas lighting for the town during the winter months. They offered to put up fifteen street lamps and to subscribe £20 a year towards the running costs provided the townspeople also agreed to contribute.[18] When in later years the gas burners gave trouble, it was the Feoffees who organised replacements and repairs, on the understanding that these were paid for by those inhabitants of Colyton who could afford it, just as it was the Feoffees who employed the lamplighter.

The administration of the thirty-five allotment gardens opened up at Ridgeway Green by the Feoffees in 1850 for the benefit of poor families also took up a certain amount of time each year, as the plots were much in demand and there were always a number of applications for any vacancy, particularly in the 1880s, when the depression bit hard, while the half-yearly rents of 2s 6d per plot had to be collected, and arguments between neighbouring allotment holders settled.[19] In addition, as managers of the fairs and markets, the Feoffees set the tolls to be charged on the livestock and cheeses brought for sale, though they auctioned the right to collect these charges to the highest bidder; while at almost every meeting some question concerning the upkeep of the trust's properties was under discussion.

These were all matters of business which continued from year to year, along with measures to relieve poverty and to keep the grammar school running, but many shorter-term issues were dealt with. In order to get through the work load, the chamber met on average from fourteen to fifteen times a year. These general meetings, however, by no means encompassed all that the members had to do, since it was usual to set up a subcommittee, which would draw up plans, or oversee agreed schemes as the case might be, and then report back to the chamber. As a result, a system of checks and balances was in place, and no one person was in a position to commit the trust's money to a scheme without the agreement of others.

The meeting held on 7 March 1851 is a good example of how the system worked. The chamber accepted the recommendations of a subcommittee on the best way of preserving the archives, including the original Deed of Enfeoffment signed by the king in 1546, and appointed a new subcommittee to be responsible for putting these recommendations into effect. Next, the proposals of a subcommittee concerning the water supply to parts of Colyton town were discussed and approved, and another subcommittee set up to arrange for and oversee the necessary work. Finally, the report of yet another subcommittee on the desirability or otherwise of providing the town with a public room was considered, and the conclusion reached that such a room was not necessary.[20]

Clearly, by the middle of the nineteenth century the committee system had a powerful hold in Colyton, and similarities with the rural district councils and county councils which now perform many of the tasks undertaken by the Feoffees come to mind. But, quite apart from differences in the scale of operations, comparison breaks down in two important respects. First, local government nowadays is controlled by representatives elected by the community, while the chamber was entirely self-perpetuating; and second, district and county councils today have an army of paid employees to implement policy decisions, whereas the Feoffees and Twentymen had only one paid helper, the bailiff.

To read the minutes of chamber meetings over the forty years from 1851 must be to conclude that the resident Feoffees and their helpers were hardworking men of integrity, who identified themselves whole-heartedly with the trust and its long history, putting its interests before their own. That having been said, they were men of their time in that they were certainly paternalistic in their outlook, especially towards the poor. They also considered the respect of parishioners was their due, although they did not always receive it, as evidenced by Hermon Anning, a mason, who was heard using abusive language about them and who as a result was denied future employment by the chamber.[21] Nor were their decisions always wise. Efforts to cut costs were made at all times, resulting in very hard bargains being struck with those they employed, but on one occasion at least they overreached themselves. Having asked Asa Richards and Samuel Restorick to erect an outbuilding on one of its farms, the chamber queried the resultant bill and brought in its own valuer to produce a revised, and much lower, total. Richards and Restorick stood firm, however, and finally both sides agreed to independent arbitration. To the Feoffees' consternation, the arbitrator arrived at a sum which left the trust worse off that it would have been if the bill had been paid without argument in the first place.[22]

A thread running through the whole period was the cooperation between the Feoffees on the one hand and the parish officers appointed by the Vestry on the other. As a present-day Feoffee has said, the aim of the chamber has always been to prime the pump, rather than to provide total funding, and so although the Feoffees often took the initiative in administering projects, the parish was also involved, even if only by subscribing towards the costs. The comprehensive nature of the Feoffees' archives makes it easy to overestimate the importance of the chamber compared with that of the parish officers, and also perhaps to put rather too high a value on the efficiency with which the ventures it undertook were run, since the minutes of its meetings were unlikely to contain references to any public dissatisfaction that might have been expressed.[23] Nevertheless, as the parish officers were often also either Feoffees or Twentymen, cooperation between the Vestry and the chamber came naturally. All this was to change with the arrival of elected parish councils in 1894.

By early 1895, the new parish council in Colyton was querying the Feoffees' letting of the Ridgeway allotments, and seeking information on the workings of the trust. This rather heavy-handed approach was not at all well received by the chamber, which instructed the bailiff to reply that it was unaware of any grounds on which the parish council was entitled either to interfere with the allotments or to receive the information for which it had asked.[24] The parish council did not give up, however, and some years later held a special meeting to discuss what could be done in order to gain representation in the chamber, one councillor stating that as things then stood, the Feoffees were members of a kind of Freemasonry.[25] Finally, in 1904 the Charity Commissioners allowed the parish council to appoint five additional Feoffees, and a measure of cooperation rather than confrontation within the parish returned.[26]

Two further bodies had a considerable influence on the administration of the parish, but both were district organisations based in Axminster. The first was the bench of magistrates sitting at petty sessions, before whom offenders from Colyton were brought. It is no surprise to learn that one of these magistrates was a Feoffee, as well as at different times a Guardian of the Poor, an inspector of police, an inspector of nuisances, a member of the burial board, president of the Colyton District Agricultural Society, president of the Chamber of Agriculture, and president of the Coly Fishing Association, which last appointment should perhaps have made him ineligible to try poaching cases, though in practice it did not do so.

The second district organisation of great importance to Colytonians was the Board of Guardians of the Poor, parish input coming from the guardians elected by the ratepayers. The work of the board will be discussed more fully later. Here it need only be said first, that three of the eleven guardians from Colyton serving between 1851 and 1861 were also Feoffees or Twentymen, and second, that the board was responsible to the government department in London known as the Poor Law Board up to 1871, when it became the Local Government Board. Just as the activities of the Feoffees were ultimately governed by the national Charity Commission, so the Guardians of the Poor were subject to a national organisation responsible to parliament. In these ways outside influences were felt in parish affairs, in the days before county councils and rural district councils were set up.[27]

Notes

1. Public Record Office, 1R 29/9. Colyton land apportionment, 1844. In that year, Colyton parish covered 6,430 acres, of which 5,680 acres were titheable. The de la Pole estate held 2,684 acres, and that of Sir Edward Elton 1,095 acres. I am grateful to Leigh Shaw-Taylor of the Cambridge Group for the History of Population and Social Structure, who compiled these figures.

2. *Devon Weekly Times* (hereafter *D.W.T.*), 5.2.1869.

3. Ibid., 5.4.1867.

4. Sir William de la Pole, who succeeded Sir John in 1874, is recorded as owning 5,846 acres in Devon, with a gross annual value of £7,416, and an unstated area in Berkshire, with a gross annual value of £370. See J. Bateman, *The Great Landowners of Great Britain and Ireland*, New York, 1971, p. 362.

5. J. Richardson, *The Local Historian's Encyclopedia*, New Barnet, 1974, B229–231, B137.

6. N. Hoare, 'The community of Colyton and its poor, 1800–1850'. Unpublished MA dissertation, 1972–1973, Department of English Local History, University of Leicester, p. 31.

7. R.G. White, *The History of the Feoffees of Colyton, 1546–1946*, Bridport, 1951, p. 13.

8. N. Hoare, 'The community of Colyton', 1972–1973, pp. 27–8.

9. The bailiff's salary was reduced to £17 15s per annum during the depression of the 1880s. See Devon Record Office (hereafter D.R.O.), F17/8 16.3.1888.

11. D.R.O., F17/8, 11.12.1882.

12. D.R.O. F17/7, 20.8.1851.

13. D.R.O. F17/8, 29.4.1874.

14. Ibid., 11.12.1876.

15. D.R.O. F 17/2 includes the trust's receipts and payments.

16. This sum was calculated from C.H. Feinstein, 'A new look at the cost of living, 1870–1914', in J. Foreman-Peck, ed., *Reinterpreting the Victorian economy*, Cambridge, 1990, table 6.4, pp. 170–71; B.R. Mitchell, *British Historical Statistics*, Cambridge, 1988, Indices of retail prices, 1915–1980; and the Retail Price Index published in the *Monthly Digest of Statistics, 1981–1995*, table 18.

17. The Colyton land apportionment, 1844, shows that the Feoffees of Colyton held 298 acres within the parish.

18. D.R.O. F 17/8, 11.9.1854.

19. Ibid., 11.10.1856.

20. D.R.O. F 17/12–13. Records of garden allotments.

21. D.R.O. F 17/ 7, 7.3.1851.

22. D.R.O. F 17/8, 12.11.1857.

23. Ibid., 12.12.1879, 6.2.1880, 4.3.1880, 1.4.1880.

24. Letters in the press indicated some dissatisfaction with the state of the gas lighting. See *D.W.T.*, 23.10.1863 and 6.11.1863.

25. R.G. White, The History of the Feoffees of Colyton, 1951, pp. 31–2.

26. Undated newspaper cutting contained in the Feoffees' minute book.

27. R.G. White, *The History of the Feoffees of Colyton*, 1951, p. 32.

28. County councils were established by the Local Government Act of 1888, and district councils by the Local Government Act of 1894.

Chapter 3

High Church or Low Church?

Although the Feoffees, with their considerable financial resources, were the major agents in the day-to-day administration of the parish, the Vestry came into its own where ecclesiastical matters were concerned.

It is difficult to realise nowadays how large an influence the church had over all sections of society. Those who rented allotments from the Feoffees were forbidden to cultivate their plots on Sundays, even though it was the only free day of the week for many working men, and they were not even allowed to visit their allotments during the hours of Divine Service. Members of the Colyton Mutual and Providential Society, whatever their religious persuasion, had to attend a church service, with a sermon, before they could enjoy a procession led by military bands, a dinner and finally a dance in the Assembly Rooms.[1] The Jubilee celebrations held in June 1887 were marked by not one, but two services in the parish church. Holy Communion was celebrated at 9.30 a.m. and a special service was held in the afternoon, attended by the Volunteer Band, the Friendly Societies wearing their insignia, the Sunday schools and many of the general public, after they had processed round the town.[2]

In 1851 Colytonians drawn to the Church of England could go to the parish church of St Andrew, so graphically described by Samuel Seaward in his walk around Colyton, while the Unitarians gathered in George's meeting-house. A separate Nonconformist group was accommodated in the Independent Chapel, and small groups of Wesleyans and Baptists also met in their own places of worship. Roughly two-thirds of the population, drawn from all sections of society, adhered to the Church of England, while the Unitarians, who comprised a number of mainly upper-middle and middle-class families, and the other Nonconformists, who came very largely from the working classes, made up the remaining third of church or chapel goers.[3]

Before 1860, the members of these varying religious groups seem to have lived in reasonable harmony, partly because the Reverend Frederick Barnes, Vicar of Colyton, belonged to the Protestant tradition, and so was not too far removed from the dissenters and Nonconformists, and partly because the leaders of the different groups liked and were tolerant of each other. Dr Barnes was only in Colyton for some three months a year, being also a Canon and Sub-dean of Christ Church Cathedral, Oxford, and his curates looked after Colyton and the other two parishes of which he held the living, namely Shute and Monckton, during his absence. But in spite of his comparatively short stays in

Colyton, or perhaps even because of them, Dr Barnes continued to be liked and respected by his parishioners. In the early days of his ministry he struck up a close friendship with the Unitarian minister, the Reverend Joseph Cornish, the two of them holding whist parties alternately at the vicarage and the parsonage,[4] and good relations between Anglicans and Unitarians continued after Cornish's death. The Reverend Jacob Pady, who preached at the Independent Chapel of the Congregationalists, was also reported as being not too bigoted to be seen occasionally at a church service.[5]

All this, however, was to change in 1860 when the Rev. Mamerto Gueritz was appointed to replace Canon Barnes by the Dean and Chapter at Exeter, patrons of the living at Colyton. The parishioners, steeped in Protestantism for at least two and a half centuries, as the history of the parish has shown, found themselves faced with an ardent Anglo-Catholic vicar, whose background was quite different from anything to which they were accustomed, and who was determined to bring spiritual renewal to the parish and to enrich the church services with the colour and music beloved of the Oxford Movement, to which he belonged.

As his first name would suggest, Mamerto Gueritz was born in Spain.[6] His grandfather, a young lawyer from Louvain in Belgium, killed a man in a duel, and had to flee the country. He went to Spain, joined the Royal Walloon Guard, in which he attained the rank of captain, married, and was killed at the battle of Baylen in 1808 when his eldest son, José, was ten years old. José was at once enlisted into the regiment, a not uncommon way of providing for its orphans.

As he grew up, José became a supporter of those who wished to restore the Spanish constitution, revoked by King Ferdinand in 1814, and he must have felt relief when Ferdinand was ousted by the revolution of 1820. Shortly after this, he married a lady of Madrid, and transferred to the Provincial Militia of Jativa in Valencia. Here Mamerto was born in 1823, shortly before a French army marched into Spain and put Ferdinand back in power. José was arrested and sentenced to life imprisonment as a Constitutionalist, but he escaped and managed to reach London. As he had served with the Spanish troops under Wellington at Waterloo, the British Government granted him a military pension for life, and this enabled him to send for his wife and Mamerto, who sailed from Alicante in a small English ship carrying a cargo of oranges, landing at Axmouth in Devon. The family then settled in Plymouth, the cost of living being lower than in London, and converted to the Protestant religion.

José died of consumption in 1832, when Mamerto was only nine years old, but friends and supporters kept the boy at school until he was thirteen. He was then apprenticed for seven years to a major wine importer in Plymouth. During this time, he helped in a Sunday school for poor children and through this work he became convinced that he had a calling to the priesthood.

There was no chance of the young Gueritz being able to afford the cost of training for holy orders without outside help, but a Protestant society in Bristol supported him, and sent him up to St Edmund's Hall, Oxford, where he worked extremely hard in order to overcome his lack of a public school education. It is reported that when he was disturbed by a rowdy group of students outside his window, he simply poured water over their heads to disperse them and then went back to his books. Unfortunately, he was unable to sit his final examinations, having suffering a breakdown which was ascribed to overwork, so that he left Oxford with only a pass degree.

Unfortunately, too, from the point of view of the Protestant society which funded him, Gueritz became influenced by the High Church Oxford Movement while he was an undergraduate, and from being an evangelical Protestant he became a Tractarian, or an Anglo-Catholic as he might be called today. The Tractarians, unlike some Protestant churchmen, did not believe that education, civilization and reason would cure the evils and sorrows of mankind. They thought the church needed spiritual regeneration, and in order to accomplish this, they developed a two-pronged attack, first by attempting to evangelize the poor, particularly in the large towns, and second by raising the standard of worship through beautifying services by the use of music for the ear, and colour for the eye.[7]

A year after his first clerical appointment, Mamerto Gueritz married Ann Derby of Plymouth. For the next eleven years he served as a curate in various parishes in Devon and Cornwall, where he experienced some of the difficulties that could arise when attempting to alter long-standing church practices. Nevertheless, when he became Vicar of Colyton in 1860, he lost no time in putting Tractarian principles into effect. Colyton might not rival Liverpool or the East End of London in the extent of its slums, but the poor were present in rural areas as well as in large conurbations, and Gueritz was prepared to speak up for them.

In October 1862, Gueritz addressed the guests at a dinner which followed the inaugural meeting of the Colyton District Agricultural Society. He was reported in the press as saying that the society had not been founded merely to help the farmers, who were able to look after themselves, but to improve the lot of the labourer. In his view, the labourers of Devon and Somerset were too badly fed and housed to be able to do a good day's work. He ended by asserting that he would be glad to assist the society 'by heart and by purse' as far as was in his power, so long as it continued to work for the improvement of the labouring classes as well as the farmers.[8] Again, in 1863, Gueritz reported to the Commissioners on Children's Employment on the conditions of work of the young female lacemakers in Colyton, which he considered injurious to their health.[9]

There is no record of any public response to Gueritz's support for the labouring classes, although the farmers may not fully have appreciated it, but his reforms in the church services met with overt hostility. Under the previous vicar and his curates the main services had been matins and evensong, with saints' days seldom observed and Holy Communion only infrequently celebrated. Under Gueritz, however, services on saints' days became a regular occurrence, Holy Communion was celebrated every Sunday morning, except for the first Sunday in the month, matins was said daily at 9 a.m. and choral singing was introduced.[10]

Battle lines were soon drawn. Only six months after Gueritz's arrival in Colyton, the Unitarian minister delivered a series of lectures in the course of which he advised parents not to send their children to the new national day school, which had replaced the Church of England Sunday school, because it was run by Puseyite priests.[11] By 1862, the Vestry meeting was raising objections to the numbers and cost of candles used on saints' nights and at midnight services, and attempting to reduce the parish clerk's salary from the 10 guineas a year he currently earned, 'his services being considered by a large number present perfectly unnecessary in the present quasi-choral service attempted in our church'.[12] Candles, indeed, were a constant source of complaint, some members of the Vestry remarking that they 'certainly did require more light in the church, but not of this sort'.[13]

It must be remembered that all payers of the poor rate, whatever their denomination, were not only entitled to vote for Vestry members, but were also able to serve on the Vestry themselves, if elected to do so. The Unitarians in Colyton came largely from the well-to-do classes, and formed a powerful group of electors. Some of them were indeed Vestry members, so that from the start of his incumbency the new vicar was faced with a rebellious element within the parish body responsible for ecclesiastical affairs. In addition, at this time a church rate as well as a poor rate was levied on all parishioners who had the appropriate property qualifications, and so Colytonians who were not members of the Church of England were contributers to the upkeep of the parish church.[14] This gave rise to the feeling that St Andrew's was not the domain of the vicar alone, but in some measure belonged to the whole parish, a feeling that was intensified in a number of Unitarians because they, or their forebears, had actually bought pews in the church at a cost of £25 each when the previous vicar was trying to raise money to provide free seating in the north aisle.[15]

Nowhere is this sense of ownership better illustrated than in the long-running case of the church bells. It is not clear exactly why such action was taken, but some friction must have been present, because in 1864 the vicar prohibited the customary bell-ringing before leaving the parish for a few months 'to recover his equilibrium'.[16] By 1867 the old team of bell-ringers had rebelled, and had been replaced by young and inexperienced men, and the ears of Colytonians were described as 'tortured by the discordant jinglings of these tyro campanologists'.[17] Nine months later, on New Year's Eve, the old ringers temporarily reclaimed the bell tower and rang what was described as one of the best and most correct peals ever heard in Colyton for one hour and five minutes from 11.30 p.m. The account of this event which was sent to the press concluded by saying that the bells were the property of the parish, not of the incumbent, and that their control was therefore in the hands of the churchwardens, both of whom the parishioners should take care to elect.[18]

The changed use of the bells, increasing emphasis on the sacraments, the introduction of candles, surplices and stoles, a robed choir, Gregorian chanting – all these innovations were greeted by complaints which found their way, anonymously, into the papers. The consistently acid style of the reports indicate that only one or two correspondents may have been involved, but other incidents occurred which showed that opposition to the new ways was not confined to a vocal few.

A major dispute developed in 1863, when Gueritz refused to marry his parishioners during Lent, thinking it absolutely wrong to do so. As it happened, the marriage of the Prince of Wales took place in Lent that year, and Gueritz wrote to the queen to protest at the bad example being set to the nation.[19] This infuriated a large number of Colytonians, who demonstrated their displeasure by erecting a pump at the top of Market Place, inscribed with the words 'The Surplus of a fund collected to commemorate the wedding of HRH the Prince of Wales during Lent, March 1863, has been devoted to the erection of this fountain by the patriotic Protestants of Colyton, as a permanent memorial of That National Triumph and in vindication of their own loyalty by vote of committee'. The pump is still standing in Colyton for all to see.[20]

The following year brought another clash, this time between the vicar and the Unitarians, news of which reached the press. A poor but much respected parishioner called John Pavey died, and his family assumed that he would be buried in the churchyard of the parish church, next to his wife who had predeceased him. But John Pavey was a Unitarian, and therefore not a Christian at all in the eyes of Gueritz, because Unitarians did not believe in the divinity of Christ and consequently did not accept the doctrine of the Holy Trinity. The vicar felt that he could not conscientiously perform the burial service, during which the name of the Holy Trinity is invoked. After much pressure, he agreed to bury Mr Pavey, not next to his wife, but in the place generally reserved for suicides. Once again, the stubborn independence typical of Colytonians came to the fore. The sexton dug the grave next to John Pavey's wife, the vicar refused to read the service, and the Unitarian minister proceeded to do so, standing outside the churchyard wall, while the vicar's supporters stood inside, with their hats on, 'in evident token of derision and contempt'. By his actions in this episode, the vicar was said to have contrived to 'outrage the feelings of the dissenters, to insult the dead, and to disgust the parishioners generally'.[21]

Complaints about the incident were made to the Bishop of Exeter, a commission of enquiry was set up, and as a result Gueritz was admonished, and charged with the costs of the enquiry. A poem, published anonymously in the press soon after this finding was released, demonstrates the glee with which it was received in Colyton. Just one verse will serve to give its flavour.

O Reverend M. Gueritz,
Your merits, your merits
In bigotry's annals have found their award!
And spite of yr. nonsense,
Your cant and yr. conscience,
You've got a good lash from your Spiritual Lord![22]

By 1866, matters had reached such a pass that effigies of Gueritz and his curate were burnt in the streets of Colyton, following the celebration of a mass in Colyton Church.[23] Years later, the vicar's granddaughter wrote, 'Grandpa was burnt in effigy in a Colyton bonfire for wearing vestments! (but the curate wouldn't burn though Grandpa did)'.[24]

The curate in question, the Reverend W.H.B. Proby, exacerbated rather than ameliorated the vicar's troubles. In the last three years of the 1860s, Gueritz spent a considerable amount of time in London, immersing himself in the worship of churches congenial to him, and assisting the parish priest at St Matthias', Stoke Newington. During his absence Proby's tactless behaviour, coupled with his devotion to the Ritual revival, led nearly 200 adult members of the Church of England in Colyton to send a memorial to the queen in 1867 asking for an investigation into the Ritualistic innovations which were being made.[25]

Warfare continued sporadically throughout the 1870s, with Proby starting the decade by circulating pamphlets against Protestantism which divided churchgoers from dissenters even further.[26] However, the Unitarians themselves were facing problems at this time and for a while turned in on themselves. The years between 1873 and 1876 were described as 'a time of storm and stress, civil war raging more or less between various persons connected with the society'.[27] The Unitarians, though, were considerably more successful than the supporters of Gueritz in keeping their difficulties out of the newspapers, and no detailed account of these troubles has been found. Gradually, however, the vicar began to gain a measure of acceptance, and he was elected a Feoffee in 1873, thirteen years after his arrival in Colyton. The choir went from strength to strength, and became a source of pride to the parish when the vicar and his son, the Reverend José Gueritz, took twenty-six surpliced choristers, and twelve unsurpliced, to Axminster to take part in the East Devon Choral Festival, where they acquitted themselves well.[28]

Gueritz had never been a killjoy, and from the start of his incumbency he used his feeling for music and colour to enliven events outside the church as well as within it. In this respect, it is instructive to compare accounts of the treats given to Sunday scholars by the different denominations. The Independent Chapel, with a congregation drawn mainly from the poor, could manage little more than tea-meetings, although the Bible class did present a silver cruet stand 'of a very chaste design' to their pastor, as a token of 'their love and esteem for his valuable labours'.[29] The Unitarians also favoured tea-meetings, at one of which 100 copies of 'Hymns for the Christian church and home' were handed to the children for use in George's meeting.[30] On another occasion, their Sunday-school treat was held out of doors and 'innocent games were heartily engaged in by the young, while the aged watched with delight their youthful gambols and wandered through the grounds charmed with the mingled beauty of the place'.[31] But the Church of England Sunday school treat was a considerably more robust affair.   After prayers and a sermon, a procession bearing evergreens, arches, floral devices, flags and banners marched behind a brass band to the Dolphin Inn, where tea was served in the yard, before moving on to the vicar's field to enjoy evening sports, with prizes, and dancing.[32]

By the mid-1880s, Gueritz's battle was largely won. His work with the children of the parish meant that a generation within the Church of England had grown up to whom the Anglo-Catholic ritual was the only known form of worship, and who accepted it without question. On one matter dear to his heart, however, he was not to meet success until the 1890s, and that was the re-ordering of the interior of St Andrew's from the state described by Samuel Seaward, where the pews were occupied largely by the well-to-do while the poor parishioners sat in galleries along the walls, to one where all the worshippers could see and hear the services from free seats and where access to the altar was unimpeded. His first attempt at change came in 1866, but was voted down by the Vestry, as were further moves in 1869 and 1876. In 1892, however, a Vestry meeting was held in the absence of Gueritz's principal opponent, and the wholesale alterations proposed were unanimously agreed. By 1900 the galleries had been removed, along with the private pews, and all the seats in the church were free. This triumph was celebrated by a fully choral service attended by the Bishop of Exeter, who preached a sermon which gave thanks as much for Gueritz's forty years in the parish as for the completed changes to the interior of the church.[33]

It was not Gueritz's personality which initially upset his parishioners, but his sincere conviction that it was his duty to change their long-established ways of worship, as well as some of their equally sincerely-held religious beliefs. It is a measure of his success that once the new ways had become the established ways, he gained the affection of Colytonians. When he and his wife celebrated their golden wedding, a number of presentations were made to them, including a handsome reading lamp from none other than 'The Ringers of the Parish Church', and when he finally retired in 1901 through ill health, the people of Colyton made him a gift of £120, the present-day equivalent of £4,800 or more. He spent his last years living with his widowed daughter in Colyton, where he died in 1912, aged eighty-nine.[34]

Notes

1. *Devon Weekly Times* (hereafter *D.W.T.*), 10.6.1887.

2. Ibid., 24.6.1887.

3. The *Ecclesiastical Census of 1851* for Devon (Public Record Office 129/279 H.O.) shows that on Sunday, 30 March 1851, 54 per cent of the church-going public in Colyton attended Church of England services, 14 per cent Unitarian, 27 per cent Independent and 5 per cent Wesleyan and Baptist. These figures are misleading, however, in that they represent the total attendances at all services, so that one individual who attended three services in the course of the day would be counted three times. A better guide is the parish burial book, which shows that 31.5 per cent of all burial services between 1868 and 1891 were taken by Nonconformist ministers.

4. G.E. Evans, *Colytonia: a chapter in the history of Devon*, Liverpool, 1898, p. 22.

5. Ibid., p. 124.

6. D.A. Gunn-Johnson, 'A Country Catholic: a study of the emergence of the Oxford Movement in an East Devon Parish'. Unpublished thesis accepted for the Archbishop of Canterbury's MA degree, December 1994, p. 206. All the following biographical information has been taken from the Reverend Gunn-Johnson's thesis, which has also provided many insights into the religious controversies which raged in Colyton in the 1860s and 1870s.

7. S.L. Ollard, in J. Hastings, ed., *Encyclopaedia of Religion and Ethics*, vol. IX, Edinburgh 1917, pp. 585–9.

8. *D.W.T.*, 31.10.1862.

9. *Report of the Commissioners on Children's Employment*, 1863, HC vol. XVIII, pp. 248–52.

10. D.A. Gunn-Johnson, 'A Country Catholic', 1994, pp. 91 and 134.

11. Ibid., p. 136. Pusey was a leading figure in the Oxford Movement.

12. *D.W.T.*, 9.5.1862. The clerk's pay was reduced to 5 guineas a year at a later Vestry meeting (see Ibid., 26.6.1863).

13. Ibid., 24.6.64.

14. In 1869, it was proposed at a Vestry meeting that funds for the church should be collected by a monthly offertory. The church rate in Colyton was discontinued from this time onwards (D. Gunn-Johnson, 'A Country Catholic', 1994, p. 162).

15. Ibid., p. 91.

16. D.W.T., 14.10.1864.

17. Ibid., 5.4.1867.

18. Ibid., 10.1.1868.

19. D.A. Gunn-Johnson, 'A Country Catholic', 1994, p. 136.

20. Colyton County Primary School, *Walk around Colyton*, Regional Resources Centre, 1976.

21. *D.W.T.*, 16.9.1864.

22. Ibid., 24.5.1865, 16.6.1865, and 23.6.1865.

23. Ibid., 23.11.1866. A dialect poem described the burning of 'Pope Gurtz's' effigy.

24. D.A. Gunn-Johnson, 'A Country Catholic', 1994, p. 143.

25. Ibid., p. 140.

26. Ibid., p. 142.

27. G. Evans, *Colytonia*, 1896, p. 48.

28. *D.W.T.*, 1.8.1879.

29. Ibid., 3.1.1868.

30. Ibid., 12.8.1864.

31. Ibid., 11.9.1868.

32. Ibid., 6.8.1869.

33. D.A. Gunn-Johnson, 'A Country Catholic', 1994, pp. 161–70.

34. Ibid., pp. 197–8.

Chapter 4

Life and Death in the Family

Now that the background to Colyton's community between 1851 and 1891 has been reviewed, it is time to examine the life experiences of its people.

Even during this brief period of forty years, in a parish of only 2,500 inhabitants, examples can be found of such dramatic events as infanticide, evidenced by the burial of an unknown child, aged about three weeks, found floating in the River Coly;[1] suicide, as in the case of the landlord of the Three Horse Shoes, who drowned himself in a water-butt;[2] death by violence, to be described in chapter 15, when law and order will be discussed; and even necrophilia, or morbid attraction to corpses, which was practised by a well-to-do Unitarian, who, incidentally, was the principal adversary of the vicar, Mamerto Gueritz, in the religious controversies already described. According to an unattributed account in the local newspaper,[3] this eccentric individual kept the unburied body of his mother in a leaden coffin, with a glass plate let into it, in an outbuilding on his property, which he visited from time to time in order to gaze at her face. Thirty-five years later, his wife died, and she too, along with her mother-in-law, remained unburied. Finally, after the death of the man himself in 1903, both women were interred in Colyton's cemetery,[4] his mother after a lapse of forty-five years.

Fortunately these kinds of event, though newsworthy, were rare. To put them in their true perspective, it is necessary to consider society as a whole, and to investigate the lives not only of the headline-makers but of the silent majority from childhood through the middle years to old age. In this chapter, it is proposed to begin the process by examining the family groupings and households to be found in Colyton in 1851, from the point of view of all the children of less than ten years of age who were living in the parish in that year. For the sake of conciseness, this body of boys and girls will from now on be referred to as 'the cohort'.[5]

There were 633 such children in 1851, with boys slightly outnumbering girls, and they fell into five main groups, depending on the economic status of their parents. A small minority, amounting to between 2 and 3 per cent of the whole, were the offspring of well-to-do persons of independent means or members of the professions, and so lived their early years in financial security. The sons and daughters of farmers and dairymen made up a further 9 per cent, and although their parents' prosperity varied with the size of their farm or dairy herd, these children in the main were not poor by the standards of the time.

Just over a fifth of the cohort belonged to families where the head was either a business owner, a school teacher, or a self-employed person of some substance.   Here again, although misfortune could at any time alter circumstances, the boys and girls in this group in general did not go hungry. But for the quarter of all the children whose fathers were wage-earning craftsmen and tradesmen, and the more than four out of ten who were the offspring of agricultural and other labourers, poverty was an ever-present threat.   Between them, the children in these two classes made up two-thirds of all those under ten years of age in 1851, and they were brought up under conditions where little could be looked for in material terms other than basic food, shelter and clothing, together with sufficient heat to get them through periods of cold weather.   Even these necessities could not always be provided by their parents alone.   These were the children whose mothers went to the winter soup kitchen set up by the Feoffees and the Vestry, to buy meat soup at 2d a gallon, and whose fathers in times of illness or unemployment had to seek relief from the Feoffees or the Poor Law.   Indeed, more than eight out of every ten fathers of children in these two groups received such help at one time or another.

Nevertheless, although the children of well-to-do and middle-class parents were spared the degree of deprivation experienced by the majority of Colyton's girls and boys, the different classes lived together in close proximity, so that the effects of poverty were visible to the whole community.   Sickness was not confined to the poor alone, and death could and did strike children in all walks of life, as will be seen.

Today, the perceived decline in the importance of the family is a much discussed subject, with particular emphasis being given to the number of children being brought up by a single parent. In 1851, however, nearly 90 per cent of the children we are considering were living with a father and a mother, whether a natural or a step-parent.[6] At this time, divorce for the great majority of people was almost unknown, but if a man or women from the wage-earning or labouring classes was widowed and left with a young family, he or she needed to remarry as soon as possible, the man in order to have someone to look after his children and his own domestic needs, as he certainly could not afford to pay anyone for these services, and the woman to secure a reliable breadwinner. As a result, under eight out of 100 children were with one parent, compared with over double that proportion in the country as a whole in 1994.[7] Fewer still were with neither their father nor their mother, but with a relative, while less than one in 100 was living with unrelated persons.   Generally speaking, this pattern held good throughout the social classes, except for the small number of children with fathers in the professions, all of whom lived with two parents.

However, the fact that nearly 90 per cent of Colyton's children were living with two parents does not mean that they were all residing in simple nuclear families, comprising parents and offspring only.   Certainly this was the case for the majority, but just over a third of the children found themselves in households which had been enlarged either by the presence of relatives, ranging from grandparents or great-uncles and great-aunts down through the generations to the children's nephews or nieces, often older than themselves; or by living-in servants; or by both. In addition, a small number of families in the wage-earning and labouring classes took in lodgers. A considerable minority of children, therefore, were used to living with adults who were not their parents, and with other young people who were not their brothers or sisters.

Relatives were more numerous than either servants or lodgers in the households in which Colyton's children lived, and were to be found in all the social groups. An examination of their circumstances may throw light on the extent to which the family in Colyton made up for the deficiencies in the local welfare system. There was indeed a welfare safety net in existence at the time, either through outdoor relief under the Poor Law or indoor relief in the workhouse, but help was only given in cases of extreme need, while the Feoffees as a matter of principle confined their assistance to occasional payments, rather than to regular weekly doles. The whole subject of poverty and how it was dealt with will be discussed in later chapters. Here it is intended only to try to assess how far family members helped each other by providing a home for their kin.

Grandparents were the relatives most likely to be living in the same households as Colyton's children in 1851, but this does not imply that it was common to find married grandparents, married parents and their children all in the same household. Indeed, only one such arrangement was in existence at the time the census was taken. The other grandparents fell into two broad groups; first those widowed grandmothers and grandfathers who on balance were being helped by their children by being taken into their homes, and second the grandparents, mostly married, who gave shelter to the grandchildren, whether or not these were accompanied by a parent. Assistance between the generations is thus seen to have worked in both directions.

In the first group, grandmothers outnumbered grandfathers by more than five to one. Of course, an active grandmother could help the family in many practical ways, and some may even have contributed financially, as indeed the grandfathers may have done, but on the whole they were probably the main beneficiaries of the arrangement, particularly in the wage-earning and labouring classes, where the alternative to entering their children's homes may well have been the workhouse. More will be said on this subject in a later chapter, when the lives of the elderly will be discussed in some detail.

In the second group, positions were reversed, for here the grandparents were the heads of the household. In seven cases, they had accepted illegitimate children into their homes, along with their single mothers. Some of these mothers may in fact never have left the parental roof, and their offspring, born out of wedlock, were brought up as part of the family with their mothers' younger brothers and sisters. A number of these single parents were lacemakers and could contribute to the household budget, but even so, the support of the grandparents was of major importance both to their unmarried daughters and to the grandchildren.

In other cases, grandparents had taken in grandchildren in the absence of any parent. Two of these grandchildren are known to have been illegitimate, and others may have been. Just as the married couples who received a widowed parent into their households possibly saved the elderly person from the workhouse, so grandparents who took in illegitimate grandchildren may have rescued these boys and girls from a similar fate. In 1851, the Axminster workhouse contained eight children under ten who had been born in Colyton, four of whom are known to have been illegitimate, although in their cases their mothers were with them. There can be no doubt of the importance of grandparents to the two descendant generations in times of difficulty, and it is noteworthy that there were no examples in Colyton at that time of grandparents being forced by legal orders to undertake their grandchildren's support. Their actions in this respect may therefore be assumed to have been voluntary.

It was not only the cohort's grandparents who gave hospitality to relations, or received it from them. Single or widowed great-uncles and great-aunts were to be found in the households of their nephews and nieces. Younger uncles and aunts who had not yet married were absorbed into the households of their brothers or sisters when their parents died, leaving again on marriage, or on removing from Colyton to find work elsewhere. In one instance, a bachelor uncle who was handicapped by deafness was still living with his brother and sister-in-law and their children in 1861, providing a further example of the sustained help which some family members gave to each other at a time when state disability allowances were not available free of means-testing as of right.

It was unusual at this time for a man or woman in their twenties or thirties to be living alone in a household of their own; in this respect they resembled people in the same age group in Spain today, who generally remain with their families until they marry.[8] Only four men and three women aged between twenty and thirty-nine in the whole parish were solitary residents in their own household, and only one of these had any kin within Colyton to whom she could have turned.

Forty years on these patterns of co-residence were still being maintained in Colyton, with a number of grandparents providing a home for illegitimate grandchildren with their mothers, while the great majority of single or widowed men and women were living with other family members rather than being on their own.

At the time of the 1851 census, there were only five exceptions to the rule that children in Colyton lived with at least one parent, or with relatives, and for three of the five children involved, the separation from their parents, or parent, was only temporary. In one instance, the son of a prosperous farmer whose home was well outside the town was boarding at a Colyton school; in another, the boy was paying a visit to a childless couple living not far from his widowed mother; in a third, a recently widowed father had placed his three-year-old son with a childless couple, presumably because he was unable to look after such a young boy himself. Only two children under the age of ten had actually been abandoned by a parent.

Apparently homeless, Selina Hancock, her eleven-year-old sister and a younger brother, were boarding with an elderly market gardener and his unmarried daughter, while another three Hancock children were being cared for in the neighbouring parish of Shute. It is not clear whether these arrangements had been made by their father, Walter Hancock, but if so he could not have kept up payments for their keep, because three months later all six children were removed to the workhouse in Axminster. Meanwhile, their father had disappeared, but the police, acting as a Victorian version of the Child Support Agency, traced him to Honiton, eleven miles distant, and he was arrested and brought before the magistrates on a charge of neglecting to provide for his children. He was sentenced to a period in prison, and the Guardians of the Poor agreed that he should be made to refund the costs of his children's maintenance in the workhouse once he was released.[9]

The experience suffered by the Hancock children was indeed hard, but it was not typical. Their exceptional case does not affect the finding that, in Colyton at least, family members in general helped each other in times of difficulty. What cannot be said, for lack of evidence, is whether the familial arrangements which have been described were entered into willingly or unwillingly, or whether some of the widowed grandparents, or the single mothers with their children, might not have preferred to live independently in their own accommodation, if that had been possible. Given the circumstances prevailing at that time, however, the family provided a much used alternative to the relief available through the Poor Law.

It has already been said that some children from all the social groups in Colyton experienced living with relations in their homes, but only the boys and girls in the three most prosperous classes knew what it was like to have servants in the house.

If the term 'servants' conjures up a picture of a large domestic staff on the lines of *Upstairs, Downstairs*, it should at once be dismissed. In the first place, only one household in Colyton in 1851 had as many as four living-in domestic staff, and only 12 per cent of the children under ten had any domestic servant in their homes. In the second, the word 'servant' in the census for that year covered four quite separate groups of employee, the common factor between them being that all members were accommodated in their employers' households. In one group were apprentices and journeymen, bound by contract to their masters for a period of years, the apprentices in order to learn a trade, and the journeymen to gain working experience. Then there were the independent workers, such as shop assistants or millers' men, who lived-in for the mutual convenience of their employers and themselves. The third group covered farm workers, both male and female, and the fourth comprised domestic servants, although in the case of female workers on farms the distinction between the third and fourth groups might become a little blurred, with a house servant helping with the poultry, for example, or a dairymaid also carrying out some household duties.[10]

A closer inspection of the servants in question shows that living-in service was principally for young people. Just over eight out of ten female servants to be found in the homes of the children of Colyton, and nearly nine out of ten male servants similarly placed, were under twenty-six years of age, while the maximum number of servants for both sexes lay in the sixteen to twenty year age group. Once these young people reached their twenties, marriage and the setting up of their own homes removed them from the pool of unattached persons who found it convenient to be provided with board and lodging as part of their wages. By living-in before marriage, they were achieving the same ends as their contemporaries already described who joined their brothers' or sisters' households when their parents died, being spared the difficulties of finding affordable lodgings. At the same time, they received training from their employers.[11]

For the most part, then, servants made up a body of young people who came and went, and domestic workers in Colyton were no exception to this rule. Although some aristocratic and upper-middle class households elsewhere may have benefited from large numbers of servants, including old retainers who devoted themselves to the family over many years, such was not the case in Colyton. Only one domestic servant present in 1851 had continuity of employment through to 1861 and beyond, and he again was the exception that proved the rule. Born illegitimate, and partly deaf and dumb, he appeared in the 1841 census as servant to Mr John Snook, a Feoffee and one-time farmer of independent means. It has not proved possible to discover why he was employed in the first place, but as he was only eleven years younger than his master, there can be no question of parental obligation on Mr Snook's part to a child born out of wedlock. By 1851, the servant was in the employment of John Snook's son, who was medical officer to the parish, and he remained with that family at least until 1871, 'working about the garden' as the 1861 census described him, and becoming a familiar figure to the doctor's numerous children.

Lodgers made up the third category of persons outside the nuclear family with whom Colyton's children might be co-residing in 1851, but they were far less numerous than either relatives or servants and were attached only to the households of the two poorest classes. Like the majority of servants, more than two-thirds of the thirteen lodgers concerned were under twenty-seven years of age, and single, so they were still at the stage of the life-cycle which preceded marriage. With only two exceptions, they had no relatives in the parish with whom they could have stayed, so that lodging with unrelated people was the most practical way of obtaining a roof over their heads. The two lodgers who had families in Colyton had both lost a parent through death, and each surviving parent had married again, starting a new family and edging out the older child of the first marriage.

The mix of nuclear families, relatives, servants and lodgers under the same roof naturally resulted in some very large housefuls, a technical term which covers both households to which lodgers are attached, as well as ones where they are absent.[12] The children of the cohort in 1851 found themselves living in the company of anything from one to twelve other people. In general, the size of the houseful increased with the prosperity of the family, so that eight out of ten children in the professional families were living in a houseful of seven members or more, a proportion which declined steadily through the social classes until it reached just under four out of ten for the children of labourers.

This of course is not necessarily to say that the richer the parents, the more children they had; rather that the better off the family, the more likely it was to employ servants in increasing numbers. In fact, the average number of siblings contained in each nuclear family at the time of the 1851 census varied very little between the social classes, ranging from 3.6 children in the professional class to 3.1 children for the labourers. But these figures do not give a true impression of the average number of brothers and sisters a child might have had. In the poorer classes, older siblings could already have left home to earn a living. Among the better-off, some boys may have been away at boarding school when the census was taken. Equally, a two-year-old who was apparently an only child in 1851 might in future become the eldest of a long line of younger children. Only by discovering the total number of children born and surviving in each family over the mother's childbearing years can a realistic assessment of family size be made.

It has proved possible to find 205 families living in Colyton in 1851 where most, if not all, of the children born to the mother over her whole fertile period have been recorded, either in the parish registers or in the censuses for Colyton, or occasionally in some other source. The results show two of the great differences between the family environment of girls and boys in the second half of the nineteenth century and the present day. First, the average number of children born per family in Colyton stood at 5.7, compared with a gross fertility rate of only 1.8 for the United Kingdom as a whole in 1993,[13] so that most children then were brought up in considerably larger nuclear families than is the case now. Second, although the two poorest classes had the largest mean number of children born into each family, the figure standing at 6.9 compared to 5.0 in the professional class, they also suffered the highest number of children dying before they were seven years old, with on average at least one child for each family dying before it reached that age, with the result that the average number of children surviving per family was reduced to 5.8. Infant deaths also occurred in the farming and business classes, and although no children under seven are known to have died in the small number of professional families, one of the doctor's sons succumbed when he was ten, and a daughter when she was twenty. All Colyton's children, then, were from an early age familiar with death, either of their own brothers and sisters, or of their friends, and were faced with the personal insecurity that such an experience carries with it.

Although the family environment of the young has been explored, nothing has been said of their lives outside the home. It may come as a shock to learn that nearly half the girls aged seven to nine years in the parish in 1851 with wage-earning or labouring fathers were already at work. How this came about will be described in the next chapter.

Notes

1. Colyton Parish Council, burial book, 6.6.1882.

2. *Devon Weekly Times*, 23.1.1868.

3. Ibid., 11.8.1865.

4. D.A. Gunn-Johnson, 'A Country Catholic: a study of the emergence of the Oxford Movement in an East Devon Parish'. Unpublished thesis accepted for the Archbishop of Canterbury's MA degree, December 1994, p. 165.

5. See J. Robin, *From childhood to middle age: cohort analysis in Colyton, 1851–1891*, Cambridge Group for the History of Population and Social Structure, Working Paper Series: no. 1, 1995, for full statistical analysis of these children and their relationships.

6. Step-parents are included as parents as it is not known in all cases whether a father or mother had married again before coming to Colyton. Only six children are known to have been living with a natural parent and a step-parent.

7. In 1994 16.6 per cent of dependent children were in single parent families. J. Haskey, 'Step families and stepchildren in Great Britain', *Population Trends*, 76, 1994, table 1.

8. S. Heath and P. Minet, *Living in and out of the parental home in Spain and Great Britain: a comparative approach*. Cambridge Group for the History of Population and Social Structure, Working Paper Series: no. 2, 1996.

9. Devon Record Office (hereafter D.R.O.), P.O. 14, Colyton, 3.7.1851; D.R.O. Axminster Union Minute Book vol. 7, 25.7.1851; 4.4.1852.

10. M. Bouquet, *Family, Servants and Visitors: the farm household in nineteenth and twentieth century Devon*, Norwich, 1985, pp. 75–9.

11. See B. Reay, *Microhistories: demography, society and culture in rural England, 1800–1930*, Cambridge, 1996, pp. 25–6, for a similar life-cycle pattern experienced in nineteenth century Kent.

12. See P. Laslett, ed., *Household and Family in Past Time*, Cambridge, 1972, pp. 36–8.

13. *Population Trends*, 79, 1995, table 9, p. 54.

Chapter 5

A Working Childhood – Girls

When Queen Victoria married Prince Albert in 1840, she wore a dress made of Honiton lace. In choosing this handmade material, costing £1000, she revived a fashion and in so doing helped to renew an industry long established in East Devonshire, but one which had declined since the introduction of machine-made net in 1815 to an extent where it was difficult to find enough skilled workers to execute the royal order.

The town of Honiton, some eleven miles distant from Colyton, was the major centre of the Devonshire lace industry and gave its name to the point lace, made on a pillow with a fine thread, for which the district is famous. However, lacemakers were to be found in many other towns and villages lying between the rivers Axe and Exe, including Colyton.

The craft of pillow-lacemaking is thought to have been introduced in the late sixteenth century by Flemish refugees, escaping from persecution in their own country,[1] and certainly there is a reference as early as 1609 to a Colyford point-maker, one William Vale, who married in Colyton church in that year.[2] In the same church, a monument to Sir John Pole and his wife shows Lady Pole, who died in 1623, 'wearing a splendid cape of three rows of bone lace descending to the waist, and a cap trimmed with the same material'. Even as late as the second half of the nineteenth century, there were families in Colyton whose surnames derived from the Flemish immigrants, for example the Stockers, the Murches, the Rocketts, the Boalches, the Kettles and the Worams.[3]

During the eighteenth century, lacemaking declined in importance in the parish, in spite of the introduction of cheaper trolly lace, also made on a pillow but using coarser thread and heavier bobbins. In its heyday, this lace was made by boys as well as girls and women, and many boys up to the age of fifteen attended lace schools with their sisters, until they were old enough and strong enough to enter the more usual male occupations, such as farm work or fishing. Even as men, some would continue to make trolly lace at home in what leisure time they had, so earning a little extra money to add to the family budget.[4]

By 1851, the fashionable world's demand for Honiton lace had helped to provide employment for at least 226 people living in Colyton, but by this time male participation in the craft had almost disappeared and only three boys, all brothers, were recorded as lacemakers. The female workers, who needed good eyesight and nimble fingers, were predominantly young, with girls under the age of majority, then standing at twenty-one years, making up nearly three-fifths of the workforce.[5]

These young workers were almost exclusively drawn from the two poorest classes, only four of the 128 known lace girls in 1851 coming from the more prosperous families of the better-off self-employed or business owners. All but one were unmarried, and except for two nineteen-year-olds and one girl of fifteen with no family connections in Colyton who were lodging with older lacemakers, they were still living at home, making a contribution to the economies of their parents' households. It was this availability of paid work from an early age which resulted in nearly half the seven- to nine-year-old daughters of wage-earning craftsmen and tradesmen or labourers being described as lacemakers in the 1851 census.

In practice, these very young children were beginning to learn their craft in lace schools, which they would continue to attend until they had nothing more to learn from their teacher, a stage they were likely to reach in their mid-'teens. In nearly all schools, the children would also be taught reading from the Bible, and possibly writing as well.[6]

The evidence given in 1863 to the Commissioners on Children's Employment by Colyton's vicar, the Reverend Mamerto Gueritz, and by other witnesses from nearby towns and villages gives some idea of the conditions under which the girls worked. The youngest children were only required to attend for two or three hours a day at first, unless they were very quick at learning, but a lace schoolmistress from Sidbury considered that after six months' training they were usually sufficiently skilled to work a full day, from 8 a.m. to 6 p.m., with an hour off for dinner. In the winter, they would go home to tea, but come back to school afterwards until 7 p.m. Some children brought breakfast with them, because sitting for long periods without eating made them very cold.

In Colyton, where there were six or seven lace schools, the vicar claimed that the older lace girls worked until eight or nine in the evening, 'when they would be seen coming out to walk'. Other witnesses stated that it was not unusual for lacemakers to work by candlelight through the night to complete an urgent order. The lace schools themselves were often overcrowded and airless rooms in the teachers' cottages. One school in Sidbury was described as containing eighteen girls and their mistress in 'a room 9 ft. 4" by a little less, and 7 ft. high'. There was no fire, even though it was early in February.[7]

Mrs Palliser, author of the comprehensive *History of Lace*, visited many Devonshire lace schools in 1875, and held a rather more optimistic view of conditions, stating that 'though it might be desired that some philanthropist would introduce the infant school system of allowing the pupils to march and stretch their legs at the expiration of every hour, the children, notwithstanding, looked ruddy as the apples in their native orchards; and though the lace worker may be less robust in appearance than the farm servant or the Cheshire milkmaid, her life is more healthy far than the female operatives in our northern manufactories'.

When it came to wages for the lace workers, Mrs Palliser was again more optimistic than those reporting to the Commissioners on Children's Employment, for she maintained that a good lacemaker easily earned 1s a day.[8] This may have been possible for exceptionally skilled older workers, but a lace schoolmistress addressing the commission in 1863 reported that after three or four years of training a good worker could expect to make 3s to 4s a week, while a girl of eight, after paying for her schooling, thread and patterns would not clear more than 5s in her first year.[9] What was agreed by all was that the infamous system of paying the lace workers with goods rather than with money was in general use, in spite of an Act of Parliament passed in 1831 which was designed to prevent the practice.

This method of payment, known as the truck system, was to the benefit of those who collected the finished lace from those who made it. Nearly all these middlemen, or lace manufactors as they were called, owned general shops, the source of the goods with which payment was made. The girls were forced to take what the manufactors chose to give them, and often two loaves of bread and half a pound of butter formed part of a common weekly allowance. In addition, unfair prices were charged for the goods supplied to the lacemakers. In the words of one of the witnesses to the commissioners, 'I know of boots bought at a shop for 2s being sold to the lace girls for 10s 6d. Calico which I get for 7d would be 9d or 10d to a lace girl, lump sugar instead of 6½d the lb. would be 8d; candles ditto; bacon always 1d or 2d a pound dearer to them; and other things in like manner, and all the year round'.[10] The more respectable shops receiving lace might give the lace girls half their earnings in money, but only a few paid entirely in cash.[11]

It cannot be said with certainty how the girls of Colyton were paid, although the town contained two lace manufactors in 1851. One ran a drapery and grocer's shop, and the wife of the other was also a draper, so it is likely that the truck system was at least partly in use.

As well as describing the working conditions of the lace girls, the vicar made three general points to the commissioners in his evidence. First, he held that the earnings of the lacemakers diminished the wages of Colyton's men, whose employers knew that family incomes could be supplemented by work in the lace industry which was widely available to wives and daughters. Second, he believed that the employment lowered morals, by making children independent at an early age, so that girls of sixteen and seventeen years could go off and live by themselves. Finally, he considered lacemaking was damaging to health, and that long hours spent sitting in crowded, airless rooms stooping over a lace-pillow led to consumption, better known as tuberculosis, which was a common illness in the town. By using the censuses and the parish registers, it is possible to find some evidence as to whether his claims were justified.

The Turner family provide an illustration of the vicar's first contention. In 1851, Edward Turner, an agricultural labourer, and his wife Susan, a washerwoman, had six children living at home. One of these was a sixteen-year-old boy, unemployed, who later in the year was on two occasions to be in trouble with one of the constabulary watchmen, but the other five offspring were girls, ranging in age from nine to twenty-three years, and all were working as lacemakers. On the assumption that at the very least the two elder daughters earned 4s a week each, and the three younger made 5s a week between them, the daughters taken together would bring into the house more than their father's average wage for a farmworker of 12s 6d a week, including benefits in kind. The Turners, with five daughters earning, were an extreme case, but it was not at all uncommon to find two or three sisters in one household working as lacemakers, thus lending support to the view that the wages of farm workers were kept down because of the money that could be earned by the female members of the family.

The vicar's second statement, that lacemaking had a harmful effect on lace girls' morals because financial independence enabled them to set up for themselves away from their parents, is difficult to substantiate, because it is not known how many girls left the parish in their mid- to late teens with this end in view. Certainly the 1861 census records seven lace girls under the age of majority living within the parish apart from their families, but it is far from clear how many of them were of dubious morals. The youngest in the group, who was only twelve years old, was lodging with an uncle and an aunt. Another girl had stayed behind when her family left Colyton. A third was Ellen Hancock, one of Walter Hancock's abandoned children whose removal to the workhouse has already been described. In 1861 she was lodging with the daughter of the market gardener with whom she had been boarded ten years earlier. Louisa Parsons was already married, and was in lodgings with a week-old daughter, while one girl had come into Colyton to lodge with a middle-aged farm worker and his wife. Mary Ann Richards, nineteen years of age, whose parents were still in the parish, had indeed set herself up in her own household, but she had taken in a 55-year-old widow as a lodger. She married a year later, and her first child was brought to church to be christened over a year after the wedding, so that it may be assumed that the child was conceived perfectly respectably after marriage. For only one girl is there evidence which could be used to support the vicar's fears, and even in her case the immorality, if immorality there was, may have lain with her father rather than with herself. Her name was Jane Davey, and she was eighteen years old when the census was taken in 1861.

At this point, Jane was boarding with Bridget Drower and Bridget's thirty-year-old daughter Henrietta, both lacemakers, although her own parents were living in Colyton. Bridget was a single mother and when the census was taken Henrietta, also unmarried, was pregnant with a daughter, having already borne an illegitimate son three years earlier who had lived only a few months. It might seem reasonable to assume that Jane had quarrelled with her parents and had taken up with undesirable company. However, after the death of Jane's mother some time between 1861 and 1863, her father married Henrietta Drower and gave his surname to the daughter born out of wedlock. Whether or not he was the father of the child cannot be proved, but in lodging with the Drowers, Jane was in fact turning to her future stepmother.

The social historian, writing well over a century after the event and using only documentary evidence of an impersonal nature, cannot hope to do more than guess at attitudes, emotions and motives, and without a knowledge of these is in no position fully to explain events. However, the general question as to whether or how far the availability of relatively well-paid women's employment affected the rates of pregnancy before marriage, and of actual illegitimacy, will be addressed in later chapters.

There is no occasion to doubt the vicar's final statement that tuberculosis was prevalent in Colyton, and that lacemakers were among the sufferers, for in the nineteenth century this disease killed more people, especially young adults, than any other illness,[12] but for a variety of reasons it is impossible to prove or disprove without question that lace girls were more likely to develop the then generally fatal disease than other girls in the same age group. In the first place, the cause of death was not recorded in the parish register or the Colyton burial book, so that when a young married woman died, it could have been because of complications during pregnancy, or at childbirth, and of course illnesses other than tuberculosis may well have carried off some girls and young women. Then over half the girls aged seven to twenty years in 1851 left Colyton before or at marriage, and although any of them could have died young in the places to which they went, it is not known whether or not they did so. A further difficulty is that the census enumerator responsible for the Colyford area of the parish failed to record the occupations of three-quarters of the girls in the age range under consideration, so it is not known whether those among them who died were lacemakers or not.

In the face of all these obstacles it may seem foolhardy to try to assess whether lacemakers were more likely to die young, whether or not from tuberculosis, than girls who were in other occupations or who simply stayed at home. Nevertheless, such an attempt has been made, and readers who are interested will find an account of the process in the appendix. The result of examining the life histories of all the girls positively known to have survived to 31 years and beyond, and those known to have died unmarried before that age, suggests that lace girls were in fact quite considerably less likely to die young than those in other occupations or none. The death rates in both categories were shocking by modern standards, but while 12.5 per cent of the lace girls whose histories can be traced died before they were thirty-one years old, no fewer than 23 per cent of non-lacemakers did so, or nearly double the proportion. The difference between the two groups of lacemakers and non-lacemakers is even more striking if only those girls in the two poorest classes are considered. All the lacemakers in the sample were the daughters of wage-earning craftsmen and tradesmen, or labourers, and as has already been shown, one in eight of them died young. The non-lacemakers in these two social classes were in a numerical minority, but no fewer than 45 per cent of them succumbed before they were thirty-one years old.

Unlike the lacemakers, the non-lacemakers came from all the social classes in Colyton, and daughters of landed proprietors, farmers and dairymen, and business people died young just as lacemakers did, and indeed in the same proportion, namely 12.5 per cent, yet they did not have to work long hours in crowded cottages, and were unlikely to be short of fresh air and good food. Nothing can be certain without knowing the causes of their deaths, but it is possible that they too became infected with tuberculosis, through drinking unpasteurized milk from tubercular dairy herds.[13] Whatever the reasons, the loss of these comparatively well-to-do girls reinforces the view expressed earlier that death came to young people from all sections of society.

It is clear that with the limited information available too much should not be read into statistics based on a small number of individuals. But if the occupational issue is ignored, and those girls who died are considered on a class basis only, then two major differences between the better-off and the poor emerge. First, the girls in the three more prosperous classes lived longer than their poorer contemporaries, their mean age at death standing at 20.8 years, compared with 14.19 years for the daughters of wage-earners and labourers. Second, taking lacemakers and non-lacemakers together, 21 per cent of poor girls died young, compared with 12.5 per cent of the well-to-do. These figures must lead to the conclusion that while disease appeared in all classes, it was the conditions created by poverty rather than occupation which caused it to spread more rapidly.

Lacemaking, though the most important, was not the only source of work for girls in Colyton in 1851. Those who did not wish, or were unsuited, to learn the craft could fall back on domestic service as a means of earning a living.

'The general servant, or maid of all work, is perhaps the only one of her class deserving of commiseration: her life is a solitary one, and in some places her work is never done ... She starts in life, probably, a girl of thirteen, with some small tradesman's wife as her mistress, just a step above her in the social scale; and although the class contains among them many excellent, kind-hearted women, it also contains some very rough specimens of the feminine gender ... By the time she has become a tolerable servant, she is probably engaged in some respectable tradesman's house, where she has to rise with the lark, for she has to do in her own person all the work which in larger establishments is performed by cook, kitchen-maid, and housemaid, and occasionally the part of a footman's duty, which consists in carrying messages'. So wrote Mrs Beeton in her *Book of Household Management*, published in 1861,[14] and if her analysis was correct, she set out a blueprint for the lives of the majority of the living-in female domestic servants under the age of twenty-one who were in Colyton when the 1851 census was taken.

Living-in domestic service was of secondary importance compared to lacemaking as a source of employment, but it still occupied a fifth of the 200 girls at work.[15] A young person who lacked the skill, opportunity or desire to become a lacemaker and who decided to go into service in Colyton had two main options open to her. She could look for an opening in the town itself, or she could try to find a situation in the country, either on a farmstead or in a dairyman's household.

Two-thirds of the girls who had found places in the town were the only servant kept, and so fell into Mrs Beeton's category of maid of all work, but the size of the households in which they were employed varied considerably. One fifteen-year-old had the responsible but possibly dispiriting task of looking after a solitary widow in her late sixties who died the following year, while at the other extreme the youngest of the group, at fourteen years old, was the sole servant to a family of six, comprising a middle-aged tailor and draper, his wife, and their four young children. In Mrs Beeton's estimation, such a servant should manage to sit down for two or three hours on a summer's evening, and even for a short time in the afternoons on leisure days, but otherwise she would be hard at work for the rest of her waking hours.[16]

The average wage for this type of service around London varied from £9 to £14 a year, according to experience, or from £7 10s to £11 a year if extra allowances for tea, sugar and beer were given.[17] It is unlikely that maids of all work in Colyton would command as high a salary as girls working in or near the capital, but even so, it was not unusual for domestic servants in Devon who lived-in for a number of years to save enough money to supply the furniture and goods needed to set up house when they finally married.[18]

The remaining third of the girls in service in the town stood higher in the domestic hierarchy, working either as housemaids or cooks. They shared their duties with at least one other female servant, and in four households with a manservant as well. They may have been better placed and better paid than the maids of all work, but even so their working days were long. Mrs Beeton considered that a conscientious housemaid would be at her work by 6 o'clock in the morning in summer, and perhaps an hour later in winter to save on the use of candles. By breakfast time, she would be expected to have cleared out and blackleaded all the grates that had been in use the previous day, dusted and polished the sitting rooms, and swept the carpets with a brush, having first sprinkled them with used tea leaves which helped to lay the dust. She would have to take hot water upstairs to the bedrooms, and while the family dressed, she would lay the breakfast table, and then wait on the household during the meal.

After breakfast there were the beds to be made, a task which involved wrestling with feather mattresses which had to be shaken, beaten and smoothed back into shape, any feathers which escaped during this process being put back through the seam of the tick, and the hole stitched up. The housemaid was also expected to empty the slops, a task which is now considered too degrading for prisoners to perform on their own behalf. Cleaning rooms, polishing brass and silver, laying meals, waiting on table and clearing up afterwards, mending household linen, lighting lamps and tending fires filled the rest of the day until the last cans of hot water for evening washing had been carried upstairs.[19]

Domestic servants, however, were not entirely at the mercy of their employers. A maid working in Exeter who was dismissed on the spot because she refused to attend family prayers took her case to the magistrates, who awarded her a month's pay in lieu of notice, saying that attendance at prayers was no part of her contract.[20]

The girls who had found work in the country with the families of farmers and dairymen, although specifically described as house servants in the census, entered a rather different kind of service from that experienced by the girls in town. They were indeed maids of all work, in that they were the only female servants kept, but a third of them found themselves on farms where boys and young men who were employed on the land were also living-in. In such cases it was not unusual for the whole household, both family and servants, to eat together at the same table, and so the girls had the company of others in their own age group at certain times of the day.[21]

Female domestic servants on farms and dairies were usually expected to help out with work beyond the normal range of housework. For example, they might be expected to feed the calves, pigs and poultry, and help in the dairy by washing milking pails and separators.[22] On the other hand, the farmer's wife was likely to do the cooking, and his daughters who stayed at home were also accustomed to help in the house and on the farm. The country servant's work was probably rougher than the town maid's, but if she had good employers she may possibly have felt more integrated into the household.

Whatever the benefits of living-in domestic service may have been, it seems that most Colyton girls preferred the greater personal freedom which lacemaking gave them. Only one female brought up in Colyton was a domestic servant on a farm in 1851, and just five had places in town. The remaining four-fifths of living-in domestic servants under the age of twenty-one had entered the parish from outside, independently of their families, and all but three of them had left again before the 1861 census was taken, so forming part of the small army of working-class girls who needed to earn their livings but whose opportunities to do so were too limited in their own home parishes to enable them to remain there. It is of course possible, indeed probable, that some girls left Colyton to work in domestic service in other parishes. However, the experiences of the daughters of wage-earning craftsmen and labourers who were aged from five to nine years in 1851 show that a considerable majority were still living at home ten years later, when they were between fifteen and nineteen years old.[23] In these poor families it was essential that girls as well as boys should earn their livings as soon as possible, even if this meant leaving home at an early age, but the demand for lacemakers meant that Colyton girls in the 1850s could stay with their parents and be an asset rather than a burden to their families. The unpopularity of domestic service is underlined by the fact that only one girl, a nursemaid, was working on a daily basis as opposed to living-in.

In the earlier part of the nineteenth century, working class girls had opportunities for employment on farms and in dairies, not as domestics, but as living-in farm servants working for the farmer or dairyman. By 1851, however, the practice of hiring girls by the year in this fashion had almost died out in Colyton, and only three young women were so employed, two of them being dairymaids.

It was not only working-class daughters who earned their livings. Four out of ten of the girls from what is often termed the 'middling class' to distinguish it from the rather differently constituted 'middle class' of today, were employed in 1851. Apart from one who was a school assistant, they worked with their hands, but with only a few exceptions dressmaking, millinery, general sewing, and in one case shoebinding, replaced bending over the lace pillow.

Again, nearly half the daughters of farmers and dairymen of fifteen years of age and over were shown in the 1851 census as having employment. Two were dressmakers, but all the rest were assisting their parents in the home, on the farm and in the dairy. Only in the very small class of comparatively well-to-do professional men and landowners did all the daughters stay at home without occupation until marriage. Although their experience is often taken as typical of the Victorian age, they represented only 2 per cent of the seven- to twenty-year-old girls in Colyton. For the majority of females in their teenage years, if the opportunity to work was available it was taken.

Forty years of change

The years between 1851 and 1891 showed a dramatic drop in the proportion of working girls under the age of majority. Six out of ten girls aged seven or over were gainfully employed at the beginning of the period. By its end, this proportion had almost halved.[24]

The chief reason for the fall was the effect of successive changes in educational provision. In 1851, there was no compulsion to go to school, and free education for girls in Colyton was obtainable only from the Sunday schools established by the various religious denominations, leaving children who attended these with the option of working for wages during the week. However, the Education Act of 1870 provided for the setting up of elementary schools managed by elected boards, and in 1874 Colytonians sought and received board school status for the national school which had been founded by the Church of England in 1861.[25] A further Act in 1876 established the principle that all children should receive elementary education, and in 1880 school attendance up to the age of ten was made compulsory. If a child of that age had reached the necessary standard, he or she was allowed to leave, but otherwise children had to stay on until the age of thirteen.[26] As a result, a considerable number of young children had been removed from the labour force by 1891.

Provision for compulsory education was not the only instrument for change, however. Coinciding with the advance of schooling came the retreat of the lacemaking industry. Fashion, then as now, was fickle, and even though the Princess of Wales followed Queen Victoria's example and ordered Honiton lace for her own wedding dress in 1863, the demand for this expensive luxury steadily declined. A craft which had employed over 200 people of all ages in 1851 supported only a quarter of this number forty years later, and the proportion of girls under the age of majority working with lace had fallen even further, to a mere sixth of the number employed in 1851.[27] Indeed, the very nature of the work had changed, since during the 1870s a new branch of the industry, that of restoring and re-making old lace, had arrived in Devonshire. Torn scraps, even rags of lace were sent for repair, with some workers specializing in mending the net background to the pieces and others in restoring the lace motifs. According to Mrs Palliser, 'the splendid mantles, tunics and flounces which enrich the shop windows of the great lace-dealers of London are mostly concocted from old fragments by the Devonshire lace-workers'.[28]

This type of work demanded different conditions from the old cottage industry, and two lace manufactories were set up in Colyton, one for net mending and the other for lace repairing, each organisation being in charge of a forewoman. One of these forewomen was married, and employed a living-in nurse to look after her two-year-old daughter while she was at work, providing an early example of the two-income family using paid help for child care which is so familiar today.

The chief sufferers from the decline of the lace industry were the girls in the two poorest classes, for whom work was a necessity. It comes as no surprise, then, to find that those who could not obtain a vacancy in the lace manufactories had been obliged to turn to the previously rejected occupation of domestic service, and by 1891 more than half of the working-class girls who had found jobs in the parish were engaged in this type of employment, their number being split equally between those living-in and those working on a daily basis.

Girls from the middling class, on the other hand, did not suffer the same diminution in employment opportunities. Indeed, a slightly higher proportion of post school-age girls from this section of society were employed in 1891 than had been the case forty years earlier. Moreover, while in 1851 all but one had been needlewomen of one kind or another, by 1891 a growth in service industries had produced work in the post office, the board school, in a laundry run by one girl's mother, as a independent small shopkeeper, and at Colyton station as a ticket clerk. A small beginning, perhaps, but nevertheless a sign of a growing diversity in the occupations available to young women.

Notes

1. F.B. Palliser, *History of Lace*, ed. M. Jourdain and A. Dryden, 1902, reprinted East Ardsley 1976, p. 409.

2. P. Sharpe, 'Gender-specific demographic adjustment to changing economic circumstances: Colyton 1538–1837'. Unpublished PhD thesis, University of Cambridge, 1988, p. 96.

3. F.B. Palliser, *History of Lace*, 1976, p. 403, fn. 9.

4. Ibid., pp. 412–13.

5. The age range of lace workers in Colyton in 1851 was as follows:

    Total known workforce, 226. Girls aged 7–20 years, 57 per cent; women, aged 21–34 years, 21 per cent , 35–49 years, 15 per cent, 50 years and over 6 per cent; boys aged 7–12 years, 1 per cent.

    Marked under-recording of girls' occupations in the tything of Colyford suggests that the workforce was in reality even larger, and the proportion of workers under twenty-one years of age still greater.

6. F.B. Palliser, *History of Lace*, 1976, p. 414.

7. *Report of the Commissioners on Children's Employment*, 1863, HC vol. XVIII, pp. 248–52.

8. F.B. Palliser, *History of Lace*, 1976, p. 416, fn. 32.

9. *Report of the Commissioners on Children's Employment*, 1863, p. 249.

10. Ibid., p. 248.

11. F.B. Palliser, *History of Lace*, 1976, p. 416, fn. 32.

12. G. Cronjé, 'Tuberculosis and mortality decline in England and Wales, 1851–1910', in R. Woods and J. Woodward, eds, *Urban disease and mortality in nineteenth century England*, London, 1984, p. 79.

13. Ibid., p. 81.

14. I. Beeton, *Beeton's Book of Household Management*, London, 1861, p. 1001.

15. The total number of girls at work in the parish in 1851, excluding Colyford tything where occupations were greatly under-recorded, was 200. Of these, 128 or 64 per cent were lacemakers, 36 or 18 per cent were living-in domestic servants, and 36, or 18 per cent were in other occupations. Of the 36 living-in domestics, 24 were attached to households in the town and 12 were employed in farmsteads or the houses of dairymen.

16. I. Beeton, *Book of Household Management*, 1861, p. 1005.

17. Ibid., p. 8.

18. M. Bouquet, *Family, Servants and Visitors: the farm household in nineteenth and twentieth century Devon*, Norwich, 1985, pp. 78–9.

19. I. Beeton, *Book of Household Management*, 1861, pp. 987–1000.

20. *Honiton and Ottery Gazette and East Devon Advertiser*, 4.10.1884.

21. M. Bouquet, *Family, Servants and Visitors*, 1985, p. 76.

22. Ibid., p. 77.

23. See J. Robin, *From childhood to middle age: cohort analysis in Colyton, 1851–1891*, Cambridge Group for the History of Population and Social Structure, Working Paper Series: no. 1, 1995, pp. 30–34 and table 13.

24. In 1851, 62 per cent of all seven- to twenty-year-old girls were in employment. By 1891 the figure stood at 35 per cent.

25. D.A. Gunn-Johnson, 'A Country Catholic: a study of the emergence of the Oxford Movement in an East Devon parish'. Unpublished thesis accepted for the Archbishop of Canterbury's MA degree, December 1994, p. 193.

26. J. Richardson, *The Local Historian's Encyclopedia*, New Barnet, 1974, F4–8.

27. In 1851, there were 226 known lacemakers of all ages. In 1891 the figure stood at 52. In 1851, there were 128 lacemakers aged seven to twenty years in the parish, excluding Colyford tything. In 1891, there were only 20 such girls.

28. F.B. Palliser, *History of Lace*, 1976, p. 411.

Chapter 6

A Working Childhood – Boys

To have described the working lives of Colyton's girls before those of its boys is not to have shown a greater interest in one sex than the other. The girls were given priority because in 1851 they constituted the majority of the workforce of seven- to twenty-year-olds. While just half the boys in Colyton were shown in the census for that year as being in employment, the proportion of working girls was nearer two-thirds, standing at 62 per cent. [1]

Average figures for a whole group, however, may conceal marked differences between various parts of the social hierarchy, and this was certainly the case in Colyton. The position was reversed in the three more prosperous classes, where a number of parents could afford to keep their sons and daughters at school until their mid-teens, and where pressure on children to add to the family income from the earliest possible age was less strong than in the two poorest groups. Here fewer girls than boys were at work, only a quarter of the daughters having employment, compared to a third of the sons. For the considerably more numerous children whose parents were wage-earning craftsmen and tradesmen or labourers, however, matters were very different, with exactly three-quarters of the girls being at work, compared to just under half the boys.[2] This discrepancy between the two sexes was at its greatest between the ages of seven and thirteen years, but even after that, working class girls held their own in the workplace right up until the age of majority at twenty-one years.

The reason for the predominance of girls in employment was of course the availability of pillow-lacemaking, which has already been described, and this was a craft to which girls were particularly suited. If employment had been available for boys from the age of seven, then they would have taken it. The Devonshire farm labourer Charles Medway, reporting to the Poor Law Commissioners' enquiry into the employment of women and children in agriculture in 1843, stated that in the early part of the century he was 'first put out at six years old to a place to fetch cows, water, etc' and was apprenticed as a living-in farm servant when he was between seven and eight.[3] Fifty years later, agriculture remained the predominant occupation for males in Devonshire, but in Colyton at least, seven-, eight- and nine-year-old boys were not in general considered strong enough to be useful to farmers in a full-time capacity,[4] though they would certainly be able to work occasionally at odd jobs such as bird-scaring, clearing stones from the fields in spring, and helping to harvest potatoes, apples and other crops in the autumn. Evidence from the log books of the Colyton Board School and the reports of the Feoffees' grammar school shows that boys were often absent from school for some of these purposes, as will be seen when education is discussed in the next chapter.

The position at Colyton was not an exceptional one, where specialized employment for girls was available locally. Seventy years earlier in Cardington in Bedfordshire, where there were opportunities for work in pillow-lacemaking and to a lesser extent in linen- and jersey-spinning, a far higher proportion of girls than boys under the age of twenty were being employed.[5] In contrast, in the village of Elmdon in Essex, where in 1861 there was no ready source of employment for girls other than in domestic service, the position was reversed, with half the boys aged five to fourteen years contributing to their parents' household expenses through their earnings, compared with only one in ten of their sisters.[6] These comparative figures demonstrate that for the poor in Colyton, as elsewhere, child and youth employment in the second half of Queen Victoria's reign depended not on a child's sex *per se*, but on what work was available.

Once boys were old enough to start earning on a regular basis, they had the advantage over girls in that a wider range of jobs was open to them. Although agriculture was the most important single occupation for all males in 1851, and almost half the working boys were employed in it, the remainder had been able to find work as apprentices or journeymen to a variety of tradesmen, from millers and bakers to blacksmiths and carpenters, or as paid employees of builders, masons, leather workers, tailors or shop keepers. Just three boys, brothers ranging in age from seven to twelve, were described in the census as lacemakers, their elder brother at sixteen years old working as a farm labourer. These boys were the last survivors in Colyton from the time, already described, when trolley-lacemaking was an accepted occupation for boys until they were old enough to enter into more strenuous work.

Colyton's working boys in 1851, then, were divided almost equally between those on the land and those in other occupations. But there was another way in which they could be differentiated, depending on whether they were living at home with their parents or other relatives, or whether they were housed and fed within the households of their employers, like the living-in female domestic and farm servants described in the last chapter. While two-thirds of the working boys lived at home, and five of the older youths were lodging or boarding with unrelated families, a not inconsiderable three out of ten were 'in service' to their employers.[7]

By the middle of the nineteenth century, the custom of sending poor children out to live as servants in the households of others had been in place in Devonshire for at least 300 years. In 1562, Justices of the Peace were given the power to apprentice any unemployed person who was under the age of twenty-one, and by 1601 they were enabled to apprentice not only the children of vagrants and paupers, but also those of working parents who had more offspring than they could cope with.[8] In this way, destitute children were supported, and youth unemployment relieved. By the end of the eighteenth century, it was usual practice in the county to require farmers and business owners with property carrying a rental value of £20 per year or more to take turns in receiving poor apprentices sent by the parish into their households.[9]

In areas such as Colyton, where agriculture was the dominant industry, it was natural that a large proportion of these apprentices should be allocated to farmers. The intention was that the children should become part of their master's household until they were twenty-one years of age, receiving their board, lodging and clothing, and indeed all their requirements, together with training in how best to do their work, in return for their labour. In practice, apprentices bound to a bad master were likely to run away as soon as they were able to support themselves elsewhere.[10] Nevertheless, it was the opinion of Charles Vancouver, who was employed to report to the government's Board of Agriculture in 1808 on the state of husbandry in Devonshire, that 'boys so trained and instructed are uniformly found to make the best servants and to prove the steadiest and best labourers afterwards'.[11]

Running alongside the compulsory apprenticeships for poor children was the voluntary system of service in husbandry. Here, the servant would be hired by a farmer for a year, at the end of which he or she was free to renew the contract or to look for work elsewhere, possibly through a hiring session or fair. In this type of service, the younger servants would receive a small cash wage in addition to free board and lodging, and training.[12]

Lists of children apprenticed by Colyton parish survive, covering various periods between 1598 and 1830, but by the early nineteenth century the boundaries between apprenticeship and service were already becoming blurred.[13] By 1851, no farm servant of any age in Colyton was described in the census as an apprentice, and it may be assumed that the great majority of young boys taken into farmers' households were there because their work was of value to their employer, rather than because of compulsion to fulfil social obligations to the parish imposed through the law.

By this time, too, service in husbandry was in rapid decline in the south and east of England, where arable farming predominated. In these areas, farmers preferred to employ day-labourers who could be laid off, unpaid, during the seasonal periods when work was slack. Only the carters, who looked after the horses, could be sure of work the year round. In the west and north of the country, however, as in Colyton, holdings in general were smaller and livestock played an important part in the farm economy. As a result, labour was required throughout the year,[14] and it suited the farmer to have farmhands on the spot for early morning and evening milking, and for all the daily tasks associated with the care of animals, many of which could suitably be undertaken by boys rather than men. Indeed, in the early years of the nineteenth century, girl apprentices were also employed in this way, although Charles Vancouver in his report on Devonshire to the Board of Agriculture deplored their use in tasks more suited to boys. 'Scraping the roads, lanes and yards, turning over mixings and filling dung pots, is at best but a waste of time and a feeble effort of infantile strength. What can a female child at the age of ten or twelve years be expected to perform with a mattock or shovel? or how will she be able to poise, at the end of a dung-fork, any reasonable weight, so as to lift it into the dung-pots slung upon the horses' backs, for hacking out the manure to the distant parts of the farm? Even driving the horses after they are loaded is by no means an employment proper for such girls', he wrote.[15] However, he considered this work suitable for the male apprentices, and it probably formed part of the daily round for those youths in Colyton, more than three-quarters of whom were aged fourteen years or over, who were living in farmers' households in 1851.

At its best, the system of living-in farm service suited the farmer, the youthful servant, and the servant's parents. The farmer provided the servant's accommodation and keep, but paid him only a small cash wage in return for which he had the use of the servant's labour throughout the year at whatever time of day it was needed. The boy might have to find his clothing from the money paid to him, but this was his only essential expense, and he could therefore save if he wished. He also, given a good master, would eat better than he would have done at home, with wheaten bread being provided rather than the cheaper barley bread which might be all his parents could afford. Equally important, he would be receiving a sound training in the type of work which he would probably have to perform for the rest of his life. The servant's parents, on the other hand, were relieved of the expense of keeping the boy, and his absence from home would reduce overcrowding in a cottage where a large family had to be accommodated. There was also the possibility that their son would send some of his earnings home to help the rest of the family.

An example of best practice in the treatment of servants may be found in an account of their accommodation on the farm of a Member of Parliament, Mr Sotherton, written during 1849.[16] Mr Sotherton's farm lay in the south of England, where living-in service was in steep decline, and he was attempting to reverse this situation. He divided one of his barns into three apartments, comprising a dormitory with six beds, a washing room with a sink linked to the tank in the yard, and a dining hall based on one of the threshing floors. His servants came to him at sixteen years old and stayed either until they married, or left to become independent workers, and in the four years during which his scheme had been in place, no servant had been dismissed for any misconduct. Food was cooked for the boys by the bailiff's wife, who also did their washing, and the bailiff presided at meals, to which the servants were summoned by the ringing of a bell. Cleanliness and order at mealtimes were insisted upon, and prayers were read morning and evening. After work, the youths could amuse themselves by playing cricket or other games, reading and writing, or even playing the flute. Substitute 'schoolmaster' for 'bailiff', and the boys' pattern of living is surprisingly reminiscent of that to be found in an English public school in the mid-twentieth century.

The sixteen-year-olds were paid £4 a year on entry, and their wages gradually rose to £8 10s a year, while the average weekly cost of feeding them came to 5s 1½d each, a sum which covered the cost of bread, flour, butcher's meat, bacon, cheese, sugar, coffee, cocoa, rice and condiments, and included beer worth 1s. On this basis, the annual cost to Mr Sotherton of keeping a sixteen-year-old farm servant was £17 6s 6d, when an adult day labourer, if at work all year round, would have involved an expenditure of some £25 11s 5d a year in cash, excluding perquisites.[17]

Mr Sotherton's conversion of a barn to house his farm servants may have been exceptional, and his care for them represented a model rather than the norm. Certainly, the small farmers of Devonshire were more likely to accommodate their servants in the farmhouse itself, the boys sometimes sharing bedrooms with the farmers' sons, and the girls with their daughters, while the whole household would sit down together for meals. Nevertheless, the success or failure of the system of living-in service from the point of view of the individual taking up employment in this way depended largely on whether the master or mistress could be classed as a good or a bad employer. One Devonshire farmer described some of his fellows as being so mean that even a fried egg would be divided between two people.[18] Nor, according to evidence given to the Poor Law Commissioners in 1843, was it unusual for farmers to inflict corporal punishment on their young servants. No example of this has been found in Colyton itself, but if the beating or whipping was excessive, the employer could be brought up before the magistrates. The local press reported one such case from Tiverton in 1866, when the parents of a thirteen-year-old servant summoned the farmer who employed him. The youth had been put to drive two horses drawing a cart, but had lost control, so that the cart overturned. He was severely beaten by his master, who called him 'a mump-headed toad and a brute', but the magistrate, remarking that it was the man and not the boy who was a brute, imposed a fine on the employer.[19]

Just as domestic service drew in a number of girls from outside Colyton who had found it necessary to leave their own villages to earn their keep, so farm service attracted youths from other parishes. Six out of ten of the living-in farm servants under the age of majority in Colyton in 1851 had originated in other parishes within a ten-mile radius. However, their presence, and the attention given to service in husbandry as part of the upbringing of a section of Colyton's youth over many generations, must not obscure the fact that in 1851 the number of boys living-in on farms was counterbalanced by the similar number of young Colytonians working in agriculture but who were still at home with their parents. Then it must also be remembered that half the total workforce of boys in 1851 was made up of those who were earning a livelihood in crafts and trades, or in the local shops, the great majority of whom were also still with their families. Living-in service, whether on farms or elsewhere, accounted for only three out of ten of the working boys.[20]

As might be expected, a Colyton boy's prospects depended heavily on the class into which he was born. This not only affected how old he was likely to be when he started work, but also determined the age at which he would probably leave home, either to go to a living-in position elsewhere in Colyton, or to a job outside the parish. Movement of this nature was not of course special to Colyton, but had been widespread throughout the country for centuries past. In the Northampton village of Cogenhoe, for example, the most mobile group in the community in the early seventeenth century comprised the unmarried children working as servants in households other than their parents',[21] while in Cardington in Bedfordshire in 1782 only just over a fifth of the fifteen- to nineteen-year-old boys were still at home.[22] By looking at the life histories of boys who either stayed in Colyton, or left it independently of their parents, it is possible to estimate the ages at which these events usually occurred in the different social classes in the last half of the nineteenth century.[23]

There were 337 boys in Colyton who were under ten years of age in 1851. A decade later, four out of ten of these boys had left the parish, half of them going as part of a migrating family group, but the other half setting out on their own, leaving their parents behind. A study of the boys whose families remained in Colyton confirms the differences between the classes. There were only seven boys under the age of ten in the professional and landowning class in 1851, a number too small to be significant statistically, but although two appeared to have left home by their early teens, it is more than likely that they were at boarding-school when the 1861 census was taken, while a third, aged nineteen, who was with his parents, was in fact a medical student, visiting home on holiday. In this class, boys were likely to continue their education or professional training until they reached manhood. The larger number of sons of farmers and dairymen in general stayed at home, working on the family holding, until they were in a position to acquire a farm or dairy of their own, most frequently by renting it, an event which was unlikely to occur until they were well into their twenties. The boys of the business owners and better-off self employed did not usually leave their parents until they were at least sixteen years old, but from that age onwards, sons for whom there was no room in the family business or who were unable to find apprenticeships elsewhere in Colyton left home for good, to train or to gain work experience away from the parish. Youths whose parents were in the wage-earning class of craftsmen and tradesmen also tended to remain with their parents until late into their teens. It was among the labourers that the effects of economic necessity were most apparent. Parents in this group kept their boys at home up to and including the age of ten, but from then on the exodus began, with 40 per cent of the sons aged eleven and twelve leaving home, and no fewer than 70 per cent of the older boys, aged thirteen to nineteen, having gone away independently of their families. It might be thought that these young people in seeking work were following a nineteenth century injunction equivalent to the modern phrase 'on your bike'.

Leaving home did not necessarily mean leaving the parish, however, and some of these boys entered living-in farm service in Colyton, as has already been described, so links with their families could easily be maintained. In one case, a young son was a servant on the farm on which his father worked as a day-labourer. Given the extended nature of Colyton parish, children who went to farms in adjoining areas could well have been closer to their families than if they had been working at the other end of Colyton. Nor was the break from home necessarily final. Some boys returned to their parents' households when they were old enough to earn a man's wage, and stayed there until marriage.

The age at leaving home was not, of course, the same as the age at starting work. In all but the very small professional class, the majority of boys began to earn a living well before the break with their families occurred. More than half the sons of middling class fathers were employed or apprenticed by the time they were thirteen years old, three years before the usual age at which they left home. Boys in the wage-earning class began working even earlier, from the age of twelve, even though the majority stayed with their parents until they were eighteen; while just over a third of the sons of labourers were employed by the time they were ten years of age.

Early employment of both boys and girls is not to be wondered at in a society where, as will be seen in the next chapter, educational provision for those who could not afford to pay for it was scanty, to say the least. If a ten-year-old child from the working classes in the 1850s could not find employment, the most likely alternative for him or her was to remain at home the year round, most probably 'running wild' as the old phrase had it, while continuing to be a drain on the family resources.

Youth unemployment is a social problem of major concern today, particularly in relation to those in what is often referred to as the 'underclass'. It is difficult to assess the exact proportion of unemployed boys in Colyton 150 years ago, because although only two youths, aged seventeen and nineteen respectively, were described as out of work in the 1851 census, the column relating to occupation was left a blank for a number of other boys, and it is impossible to determine whether this was because the boy in question had no employment, or because the head of the household neglected to tell the enumerator that his son was working. However, omitting boys in the Colyford tything where occupations are known to have been grossly under-recorded, it is possible to say that eleven, or 15 per cent of all the fourteen- to twenty-year-old youths in the two poorest classes had no kind of employment recorded against their names in the 1851 census. Further investigation shows that at least two of these boys had good reason not to be working, as one of them was deaf and the other mentally handicapped, while two more may have been in indifferent health, for they died before 1861. If these four youths are discounted, the maximum proportion of unemployed poor boys aged fourteen to twenty years on the day the census was taken falls to one in ten of that whole age group, though the real ratio may have been less. It would be satisfactory if this figure could be directly set against the unemployment rate of 20.6 per cent for sixteen- to nineteen-year-old youths in 1996 given in *Social Trends*, 1997,[24] but unfortunately the differences between the two samples are too great for any useful comparison to be made. The figure for 1996, at double the maximum estimated youth unemployment rate in Colyton, covers the whole nation and so includes densely-populated inner-city areas, very different in character from a rural parish, while it also covers students in full-time further education who were seeking part-time work during the vacations. Indeed, it is suggested that half the 'unemployed' young people aged sixteen to nineteen fell into this category. These two factors alone make a comparison with Colyton in 1851 of little value.

Early death affected the boys and young men in Colyton to much the same extent as it did girls and young women, although without free access to the Registrar General's records, which give the cause of death, it cannot be known how many died as the result of illness, or what proportion of deaths was caused through accidents at work. Because migration from Colyton took place on a large scale, it is not possible to say how many of the seven- to twenty-year-old boys present in Colyton in 1851 died before they were thirty-one, because an unknown number of those migrating must also have died and been buried elsewhere. However, if only those boys who are known either to have survived to thirty-one years or to have died before that age are considered, it is true to say that 17 per cent of them were dead before they reached middle age, a proportion very similar to that of 18 per cent for girls and young women shown in the appendix.

Once again the death rate between the social classes varied, but while the main difference among the girls related to economic prosperity, with the boys it lay in their occupations. It was the sons of the middling class and their employees who had the highest early death rate, with more than one in four (21 per cent) dying before reaching thirty-one years of age, as against 13 per cent of boys and young men in the farming and labouring classes. It could be that the sicklier children of both sexes in Colyton, who were the most likely to die young, remained at home, so raising the death rate for those staying in the parish to a higher level than the national mortality rates for a similar age group.[25] However that may be, for those remaining in Colyton the high death rates represented reality and meant that the loss before they had reached middle age of sons or daughters, brothers or sisters, or friends, could never be discounted.[26]

Changes between 1851 and 1891

The various Education Acts described at the end of the last chapter had their effect on the proportion of boys at work in Colyton in 1891, but the resultant change was much less marked than it had been for the girls. This was because fewer boys than girls of ten years of age and under had been employed in 1851, and so a smaller number needed to be removed from the work place in order to go to school. In one respect, however, boys and girls alike had a shared experience. Both sexes suffered a decline in their major source of employment, that is to say lacemaking in the case of the girls and agriculture where the boys were concerned.

In 1851, almost half the seven- to twenty-year-old boys in Colyton who were in employment were working on the land, whether as sons or grandsons of farmers providing labour on the family holding, or as living-in farm servants, or as farm workers going to work daily from home. Forty years later, affected by two periods of depression and by an increase in mechanization, agriculture was able to employ only a third of the local male workforce under the age of majority.

One of the ways in which this situation was met in Colyton was through an increase in the allocation of what jobs were available on the land to the boys of the parish, rather than to outsiders coming in as part of the system of living-in service described earlier. While in 1851 boys from outside Colyton made up a quarter of the junior workforce on the farms, by 1891 they represented only 17 per cent of those youths working in agriculture. Nor did the decrease in employment of boys from outside Colyton lead to a corresponding decrease in living-in farm service, as might have been expected. In 1851, if farmers' sons and grandsons living at home are ignored, nearly half of all young farm workers were in living-in service. By 1891, this proportion had increased slightly to 54 per cent. Moreover, while in 1851 only 37.5 per cent of young living-in farm servants were Colytonians, the remainder being outsiders, by 1891 boys from within the parish occupied 53 per cent of the living-in posts. It could be that hard-pressed farmers continued to take young servants into their households on the grounds that they were cheaper than adult day-labourers, and under greater control than boys living at home and coming in to work for set hours would be; while the poor families from which these boys came may have been anxious for their sons to take the first job offer that came their way, rather than go looking for work further afield. Be that as it may, living-in farm service for the young was still flourishing in Colyton close to the turn of the century.

Where such a small population was concerned, it might be suggested that these apparent changes in the pattern of boys' employment in agriculture were the result of a statistical quirk, but a similar effect was apparent in relation to girls' employment. When the lacemaking industry collapsed, Colyton girls managed to find employment in domestic service within the parish, an area of work which in 1851 had been dominated by those coming in from outside. In

1851, under two out of every ten jobs in domestic service, whether in the town or on the farms, were held by Colytonians, but by 1891, their share of the much expanded domestic job market had increased to two-thirds, at the expense of girls from other parishes. Once again, it seems that Colyton looked after its own.

As agriculture declined in importance, so small businesses and service industries expanded. While in 1851 there were two doctors in Colyton, forty years later patients had a choice between four physicians and surgeons. Two of these medical men lived in a joint household and employed a butler – a new departure for the town. Two solicitors were to be found in 1891 where none had been present in 1851. Insurance agents, a shop run for the Society for the Promulgation of Christian Knowledge and other new enterprises had appeared. Boys under the age of majority were employed in a whole range of activities which had not been available forty years earlier. Basket-making, artists' brush-making, work in the telegraph office, pupil-teaching at the board school, selling sewing machines, gardening as part of a business which employed staff, flower-gathering, box-making, and acting as a coal merchant's agent were all new occupations for boys.

These employments, joined to the wide range of businesses already described in chapter 1, were evidence of an increasingly middle-class community. Although the total population of Colyton declined by 14 per cent between 1851 and 1891, the actual number of seven- to twenty-year-old boys in the three most prosperous classes of landowners and professional men, farmers, and business owners increased in real terms and remained almost static in the wage-earning class. It was the farm labourers who were forced out of the parish by the adverse conditions brought about through the agricultural depressions, and the number of their sons in the same age range declined by more than a quarter. For some of those who remained, however, the benefits of compulsory education, resulting in a spread of literacy and numeracy hitherto unknown in the poorest class, allowed them to leave farm work and other labouring jobs altogether, to take advantage of the expanding opportunities around them. By 1891, nearly half the sons of labourers in the juvenile workforce were employed in occupations other than agriculture or general labouring. The development of education, which made this possible, is the subject of the next chapter.

Notes

1. Those living in Colyford tything have again been omitted, here and throughout the chapter, because of under-registration of employment there by the 1851 census enumerator. Of the 302 boys aged seven to twenty in the rest of the parish, 152, or 50 per cent, were employed, compared to 200, or 62 per cent, of the 324 girls.

2.   In social classes I, II and III, 28 out of 87 boys aged seven to twenty, or 32 per cent, were
     employed in 1851, compared to 25 girls out of 102, or 25 per cent. In social classes IV and V,
     84 out of 175 boys, or 48 per cent, were at work, compared to 135 out of 180 girls, or 75 per
     cent. The workforce was increased by 40 boys and 40 girls coming into Colyton to work
     from elsewhere, whose parentage is not known. In addition, two incoming girls had no
     occupation.

3.   W.G. Hoskins, 'The farm-labourer through four centuries' in W.G. Hoskins and H.P.R.
     Finberg, eds, *Devonshire Studies*, London, 1952, p. 431.

4.   Only two nine-year-old boys were shown to be working on farms in Colyton in 1851, and
     both were living at home.

5.   R.S. Schofield, 'Age specific mobility in an eighteenth-century rural English parish' in P.
     Clark and D. Souden, eds, *Migration and Society in Early Modern England*, London,
     1987, pp. 256–9.

6.   J. Robin, *Elmdon. Continuity and change in a north-west Essex village, 1861–1964*,
     Cambridge, 1980, table 5, p. 21.

7.   The 152 working boys aged seven to twenty in 1851 were employed as follows:

	Total	
	No.	%
Agriculture: living-in farm servants, 32; living-out farm workers, 34;		
sons or grandsons of farmers, working on the family farms, 8	74	48.5
Apprentices to crafts or trades: living-in, 5; living at home, 13	18	12.0
Living-in journeymen	9	6.0
Workers in other occupations: living at home, 46; boarding or		
lodging, 5	51	33.5
Total	152	100.0

8.   P. Sharpe, 'Gender-specific demographic adjustment to changing economic circumstances,
     Colyton 1538–1837'. Unpublished PhD thesis, University of Cambridge, 1988, p. 217.

9.   C. Vancouver, *General view of agriculture of the county of Devon*, 1808, reprinted
     Newton Abbot, 1969, p. 360.

10. G. Mingay, *The Agricultural Revolution: changes in agriculture, 1650–1880*, London
     1977, pp. 200–201.

11. C. Vancouver, *The Agriculture of Devon*, 1969, pp. 359–61.

12. A. Kussmaul, *Servants in husbandry in early modern England*, Cambridge, 1981, p. 122.

13. P. Sharpe, 'Gender-specific demographic adjustment', 1988, pp. 268 and 292.

14. A. Kussmaul, *Servants in husbandry*, 1981, p. 122.

15. C. Vancouver, *The Agriculture of Devon*, 1969, p. 360.

16. Appearing in G.E. Mingay, *The Agricultural Revolution*, 1977, pp. 250–53.

17. This figure is based on the estimate of the cash wages of farm workers in the southern county of Hampshire, 1833–45, made by E.H. Hunt in 'Industrialization and regional inequality. Wages in Britain 1750–1914', *Journal of Economic History*, XLVI (4), table 6, p. 965.

18. M. Bouquet, *Family, Servants and Visitors: the farm household in nineteenth and twentieth century Devon*, Norwich, 1985 p. 76.

19. *Devon Weekly Times*, 23.3.1866.

20. See endnote 7.

21. P. Laslett, 'Clayworth and Cogenhoe' in H.E. Bell and R. Ollard, eds, *Historical essays, 1680–1750*, London, 1963, pp. 157–84.

22. R.S. Schofield, 'Age-specific mobility' in P. Clark and D. Souden, eds, *Migration and Society*, London 1987, p. 258.

23. A full account is given in J. Robin, *From childhood to middle age: cohort analysis in Colyton, 1851–1891*, Cambridge Group for the History of Population and Social Structure, Working Paper Series: no. 1, 1995, pp. 32–4 and tables 13 and 14.

24. *Social Trends*, 27, 1997, table 4.23, p. 84.

25. The national mortality rates for girls and boys aged ten to thirty in 1851 stood at 12 per cent and 13 per cent respectively. I am grateful to Jim Oeppen of the Cambridge Group for these figures, derived from R.A.M. Case et al., *The Chester Beatty Research Institute Serial Abridged Life Tables, 1841–1960*, part 1, London, 1962.

26. The relation between actual and perceived risks of death is discussed in D.S. Smith and J.D. Hacker, 'Cultural demography: New England deaths and the Puritan perception of risk', *Journal of Interdisciplinary History*, XXVI (3), 1995–1996, pp. 367–92.

Chapter 7

From Sunday School
to Universal Education

So far, the working lives of those under the age of majority have been examined, but educational provision has barely been touched upon. In this respect, the forty years from 1851 to 1891 were momentous ones in Colyton. They saw the transition from a time when there was no compulsion to attend any school in the parish, whether it be provided by the private sector, by the voluntary organisation of the Feoffees in the shape of their grammar school, or by the churches through their Sunday schools, to one where, following a series of Education Acts, elementary school attendance in 1891 was not only compulsory, but was available free of charge in a secular, non-denominational school run by the local authority through a school board elected by the parish ratepayers.

The freedom of parents to choose the school within the state system which they feel is best suited to their child has today become a political issue. In Colyton in 1851, choice for the better-off was governed by the size of the family income; for the poor, education depended very largely, though not entirely, on religious affiliation.

There were a number of schools in Colyton town in 1851 for those who could afford the fees and who were unable, or unwilling, to employ a governess to teach their children at home. At the bottom of the scale were the dame schools, similar to the one held in Mrs Chown's kitchen where the pupils sat round on small stools, as Samuel Seaward remembered when he took the imaginary walk around Colyton described in chapter 1.[1] Next came a large establishment directed by the Misses Betsy and Mary Seaward, which taught girls the three R's, fine arts and deportment throughout their schooldays[2] and also acted as a preparatory school for boys. This school included eighteen boarders, the boys ranging in age from four to eight years, and the girls from seven to thirteen , at the time when the 1851 census was taken. Forty years on the school was still in existence, under the name of Riversleigh House School, with the Misses Seawards' nephew and his wife acting as joint principals. A newspaper report describes how the pupils put on a Christmas entertainment at the end of term, featuring a play called 'Fairy Gifts' which demonstrated the triumph of virtue and humility, and the downfall of pride. This was followed by a programme of songs, and a mélange entitled 'Nurseryrhymia' which evoked tremendous applause from the audience.[3]

Boys moving on to other fee-paying establishments in the town in 1851 could join the school run by Mr Tett where, according to Samuel Seaward, much the same curriculum was followed as that in place at the Misses Seaward's school, with the difference that the teaching was reinforced by the use of the cane. Mr Tett combined his duties as a schoolmaster with those of Post Master for Colyton, and the post office occupied the partitioned-off front part of the schoolroom. In 1851, he had attracted four boarders, the eldest being fourteen years of age, in addition to his day-pupils.

A serious rival to Mr Tett appeared in 1850, in the shape of the Reverend David Lewis Evans, who was appointed as Colyton's Unitarian minister in that year. He arrived from Wales, having wound up the Bridgend Academy which he had been directing, and bringing some of his former pupils with him as boarders. On arrival in the town, he opened the Colyton Academy and during the eight or more years of its life, he taught at least twenty-one Colyton boys, as well as a number of others coming from afar. It is likely that the curriculum in his school was the broadest available in the parish, because when he left Colyton in December 1863, it was to take up the Chair of Hebrew and Mathematics at his old Presbyterian College at Caermarthen.[4]

These opportunities were beyond the reach of the poor. There was, however, one free day-school for boys in Colyton, namely the Feoffees' grammar school which by 1851 had been in existence for over 300 years. This school provided two or three years' education for up to thirty boys. In March 1851 there were twenty-seven scholars on its books, drawn from all walks of life with the exception of the landowning and professional class, but the majority of the pupils were from the families of the two poorest groups of wage-earning craftsmen and tradesmen, and labourers.

The master of the grammar school, the genial Mr Stirling, was remembered by Samuel Seaward as sitting with his feet up on his desk during the boys' playtime, a mug of cider in his hand while he smoked his pipe. If this description does something to destroy the image which the term 'grammar school' conjures up today, then to learn of the curriculum in force in the 1850's may complete the disillusionment. Reading, writing and arithmetic were the only subjects to figure in the school examinations, which Mr Stirling carried out at frequent intervals. His comments against the names of individual pupils rarely concerned academic progress from one term to the next, but were usually confined to remarks on attendance and general behaviour. 'Careless, inattention [sic] and attendance irregular', he wrote of one boy, and 'Very backward, to be tried for one month longer', of another. He also noted that J. Sweetland, aged nine and a quarter, had left the school in consequence of having found work. The attendance record shows that boys were often absent in order to perform tasks such as apple-picking or potato-harvesting. The whole school was given three weeks' holiday over the grain harvest so that the boys could go gleaning. Nor does it seem that potential pupils were always clamouring for admission to the school. In September 1851 Mr Stirling recorded the somewhat dictatorial decision of the Feoffees that 'There being no candidates for entry into the School, it is resolved that those boys who have been already two years in the School are to remain until candidates offer'. At this time, enrolment was down to twenty-four pupils.[5]

The grammar school, even when full, could only take a fraction of Colyton's most needy boys. In March 1851 it was educating nineteen scholars from the two poorest classes, the youngest being seven years of age, and the eldest, eleven. Yet the census, taken in the same month, shows that there were 101 boys from these classes who were within the same age group living in the parish. Educationally, the girls were in an even worse state, because the free grammar school was for boys only. It is of course possible, as suggested in an earlier chapter, that lace girls were taught to read the Bible, and perhaps to write, in their lace schools, although it is not clear whether this was the case in Colyton. The great majority of parents who wished their children to receive an education but could not afford to pay for it had to look for help to the Sunday schools run by the various religious groups. These schools were in practice very different from those of today, although then, as now, their motivation was religious.

The Sunday School Movement was founded in the late eighteenth century by Robert Raikes in order to teach reading, the catechism and the Christian life style, and as time went on, some schools added lessons in writing, spelling and even arithmetic.[6] By the early years of the nineteenth century, however, the Evangelicals, whether Methodist, Congregationalist or low church adherents of the Church of England, began to question this broadening of the curriculum. They felt that although reading was an accomplishment which was absolutely necessary for Bible study, the other subjects did nothing to promote man's salvation, and so constituted 'work', which profaned the Lord's day instead of keeping it holy. This granted, the evangelicals considered it not only permissible, but desirable, that writing should be taught in weekday evening classes.[7]

Whatever the curriculum, in practice Sunday school children had a long day in front of them. It was usual for the morning session to begin at nine or nine-thirty, and classes started again at two in the afternoon. In the average school, there would be an infants' class for children between three and six years of age, an ordinary class for the six- to fourteen-year-olds, divided into sections according to their ability to read, and a senior class for persons of fifteen and over.[8]

A very popular teaching aid for those learning to read was a box containing moveable letters. These would be used to set up a verse from the Bible in a rack attached to the underside of the lid, and the verse would then be repeated until it was impressed on the children's minds – an early version of the 'look and say' method of teaching reading.[9]

Improving tracts were also used. One such, printed in 1840, was entitled 'The Dying Christian entering the World of Glory', while another, produced earlier in the century, went through the alphabet, with a verse or verses printed beneath each letter. But instead of the innocuous 'D for Dog' which today's pupil might encounter, the nineteenth-century Sunday-school child would learn that D stood for Death, and read the verses:

> I look upon the letter D
> And quickly draw my breath;
> For solemn is the thought it brings,
> The day and hour of Death.

> However young, fail not to keep
> Thy latter end in view;
> If ought be certain in thy life
> Death is as certain too ...

The verse below the letter E followed the same theme, for in this tract, E stood for Eternity.[10]

Before dismissing this approach as morbid, it should be remembered that unlike today, the early death of a brother or sister was a common experience in the nineteenth century. It has already been shown that child mortality occurred in all classes in Colyton, and that on average at least one boy or girl for each family in the two poorest classes died before reaching the age of seven. The emphasis on death in some of the Sunday school literature, followed by the promise of eternal life for the Christian, may have been an attempt to meet the emotional stress caused by these tragedies, just as nowadays children are often offered counselling if one of their schoolfellows dies.

However gloomy such a Sunday school may appear to young people today, it did present an opportunity to children who may have been idle throughout the week at least to learn to read, and possibly to write. In addition there were the Sunday school treats to look forward to, of the kind enjoyed by Colyton children which have already been described in chapter 3, while rewards were given for good attendance. These were usually in the form of tiny pictorial reward books, costing the school a farthing each. More expensive books, such as *The Dairyman's Daughter* at 1d, or *The History of Little George and his Penny* at 2d, were also given as prizes.[11]

The importance of the Sunday schools in combating illiteracy is confirmed by the 1851 census, which shows that nationally they contained more scholars than did all the day-schools put together, while in the Axminster district of which Colyton was a part there were 2,281 scholars in public and private day schools, compared to 2,551 children in Sunday schools. Two-thirds of these Sunday scholars were in schools run by the Church of England.[12]

In Colyton, the National Society for Promoting the Education of the Poor in the Principles of the Established Church, with the help of public subscriptions, built a two-storey Sunday school close to the church, which was free to all children and opened its doors in 1835.[13] Even in 1863, by which time a day school had become available, it still had 250 scholars on its roll.[14] The Unitarians and Independents also ran Sunday schools for their own adherents.

Such was the educational provision in Colyton in 1851. The census shows that just over a third of the girls in the parish who were aged from three to fourteen years were receiving some kind of education, while the proportion of boys in the same range who were recorded as scholars was rather higher, standing at 45 per cent. If only those children in the two poorest classes are considered, however, the proportion of girls listed as scholars fell to just under a quarter, because so many were already working as lacemakers. The boys did rather better, with nearly four out of ten being educated in some way.[15] However, schooldays were in any case short, even the grammar school keeping its pupils for three years at the most, so some of those children shown as being of no occupation in the census may have been at school before 1851, or have attended after that year.

It is difficult to assess how successful the education available in 1851 was in improving the material fortunes of those receiving it. As far as the private sector was concerned, a published list of the Reverend David Evans' pupils from the parish over the short life of the Colyton Academy shows that in the great majority of cases boys on leaving school followed a similar course to the one taken by their fathers. Farmers' sons remained working in agriculture, and tradesmen's sons in trade. One exception was Albert Edwards, who may have been an orphan as he spent his childhood in the household of his uncle, a shoemaker. Although Albert became a shoemaker in his turn, and remained one at least until 1881, by 1891 he had broken away from the business and was supporting himself by a variety of part-time jobs, including those of organist, parish clerk, assistant overseer, and bailiff to the Feoffees,[16] in all of which it was an advantage to be an educated man.

The careers of the class of 1851 at the grammar school followed a very similar pattern. Although more than half the boys who can be traced had either left Colyton or died before the 1861 census was taken, those who remained showed the same propensity either to follow exactly the same type of work as their fathers, or in two cases, to enter a different trade but one of similar standing. However, two boys whose fathers were wage-earning tradesmen became labourers.

When considering the two poorest classes as a whole, probably the best way to assess the efficacy of their education after the custom-built Church of England Sunday school opened in 1835 is to examine the parish register of marriages between 1861 and 1870, with a view to finding out what proportion of men and women marrying were literate or illiterate. This investigation shows that of forty-two poor Colyton men who had spent their childhood in the parish, and who were under thirty years of age so that all would have had the opportunity to attend the new Sunday school, 55 per cent could sign their names, even though some signatures were written in a distinctly shaky hand, but 45 per cent could not. The proportion of the fifty-eight poor women fulfilling the same conditions who were able to sign their names was slightly higher, standing at 60 per cent, but even so, four out of ten had to make a cross. It would appear that much needed to be done if the population as a whole was to be raised even to semi-literacy.

A step towards improving educational facilities was taken when Mamerto Gueritz became Vicar of Colyton in 1860. Within months of his arrival he was asking the chamber of the Feoffees for help towards the maintenance and support of a Church of England day-school to be established under government authority. The chamber generously donated £40 towards building costs, with the promise of an annual subvention of £10 towards the master's salary.[17] As so often happened in Colyton, however, nothing went smoothly. This was the school that the Unitarian minister had advised his congregation to boycott, on the grounds that it was run by Puseyite priests, and a week after the chamber agreed their donation, a Feoffee and three Twentymen, two of whom were prominent Unitarians, protested against the decision, considering that there was no need for a new school as existing provision was sufficient, while in any case the Feoffees possessed the power to enlarge their own school if it were necessary to do so.[18] However, the new day-school opened in the Sunday school rooms, and its intake built up to some 140 pupils.[19] A further attempt by dissident chamber members to stop the annual grant to the school was defeated two years later.[20]

Meanwhile there were also changes in the Feoffees' own school. Mr Stirling, the cider-drinking master, died in post in 1863 at the age of seventy-two years, and was replaced by Mr Tett, who had previously been running his own private school. Mr Tett's contract is of some interest in showing his financial standing compared to those in other occupations. He was to be paid £37 10s a year, and given the use of part of the Feoffees' house, in return for teaching twenty-five boys nominated by the Feoffees. Out of his salary he agreed to provide 'a fair and proper quantity of pens, paper, copy books and ciphering books' for the pupils, and he was also made financially responsible for replacing any windows which might be broken in the school house.[21] He was certainly better off than the average farm labourer, whose cash income of 8s a week exclusive of harvest payments and subsidized or free housing came to £20 8s a year,[22] but both the police constable on £59 8s a year and perquisites,[23] and a wage-earning mason on £57 2s a year,[24] were better off than he was. It is noteworthy that his unmarried sister, who had been living with him until his death, herself died in the workhouse.

The Education Act of 1870 provided that England should be divided into districts, and that elementary schools should be set up where school provision was insufficient. At the written request of at least fifty ratepayers, school boards could be elected by all ratepayers to act much as school governors do nowadays.[25]   In Colyton such a request to turn the Church day-school into a board school was made in 1874, and the search for a new site began.

Once again, the parish was riven by dissension. The school board, whose members were predominantly Unitarian, bought a property for the considerable sum of £785, in spite of a ratepayers' meeting held in July 1875, at which protests were made against the purchase, and a resolution was put forward to the effect that the price to be paid was excessive, that there would be further heavy costs, and that the site was unhealthy. Two Unitarians put forward an amendment that the site was a desirable one, but the chairman put neither the resolution nor the amendment to the vote, and the meeting broke up 'in the greatest tumult and disorder'. Even as late as 1880, allegations of what would today be called 'sleaze' were being made, with the vicar and churchwardens issuing posters claiming that the church would have provided land for £80 instead of the £785 spent, and that voters in the current school board elections were being coerced.[26]

Posters and billboards appeared all over the parish with claims and counter-claims from the two sides, but in spite of all the difficulties, the school was built on the site where the present day county primary school stands, and state education arrived in Colyton, being reinforced by the Education Act of 1876 which established the principle that all children should receive elementary education.

Unfortunately, the official records of the Colyton school board have not survived, but even a small number of press reports describing its meetings show that almost from the start the school faced many of the problems that beset education in the 1990s.

Shortage of teachers is a common complaint nowadays, yet in January 1879, the board was asked to cancel the indentures of a pupil-teacher at the school who was suffering from ill health brought on by overstudying, while the headmistress complained of lack of staff.[27]   A month later, the board was able to appoint an assistant mistress, brought in from Market Drayton in Shropshire, at a salary of £40 a year, but this new appointment coincided with the resignation of another pupil-teacher, so numerically the teaching situation did not improve.[28]

Examinations were also a worry. At the same meeting, the schoolmistress reported that eighty-eight of her pupils were being entered for examination, but that the list included 'a large number of dunces', so that a higher proportion of failures must be expected on that account, as well as because of under-staffing.[29]

School finances, too, were a problem then as they are today. The board school was supported by a government grant based on a capitation fee, which in turn depended on the attendance records of the children. At its meeting in June 1881, the board learnt that the headmistress had resigned, following the discovery by the Education Department that she had falsified the attendance figures in order to acquire a larger grant for the school. As a result, a considerable reduction in the next year's subvention was expected. To meet this, one member of the board suggested that £25 a year could be saved if an assistant mistress were to be removed, but as the capitation fee would decrease by 2s a head if the infants were taught by a pupil-teacher rather than an assistant mistress, the rest of the board rejected his proposal.[30]

A week or two later the board received HM Inspector's report on the school, and learned that the headmistress's certificate to teach was to be suspended for a year, while any irregularities of registration would in future be punished by a reduction in the grants. As it was, the government would provide £87 2s for the boys' section of the school, and £65 11s for the girls. At this time, an average of 92 boys, 61 girls and 41 infants were being taught.[31]

Government grants were not the only source of income for the school, because although children were legally bound to attend, they also had to pay a weekly fee to do so. It is not known what the charge in Colyton was, but it was likely to lie between 1d and 3d a week for each child. This was particularly hard on the poor who were in regular employment, because they had to find the money from their already tight budgets, while after the 1870 Education Act, those receiving parish relief were given an extra allowance of up to 3d a week per child to pay the fee.[32]

Such financial pressure led some parents to keep their children at home, and persistent truancy became a problem for the authorities, not only because of its effect on the offender's education, but also because it was relevant to the cash flow of the school through its effect on the capitation fees.

The method used to combat truancy was to place responsibility for a child's attendance directly upon the parents. A School Attendance Officer was employed on a part-time basis to track down absentees, and if necessary to go to the magistrates to secure an attendance order to be served on the truant's parents. At one sitting of petty sessions in 1879, George Crabb was summoned for failing to respond to an order to send his two children to school. His wife appeared in court on his behalf, and told the magistrates that she could not afford to pay the fees. The law being the law, the magistrates fined her, but set the sum at 1d, although she had to find the far more substantial amount of 4s for costs. At the same sitting, the magistrates were asked to serve attendance orders on William Long, Thomas West, John Hoare and William Restorick to compel them to send their children to school. Mrs. Restorick was in court to contest the application, saying that one of her children was not well, and the other, now twelve years old, had been put out to earn something. The Chairman of the Bench remarked that it was impolitic to require the attendance of a twelve-year-old capable of earning, but nevertheless the order was made.[33]

It was difficult for poor parents, who had received little or no education themselves and who had started their working lives as young as seven years old in the case of the lacemakers, to accept that, following the 1880 Education Act, they must pay for their children to stay at school in all cases until they were ten years old, and even longer if they had not passed Standard IV, which was then the acceptable school-leaving examination. The board school log book for girls in 1880 shows that girls under ten years of age, as well as some who were older but had not passed Standard IV, were working in the lace manufactory. They were quickly traced, and made to return to school.[34] It was not until the 1890 Education Act was passed that elementary education became free.

Short-term absence from school was a different matter, and was accepted as inevitable in a parish where agriculture was a major industry. In 1876, the log book for boys recorded on 5 May that many children had been away during the week, their parents requiring their help in the gardens. In June it was hay-making that reduced attendances, and in late October, gathering apples and potatoes. In harmony with the Feoffees' grammar school, the board school timed the summer holidays to coincide with the grain harvest.

It appears, then, that problems facing present-day schools of staff shortages, league tables depending on examination results, lack of resources, and truancy were all present to some degree in Colyton almost from the start of compulsory education. There is even an example of a confrontation between parent and teacher over a pupil. The school board received a complaint from a father that his boy had been improperly treated by the master. The board held that the facts showed the boy to be very violent, and the nature of his punishment to have been greatly exaggerated. As a result of the enquiry, the parent agreed to resume sending his boy to school.[35] Bad behaviour outside class was also recorded. When boys ran over Mr Strawbridge's garden during the dinner break, he brought the town's policeman to the school to warn the boys of the consequences of repeating their actions, providing an early example of the newly fashionable policy of zero tolerance.[36]

The subjects taught in the board school were reading, writing, spelling, arithmetic and singing, a syllabus very similar to that of the Feoffees' grammar school before the board school came into existence.[37] The Feoffees were therefore faced with the problem of how to differentiate their school from the one provided by the state. Their opportunity came in 1875, when Mr Tett resigned as master, probably on the grounds of ill health, as he died six months later. The grammar school pupils were temporarily dispatched to the board school, while the Feoffees approached the Endowed School Commissioners with a view to establishing a public school of as high a class as the commissioners might think fit. As a result, six months later the Feoffees resolved that the school should be re-established as a day- and boarding-school, to give a good education to six scholarship boys, and to the sons of parish residents whose parents were ready to pay 4 guineas a year. Latin and French were added to the curriculum, thus differentiating the grammar school from the board school. Other things being equal, preference would be given to a graduate as master. By August, the post had been advertised, and sixty-five applications were received. Eleven candidates were interviewed, at some cost as their rail fares were paid by the Feoffees, and from these the Reverend H.J. Dodwell from Brighton was elected.[38]

The trials faced by the school board when the headmistress falsified the attendance figures were as nothing compared to the tribulations heaped on the Feoffees as a result of their unfortunate choice of applicant. Soon after his appointment, Mr Dodwell was seen drunk at the Colcombe Castle Hotel, bringing on himself 'the contempt and derision of persons there present'. In school, he laid about him with the cane, flogging and otherwise cruelly mistreating not only the free boys, but the fee-paying ones as well. He neglected his teaching duties, and closed the school to certain boys. As a result, while the school opened on 31 January 1876 with eleven pupils, to whom another was added soon afterwards, bringing the total to twelve, five months later only one intrepid boy remained. In addition to all these misdemeanours, Mr Dodwell resolutely refused either to resign, or to sign his contract with the Feoffees unless it included a clause that he should not be dismissed except for reasonable cause.[39]

Clearly the Feoffees had to be rid of Mr Dodwell. After consulting the Charity Commissioners and their lawyers, they resolved to dismiss him from 24 June, paying him £40, his salary to that date, and requiring him to vacate the school house immediately. Unfortunately, Mr Dodwell refused to go, and indeed stayed on for a further five and a half months until he was finally ejected after a law suit which resulted in the Master of the Rolls finding against him. Even this did not end the matter, because Mr Dodwell appealed against the judgement, involving the Feoffees in further costs. Indeed, the total of the solicitors' fees incurred amounted to nearly half the trust's annual income, and so for a time severely restricted their expenditure on more desirable causes.[40]

In spite of this reverse, in January 1877 the grammar school reopened, this time with twelve scholarship boys. The Feoffees had no wish to risk repeating their former mistake, and chose a candidate whom they knew to be respectable as master. He was the Reverend José Gueritz, the vicar's son, but even so, the Feoffees insisted that he signed his contract with them before taking up his post. He stayed for only eighteen months, but the next incumbent, the Reverend James Fowler who was a graduate of King's College, Cambridge, remained at the school until 1887. It was during his tenure that the free places were abolished, and the school became open only to fee-paying pupils, although subsidized by the Feoffees through a capitation fee paid for scholars living in the parish.[41]

School inspections were carried out by Dr Dangar of the Exeter Training College in 1889 and 1890, by which time Mr MacKaig had become master. The reports show that Mr MacKaig was teaching thirty-five boys of different ages and abilities not only the basic reading, writing, spelling and arithmetic, but Latin, French, geography, history, religious knowledge, English grammar, algebra and Euclid, and drawing. The inspector was greatly impressed by Mr MacKaig's work, as well he might be, but recommended that an assistant master be appointed, as it was impossible for one man to attend to more than two divisions at a time, and the age range of the pupils meant that several divisions were needed if all pupils were to receive the basic grounding that they needed. As it was, Latin and French were being better taught than elementary reading. In spite of the favourable reports, however, the Feoffees rejected Mr MacKaig's request for an increase in his salary, nor did they grant him an assistant immediately.[42]

As a postscript, the further history of the grammar school is of some interest. In 1924, the County Educational Committee suggested that the school should become an endowed secondary school under county control, catering for pupils not only from Colyton but from a wider area. The Feoffees agreed to this proposal, new buildings were erected on a site in Colyford, and in 1927 the state-controlled Colyton grammar school came into being, although the Feoffees were and are still represented on the Board of Governors.[43] In 1996 the school, now selective, and taking students of both sexes from eleven to eighteen years of age, held the leading place in the league table of all Devonshire schools, and came twenty-eighth of all state schools in the country in its A-level results – a far cry from the days of Mr Dodwell.[44]

Notes

1.   S. Seaward. 'Old Colyton. What it was like ninety years ago. A stroll through the streets with a native'. Reminiscences of Mr Samuel Seaward, dictated to his son, Mr Basil Seaward, and kindly made available by the Reverend David Gunn-Johnson, team rector of Colyton.

2.   Ibid.

3.   *Devon Weekly Times* (hereinafter *D.W.T.*) 24.12.1886.

4.   G.E. Evans, *Colytonia: A chapter in the history of Devon*, Liverpool, 1898, pp. 39–43.

5.   Devon Record Office (hereinafter D.R.O.), F 17/14.

6.   P. Cliff, *The Rise and Development of the Sunday School Movement in England, 1780–1980*, Redhill, 1986, p. 7.

7.   Ibid., p. 78.

8.   Parliamentary Papers, 1851 Census of Great Britain, *Population*, HMSO, 1854, reprinted Shannon, 1970, vol. 11, pp. lxxi–lxxix.

9.   P. Cliff, *The Sunday School Movement*, 1986, p. 152.

10. Ibid., pp. 158–159.

11. Ibid., p. 153.

12. Parliamentary Papers, 1851 Census of Great Britain, *Population*, reprinted Shannon, 1970, vol. 11, pp. 250–51.

13. R. Bovett, *Historical Notes on Devon Schools*, Exeter, 1989.

14. *Report of the Commissioners on Children's Employment*, 1863 HC vol. XVIII, pp. 251–2.

15. The census enumerators for Colyton parish made no distinction between 'scholar' and 'Sunday scholar', although parents were instructed to record their children as 'scholars' only if they were above five years old and daily attending school, or receiving regular tuition under a master or governess at home. (E. Higgs, *Making Sense of the Census*, PRO Handbook no. 23, HMSO, 1989, p. 83). It is evident that this rule was not followed in Colyton, because a number of three- and four-year-olds from poor families were listed as scholars. The assumption must be that they were Sunday scholars. Children from the Colyford tything, where the enumerator failed to record their occupations adequately, and those coming in to Colyton to work from outside the parish, have been omitted from the sample.

16. G.E. Evans, *Colytonia*, p. 43.

17. D.R.O., F 17/8, 3.1.1861.

18. Ibid., F 17/8, 9.1.1861.

19. Communication from the Reverend David Gunn-Johnson.

20. D.R.O., F 17/8 25.2.1863.

21. Ibid., 10.2.1863.

22. Parliamentary Papers L, HMSO, 1861, p. 589.

23. D.R.O., 3483 A/PC4. Minute book of the Inspectors of Police, Colyton, 19.1.1854.

24. *D.W.T.*, 15.5.1874.

25. J. Richardson, *The Local Historian's Encyclopedia*, New Barnet, 1974, F4 and B244.

26. D.A. Gunn-Johnson, 'A Country Catholic: a study of the emergence of the Oxford Movement in an East Devon Parish'. Unpublished thesis accepted for the Archbishop of Canterbury's MA degree, December 1994, pp. 193–4.

27. *D.W.T.*, 24.1.1879.

28. *Honiton and Ottery Weekly News and General Advertiser*, 22.2.1879.

29. Ibid.

30. *D.W.T.*, 24.6.1881.

31. Ibid., 1.7.1881.

31. Ibid., 1.7.1881.

32. W.H. Dumsday, *Haddon's Relieving Officer's Handbook*, London, 1902, p. 54.

33. *D.W.T.*, 27.6.1879.

34. Colyton Board School Log Book for Girls, 1880, held in Colyton Primary School.

35. *D.W.T.*, 20.5.1881.

36. Colyton Board School Log Book for Boys, held in Colyton Primary School, 8.3.1878.

37. *D.W.T.*, 1.7.1881.

38. D.R.O., F 17/8, 4.1.1875, 16.7.1875, 12.8.1875, 13.8.1875, 17.9.1875.

39. Ibid., 20.3.1876, 22.3.1876, 5.5.1876, 26–31.5.1876, 8–16.6.1876.

40. Ibid., 20.6.1876, 14.11.1876, 11.12.1876, 16.11.1877.

41. Ibid., 13.1.1877, 17.7.1879, 4.11.1884.

42. D.R.O., F 17/9, 14.1.1890, 9.12.1890, 17.3.1891.

43. R.G. White, *The History of the Feoffees of Colyton 1546–1946*, Bridport, 1951.

44. *The Times*, Schools Report, 20.11.1996.

Chapter 8

Sex before Marriage

With childhood left behind them, the young people of Colyton entered the period of their lives when finding permanent partners of the opposite sex became of major importance. Unlike many couples today, they did not set up house together until after their wedding. Nevertheless, the majority of them had no hesitation in experiencing sex before marriage, and only entered into matrimony when it was clear that a baby was on the way.

Evidence for this is to be found in the records of the Church of England and the Nonconformist groups, which give the date on which a couple married, and the date when their first child was baptized, or in a few cases, born.[1] When the time between marriage and baptism was less than nine months, it may be assumed that the baby was conceived out of wedlock.[2] In Colyton between 1851 and 1881,[3] just over half of all the first-born children who were christened fell into this category, as against just under half who were baptized more than nine months after their parents' wedding, and who may therefore have been conceived after marriage.[4]

Sex before the wedding was nothing new in Colyton, or indeed in the country at large, but by 1849, well into Queen Victoria's reign, it had reached a higher level than at any period since the mid-sixteenth century.[5] In Colyton itself, from 1550 onwards the proportion of children conceived before marriage, set against all first-born children, never fell below 22 per cent in any one fifty-year period, and between 1800 and 1849 it rose to 44 per cent.[6] The further rise between 1851 and 1891 to 52 per cent may seem astonishing to those who still believe that in Victorian times a rigid rule of sexual behaviour was in operation throughout the country, and that transgression of that rule resulted in loss of respectability, but it does make it appear that the ideal of chastity before marriage was of little relevance to a large number of people in Colyton.

It has been suggested that some, indeed most, premarital pregnancies occurred when the process of marriage was very long drawn out. In other cases, 'shot-gun' weddings may have been brought about by the intervention of parents or other authorities. Some women may have become pregnant deliberately in order to trap a husband, or some men may have wanted to be sure of the fertility of their future wives, particularly if they owned property which they wished to hand down to the next generation.[7] This last suggestion is often put forward by members of the general public as the most compelling reason for sex before marriage in earlier centuries. A closer investigation of the couples marrying between 1851 and 1881, whether or not their first-born children were conceived before marriage, may show how far these suggested causes governed their behaviour.

Numerically, the couples marrying in Colyton between 1851 and 1881 were almost evenly divided between those who waited for a pregnancy to occur before legalizing their relationship, and those who avoided conception until after marriage. This division, however, did not run equally through all the social classes. There were no known cases of pregnancy before marriage in the professional and landowning class, although the number of bridegrooms in this group was too small to be statistically significant; while only one in five of the bridegrooms who were business owners married women who were pregnant when the ceremony took place, a figure which was well below the average for the community as a whole. Yet these were the men who were most likely to be owners of houses and land, and who, if fertility testing in relation to property inheritance really affected behaviour on a large scale, could be expected to be responsible for a higher rather than a lower rate of premarital conceptions than average. It seems more likely that they were indeed influenced by conventional ideas of respectability, which put a brake on those who might otherwise contemplate intercourse before marriage. For instance, there is evidence that one of the small number of bridegrooms in this group who indulged in premarital sex made some effort to conceal the fact. He was not only a linen and woollen draper owning house property in Colyton, but also a trustee of the Unitarian George's meeting house. His first-born child was conceived some three months before his marriage to a middle-aged schoolmistress, and was presented for baptism unusually late, eleven months after the birth, whereas his second child was baptised when two months old. It is even possible, though by no means certain, that this was an example of a 'shot-gun' marriage.

However, the professional and landowning class and the business owners between them contained only 8 per cent of the bridegrooms. The great majority were in the other three social groups, that is to say the farmers and dairymen, the wage-earning craftsmen and tradesmen, and the labourers, and in all these groups premarital pregnancies equalled or outnumbered first conceptions after marriage.

The farming class were responsible for the highest proportion of premarital pregnancies. Here more than six out of every ten first-born children had been conceived before marriage. Yet there were no easily recognisable divisions among the farmers which might help to explain why they behaved as they did, since both large and small farmers were to be found amongst those responsible for premarital pregnancies, and those who were not. Moreover, in the cases where the form of landholding can be traced, it has been found that all but one of the farms were tenanted, not owned. The sole known owner-occupier married before his first child was conceived, thus lending no credence to the theory that premarital pregnancies were the result of fertility testing in cases where property, in the sense of real estate, existed to be handed down to the next generation.

If the farmers inclined towards sex before marriage, it can be no surprise that the labouring class, nearly all of whom worked on the land, were responsible for the second highest proportion of premarital pregnancies, with 56 per cent of their first-born children falling into this category. They were closely followed by the wage-earning craftsmen and tradesmen, half of whom married wives who had conceived outside wedlock. In a low-wage economy, economic differences within these two groups were small, and no bridegroom coming from them owned land or house property when they married, while none rented accommodation of sufficient value to qualify them to appear on the Register of Electors.[8] To these men, fertility testing in relation to the transfer of property to a younger generation was an irrelevance.

There are, however, other possible motives for fertility testing, the importance of which is harder to prove or disprove. For example, some men may have been strongly influenced by a natural desire to found a family, but evidence of this kind of attitude is almost impossible to obtain. Again, it could be suggested that children were so important in providing economic support to their parents that it was essential to ensure that a prospective wife was not barren. Certainly the ability to have children has been of fundamental importance in certain countries in the Far East, such as Taiwan, where at least until the end of the Second World War the poorest classes depended on child labour from an early age to add to the family income, and adult children ensured that their parents were supported in old age. In that society, however, welfare payments from the state did not yet exist, and the family provided the only safety net in times of difficulty.[9] However, in Colyton, as in the rest of the country, childless individuals who were past work had since the middle of the sixteenth century been supported, if only to a minimum standard, by the Poor Law. In addition, by the second half of the nineteenth century, a large number of children were more likely to be a financial burden than an asset, particularly after the decline of lacemaking and the introduction of compulsory education with its attendant obligation to pay school fees, until the 1890 Education Act released parents from this necessity.

It is worth noting that the financial difficulties caused by a large family were recognised by the Guardians of the Poor for Axminster district, within which Colyton lay. In 1856 they resolved that, in addition to the 2s 6d payable when a poor woman was confined, they would grant extra relief in the form of two loaves weekly for one month to 'the person whose wife has had three children and is confined for the fourth; and four loaves for one month to be given to each person who has had four children all under ten years of age, and is confined for the fifth'.[10] Joseph Arch, the founder of the first trades union for agricultural workers, reported that when he was a ploughboy in the 1840s he earned 3s a week, but that this was not sufficient to support him, let alone buy clothes, and it was only because his mother added to his father's wages by working as a laundress that the family could keep going.[11] It therefore seems unlikely that a large family would be associated with material well-being in the minds of Colyton's poorest classes.

Economic considerations, then, probably played little part in influencing the behaviour of the majority of Colyton's men and women in relation to sex before marriage. It could, however, be suggested that a predilection towards premarital pregnancy might run in families, but the facts do not support this theory either. If all the sets of two or more brothers to be found among the bridegrooms are investigated, it appears that in two-thirds of these sets at least one brother was responsible for a conception before marriage, while another was not. A very similar result occurs for the sets of sisters to be found amongst the brides. Nor did the social position of the brides differ from those of their bridegrooms to any great extent. Exceptions to the rule may always be found, but two-thirds of the brides and grooms were of similar social standing both in the group where the bride was pregnant when she married, and in the group where she was not, while the proportions of men marrying above or below their own class were little different in either group.[12]

However, there was one respect in which the men who engaged in sex before marriage may be distinguished from those who did not, and that was their age. The bridegrooms who married after their first child had been conceived were markedly younger than those who delayed conception until after the wedding had taken place.[13] It might therefore be thought that the older men, who married later, chose not to risk a premarital conception, with a resultant earlier marriage, because they positively wanted to limit the size of their families, and therefore their economic burden while their children were young, by taking a wife of a similar age to themselves who consequently had a shorter period of fertility ahead of her. Once again, the facts do not support this explanation. The majority of both younger and older bridegrooms took their wives from the younger age groups, so that both sets of fathers were likely to have a similar number of children to rear. Adult wages did not increase with age, so that a young, fully-trained adult worker earned the same as an older man doing the same type of work. As the brides of both younger and older bridegrooms largely came from the same age group, and so were likely to have a similar fertility span, the men who married when they were older derived little economic advantage from waiting longer before marriage, except in so far as they had been able to make savings from their earnings while they were single.

It may be asked what it was, then, that made one brother engage in intercourse before marriage, while another did not. The answer seems to lie simply in individual choice. Marriage, of course, is not just a question of legalized sex. It carries with it moral as well as legal responsibilities, and in the nineteenth century divorce was not an easy option for the great majority of people. Men of a certain temperament might well agree with the old adage 'marry in haste, repent at leisure', while others, and their partners, were prepared to take the risk incurred in enjoying sexual intercourse, at a time when birth-control methods were not widely used, for as long as possible without the responsibility of a home and family, but on the understanding that when it was absolutely clear that a child was on the way, marriage would take place. This is borne out by the fact that the bride was at least three months pregnant before the wedding ceremony in nearly seven out of ten of the premarital pregnancies. The evidence would suggest that most men and women had a free choice between risking a premarital pregnancy, and therefore having to settle down at a time dictated by the conception of a child, or waiting until they were ready to take on the responsibility of a home, and probably a family. There is no evidence that a premarital pregnancy carried with it any ill effects in terms of employment or social disapproval for the great majority of the community, and indeed it is difficult to see how it could do, as the farmers who employed most of the labourers and used the services of many of the craftsmen, had themselves the highest premarital pregnancy rate of all the social groupings. Although it is possible that one or more examples of all the types of premarital pregnancy suggested at the beginning of this chapter could be found if more were known about individual attitudes, the conclusion must be drawn that in the great majority of cases it was individual choice, made in an atmosphere of social tolerance, and uninfluenced by major economic considerations, that determined whether or not a couple engaged in sex before marriage.

Notes

1. The Public Record Office holds a list of baptisms in the Independent chapel, Colyton, covering the period 1815–1857, and a further list of Unitarian baptisms in George's chapel up to 1862, while G.E. Evan's history of George's meeting house, *Colytonia: a chapter in the history of Devon*, Liverpool, 1898, includes entries of marriages, and dates of birth and baptisms from 1862 to 1898. Additional information on marriages comes from a marriage notice book for Axminster (Devon Record Office, hereafter D.R.O., R 7/8/c, 1836–1916) which names some couples intending to marry outside the Church of England. The Church of England registers are held in the D.R.O., and by the Team Rector of Colyton.

2. There was only one recorded pregnancy in Colyton between 1851 and 1891 where the interval between marriage and baptism showed an interval of more than 8½ months, the dividing line adopted by the Registrar General in 1938.

3. This chapter is a shortened and revised version of the author's paper 'Prenuptial pregnancy in a rural area of Devonshire in the mid-nineteenth century: Colyton, 1851–1881', published in *Continuity and Change*, 1 (1), 1986, pp. 113–24. Examination of the prenuptial pregnancies in Colyton from 1881 to 1891 reveals no change in the overall proportion of such pregnancies and any differences in relation to other aspects of the subject are so slight, or based on such small numbers, as to be statistically insignificant.

4. A total of 221 births recorded in the Colyton parish registers between 1851 and 1881 were identified, where it could be certain that the child was the first born of the couple

concerned, and where the dates of both baptism and marriage were known. Conception had occurred before marriage in 114 cases (52 per cent and after marriage in 107 cases (48 per cent).

5. See P.E.H. Hair, 'Bridal pregnancy in rural England in earlier centuries', *Population Studies*, 20, 1966, pp. 233–43; and P. Laslett, K. Oosterveen and R.M. Smith, eds, *Bastardy and its comparative history*, London, 1980, table 1.3, p. 23, which shows an average of 37 per cent premarital pregnancies in a widely-drawn sample of parishes.

6. P. Laslett, K. Oosterveen and R.M. Smith, eds, *Bastardy*, 1980, table 3.16, p. 109.

7. Ibid., p. 8.

8. The rental value which was sufficient to give a tenant a vote was lowered from £50 a year to £12 a year in 1869.

9. See A. Thornton and Hui-Sheng Lin, *Social Change and the Family in Taiwan*, Chicago 1994, for a full account of the changing place of the family in Taiwan. I am grateful to Dr Chyong-fang Ko for this reference.

10. D.R.O., Axminster Union Minute Book, vol. 8, 2.9.1856.

11. J.G. O'Leary, ed., *The Autobiography of Joseph Arch*, London, 1966, pp. 30–33.

12. See J. Robin, 'Prenuptial pregnancy', 1986, table 3, p. 119.

13. Ibid., table 5, p. 122.

Chapter 9

'Fallen Women'

However light-heartedly some young women may have embarked on sex before marriage, confident in the belief that their lover would marry them when a child was conceived, they were in reality taking a considerable risk in having intercourse before the wedding, at a time when abortion was illegal and infanticide a capital offence.[1] An examination of all known first births recorded in the Colyton baptismal register from 1 April 1851 to 31 March 1881, whether to a married or to a single woman, reveals that in addition to the 114 premarital pregnancies and the 107 conceptions after marriage which have already been discussed, a further fifty-seven first children were born out of wedlock altogether, and were therefore illegitimate in the eyes of the law. Thus, while only 38 per cent of known first born children in Colyton over a thirty-year period were conceived after the marriage of their parents, as many as one out of every three women known to have engaged in premarital sex resulting in the birth of a child found themselves faced with the prospect of bringing up their offspring without the help of its father. Just as women in Colyton in the second half of the nineteenth century who engaged in intercourse before marriage were carrying on a long tradition, so their contemporaries who became single mothers did not differ markedly from their predecessors living in the parish in earlier times. Illegitimacy had been a fact of life for centuries not only in Colyton, but in other parts of the country as well.[2]

Births outside marriage on this scale raise many questions about the society of which the single mothers were part, ranging from the degree of support they received as one-parent families, to the possibility that some of them may have formed an underclass whose members behaved in a way fundamentally different from those who had simply fallen in with the generally tolerated practice of intercourse before marriage, only to be let down by the man concerned, or even to have lost him through death by accident or illness. A study of the life histories of the women involved may help to answer these and other questions, if only to a limited degree.

It has been possible to trace ninety unmarried mothers between 1851 and 1881 who may be considered to be Colytonians, either because they themselves, their parents or their late husbands were born in the parish, or because they grew up there.[3] Nine of these women were widows at the time of the conception of their children, and the remainder were single women. They were to be found in all sections of society, except for the small upper-middle class, but daughters of labourers were by far the most likely to bear an illegitimate child, with more than half of all the single mothers coming from this, the poorest social group. It should be remembered, however, that illegitimacy was less likely to be recorded for those in the more prosperous classes, who would not be traceable as a result of receiving help from the Poor Law authorities when undergoing child-birth; while parents who were sufficiently well off could send their daughters away from the parish to have their babies, if they wished.

Leaving aside the widows, whose age when they had their first child outside marriage depended on how old they were when their husbands died, it appears that many single mothers began serious sexual activity rather earlier than other young women in the parish, for nearly half of them had given birth before they were twenty-one years old, while only just over a fifth of their contemporaries were married by the time they were twenty, whether or not they experienced a premarital pregnancy. However, no unmarried mother has been found to be under seventeen at the time her child was born or baptized, and there is no evidence of widespread early or mid-teenage promiscuity. Sophia Poseland did marry when she was only sixteen years old, although her age was entered as 18 in the parish register, but her first child was baptized thirteen months after the wedding, so that a premarital pregnancy leading to a forced marriage is unlikely to have occurred. This girl was herself illegitimate, and was the only known survivor of her mother's five children born out of wedlock, so it would not be surprising if she had seized the first opportunity possible to leave home. Sophia was not alone in having had brothers or sisters who had no lawful father, for nearly a third of all the women who bore illegitimate children had at least two, while some had three or even four such offspring, although only Sophia Poseland's mother is known to have reached the total of five.[4]

It may be suspected that these women with more than one illegitimate child, who will be called 'repeaters' for the sake of conciseness, did indeed belong to an underclass, and that their futures would be fundamentally different from those of the 'singletons' who had borne only one child out of wedlock. By dividing all the mothers into three groups, namely those who left the parish without having married; those who stayed, unmarried, in Colyton either until they died, or for at least ten years after the birth of their first illegitimate child; and those who ultimately married, it may be possible to see if the suspicion proves to be justified.[5]

At first sight, the nineteen women who left Colyton unmarried did appear to form a distinct group. They represented a fifth of the unmarried mothers, and all but one of them were singletons. They included two farmers' daughters and one young woman from the business class, as well as a higher proportion of wage-earning craftsmen and tradesmen's daughters and a lower proportion of labourers' daughters than would be expected from their numbers in the whole sample of mothers, so that their overall social standing was slightly higher than average. On the other hand, we cannot say what happened to this group after they had left the parish. Any of them may have married, and it would be surprising if none of them did so, while some may have had another illegitimate child in their new environment, so joining the ranks of the repeaters. What did distinguish the members of this group, however, was not so much that all but one were singletons, as that just over two-thirds of them were able to leave Colyton for a fresh start in life unencumbered by a child, since nearly half the women, including the only repeater, had lost their babies through death before the age of three years, while another fifth were able to leave their children in Colyton to be brought up by grandparents, or in one case, an uncle and aunt.

Nothing is known of the futures of these women, except for one, Eliza Purse. Her child died in the Axminster workhouse at the age of two, and seven years later, still unmarried, Eliza was sent back to the Axminster Union from St Mary Abbott's, Kensington, where she had become a charge on the parish.[6] The fact that the Axminster guardians recorded only one such removal order suggests that the other women who had left Colyton had either managed to establish themselves elsewhere for a sufficient length of time to be granted irremovability in their new abode, or had been able to avoid applying to the Poor Law authorities for relief.

A similar number of unmarried mothers remained in Colyton for at least ten years after the birth of their first illegitimate child, and most of them for longer, but they differed from those who left the parish in two main respects. First, while the group leaving Colyton was made up almost entirely of singletons, four out of every ten women who stayed were repeaters. Second, only four women out of the nineteen remaining in the parish lost all their children through death. These women were singletons, for although some of the repeaters' children died too, in no case was a repeater left without any child to bring up. For the repeaters, and for the singletons whose children survived, it was not so easy to leave Colyton for a new life, and they had to meet the challenge of bringing up a child, or children, without the help of a husband as a breadwinner.

There were two main sources of support for those unmarried mothers staying in Colyton who were unable to maintain themselves and their children unaided, namely the family, and the Guardians of the Poor. The work of the guardians, who were the local administrators of the national Poor Law, will be discussed more fully in later chapters. Here it is sufficient to say that although the New Poor Law introduced in 1834 continued to provide a safety-net for the poorest in society, it did so at a lower level than the Old Poor Law had done.[7] The relief it gave was heavily means-tested, and in Colyton, as the agricultural depressions of the 1870s and 1880s took hold, was increasingly limited to bare necessities, whether provided in the form of outdoor relief to individuals living in the community, or as accommodation in the workhouse.

The numbers involved are far too small to be statistically significant, but it is nevertheless interesting that all the women in this group, whether singletons or repeaters, who had a parent or parents in the parish were living at home with them when the next census after the birth of their first illegitimate child was taken. Furthermore, with one exception, none of these women are recorded as having had any help, medical or otherwise, from the Guardians of the Poor at this period of their lives. It is probable that the woman who did receive assistance from the guardians was in some way disabled, as she was recorded as being on parish relief in the census preceding the birth of her child, as well as in that following it, even though she was living at home with her parents on both occasions. For these women, making up three-quarters of all those who stayed on in the parish without marrying, the family provided shelter, though whether with a good heart or grudgingly it is impossible to say. What can be asserted is that in the majority of cases the unmarried mothers were not entirely a drain on their parents' resources. Nearly two-thirds of them were lacemakers, which as a home-based occupation could be combined with child-rearing and domestic duties, as could millinery and dressmaking in which two other single mothers were engaged. Nearly all of those living with their parents were in a position to make some kind of financial contribution to the household economy.

The parents of the remaining five mothers were either dead, or long-time absentees from Colyton. One woman and her child had been taken in by an uncle and aunt, and another, whose first illegitimate child had died and whose two subsequent children had not yet been born, was therefore a free agent and had found a job as a living-in dairymaid. Life was more difficult for the remaining three women who could not count on parental support. One, who had been in and out of the workhouse since her children were born, was boarding with an unrelated family, as was another who had been helped by the guardians during periods of illness, while the third, a widow, was in the Axminster workhouse with one legitimate and two illegitimate children when the census was taken.

Ten years on, the position of those women who were recorded in a second census shows that family ties remained very strong. Only one unmarried mother who still had a parent or parents living in Colyton had detached herself to set up her own independent household. She was supporting herself and her child by working as a dressmaker, while her mother, a retired grocer, lived with two adult grandchildren some distance away. Another woman was living as part of her married brother's household, but was next door to her own mother who was looking after her daughter's two illegitimate children.

The fate of the women whose parents had died in the period between the censuses depended largely on their economic status. Two better-off women, one of whom was a widow, headed their own households, but one unmarried mother, whose child had also died, had found employment as a living-in housekeeper to a 72-year-old widower, while a fourth had found it necessary to seek assistance from the Poor Law. She was described as a pauper in the census, and was boarding in the household of an 81-year-old widow, also a pauper. The authorities had almost certainly placed her there to look after the old lady, since in an unrelated case the guardians had refused outdoor relief to two 'not wholly disabled' women who were not prepared to 'attend and wait on a poor aged person, such work being suitable for each to perform'.[8]

It appears, then, that differences in life-style between the women who stayed on in Colyton, unmarried, did not depend on whether they were repeaters or singletons, but on whether or not their own parents were present in the parish. If they were, then the unmarried mothers could look to them for shelter; if not, it was difficult to avoid asking for relief from the Poor Law authorities if the child born out of wedlock survived. By receiving such relief, a measure of bureaucratic control had to be accepted.

Even though it might be thought that in Victorian England the bearing of an illegitimate child would militate against marriage, the third group of mothers shows that in Colyton at least this was not the case, since it is known that well over half of all the mothers in the sample did ultimately marry. Furthermore, although no records have been found which systematically reveal the paternity of the children, evidence drawn from the baptismal registers and the censuses makes it appear highly likely that only a handful of the mothers married the father of their child. Nor does it seem that the survival of the children was a bar to matrimony, in spite of the fact that the Guardians of the Poor held that the man who married a woman with an illegitimate child became responsible for that child's maintenance.[9] Although most of the women leaving Colyton to start a new life had either lost their children through death, or had left them to be brought up by grandparents, the opposite was the case for women marrying, since nearly seven out of ten of them entered into matrimony with at least one child still alive. Repeaters, moreover, found it no more difficult to marry than singletons – indeed, rather the reverse, since 66 per cent of all the repeaters are known to have married, compared to 53 per cent of the singletons. It must be remembered, however, that the evidence is incomplete, since the singletons leaving Colyton could very well have married in the parishes to which they went.

It would seem, then, that the majority of women who bore illegitimate children married; that the survival of their children was not a bar to matrimony; and that most of those who married were unlikely to have married the father of their child. However, two further pieces of evidence dispel any idea that most unmarried mothers went on to follow the normal marriage pattern of other women in Colyton and were in no way handicapped in the marriage market. In the first place, the mothers of illegitimate children had to wait on average four or five years between bearing their first offspring and finding a husband, so that they saw their contemporaries who had not had children marrying before them; and second, in part because of this, they found that the pool of possible husbands was much reduced. This effect was most noticeable in the case of the repeaters, since over two-thirds of them married men who were either widowers ranging from sixteen to twenty-nine years older than themselves, or bachelors who were from four to twelve years younger. A woman marrying a much older man presumably hoped that the union would provide a measure of security, at least until her child or children had become old enough to support themselves, while a husband could expect to be looked after during his old age by an active wife who would be unlikely to die before him. The long-term advantage to the mother of an illegitimate child who married a man younger, or even much younger, than herself seems clear, and it is possible that some of these marriages were examples of spouse entrapment, as in the case of the 32-year-old woman with four living illegitimate children who married a twenty-year-old man when she was two months pregnant.

These extreme age differences between husband and wife were less marked for the singletons, as well over half of them married men who were either the same age as themselves, or from one to nine years older or one to three years younger. Even so, a quarter of them married husbands who were anything from ten to twenty-eight years older. It is difficult to believe that marriages of convenience were uncommon whether for repeaters or singletons.

It was seen earlier that sex before marriage resulting in pre-nuptial pregnancy occurred sufficiently frequently in Colyton for it to carry little or no social stigma or economic disadvantage amongst a large section of the community. Attitudes to illegitimacy, however, were not always so clear cut. There is only fragmentary evidence as to how the families of the single mothers themselves felt about illegitimacy, and the censuses reveal a diversity of responses to the presence of an illegitimate child in the household. Some children were entered in the column describing the relationship of the individual to the household head as 'sons' or 'daughters' of the men their mothers ultimately married, even though in later life they used their mothers' maiden names. In other cases no attempt was made to hide the illegitimacy, and the children were recorded as 'step-sons' and 'step-daughters', retaining their mothers' names before marriage. In only one case, however, did the husband describe the child his wife brought with her into his household as 'illegitimate'.

It was easier to conceal illegitimacy, if that was thought to be desirable, when the children were living with grandparents in the absence of their mothers, as they could correctly, and unrevealingly, be entered on the census return as grandsons or granddaughters. Even so, there were cases where grandparents seem to have tried to distance the children from any hint of illegitimacy by entering them as 'sons' or 'daughters' even though the grandmothers were beyond the age at which they could have borne a child themselves.

It is not surprising that there should be a range of attitudes and social values held by individual families. The response of the Church of England was less equivocal. Colyton's vicar, Mamerto Gueritz, was living in Plymouth in

1848 when the Church of England Sisterhood of Mercy of Devonport and Plymouth was established to serve the poor, so that early in his career he became aware of the potential offered by a parochial Sisterhood.[10] He may also have been influenced by the founding in Bovey Tracey in 1863 of a community called The Devon House of Mercy, also run by Sisters, whose purpose was 'the reception and reformation of females who have sinned against the Divine law of chastity', an aim which in Colyton would have had to embrace the majority of its young women. The first statute of the house stated categorically 'That the object be ... the reception and protection of fallen women, with a view to their reformation and ultimate safe establishment ... in some respectable calling'.[11] Be that as it may, the Sisterhood of Our Lady of Compassion arrived in Colyton in the late summer of 1870 and set up house in the Tanyard. It was only a small establishment, containing three Sisters of Mercy, a child of four years, and an eleven-year-old servant, but a novice joined the Sisterhood on 2 February 1872 in a service which outraged the Nonconformist correspondent of *Pulman's Weekly News*. He reported that 'On Wednesday evening a ceremony took place in our parish which will scarcely find parallel perhaps in all the later doings of ritualistic tomfoolery – namely the *admission of a nun*. ... A Priest from Exeter ... conducted the ceremony and the poor silly girl was put through an elaborate performance – first arrayed as a bride in white, with a long white veil which had previously, with much ceremony, been presented, placed and "blessed" on the altar. She was then taken back to the vestry, whence, her hair being all cut off, she reappeared in the hideous black garments of the "order", members of which, resembling guys or scarecrows, may be daily seen stalking about the streets ...'

The black-clad Sisters engaged in parochial visiting, and cared for the poor and the sick; they also acted as sponsors for children brought for baptism and took on responsibility for their well-being, spiritual and otherwise, so that they would have been in a position to influence at least some of the unmarried mothers. The habits and customs of Colytonians were not easily to be changed, however, and within three years the Sisterhood had disappeared,[12] while the rates of premarital pregnancy and illegitimacy continued unabated.

There remains one body whose attitude towards illegitimacy was of particular importance to unmarried mothers, namely the Guardians of the Poor. Their records during the 1850s and 1860s provide no evidence that poor single mothers were treated any differently from two-parent families. Single women, like married women, were given outdoor relief if they or their children fell ill; they received the same relief at childbirth and were provided with coffins if their children died. When they were sent to the Axminster workhouse they were being treated no differently from deserted wives or poor widows who could not support themselves in the community. The greater misfortune in Colyton during the second half of the nineteenth century was not to be a single mother, but to be without a parent or parents to provide shelter and support in time of need.

By the 1870s, however, the nationwide depression was causing local authorities to look for ways of cutting back expenditure, and this almost certainly had some effect on unmarried mothers. In 1874, for example, the guardians decided 'that all widows receiving out relief who had illegitimate children since their husbands' death should have such relief discontinued and be offered the House',[13] presumably in the hope that the women in question would refuse the offer and so cease to be a charge on the parish. Three years later, the guardians were openly discriminating between the 'deserving' and 'undeserving' poor, when they granted the former group an extra 6d a week in outdoor relief during the winter months.[14] It is not known how unmarried mothers were viewed, but it is possible that the repeaters at least would fall into the second category. On the other hand, the guardians were sometimes overruled by the magistracy. In the autumn of 1875, a Colyton woman was told by the guardians to remove her illegitimate child from the workhouse. She pleaded that she could not afford to do this, but offered to pay 6d a week towards the cost of the child's keep. The guardians rejected this offer, and she was brought to court, but the magistrates found against the guardians as they considered that the mother was not in a position to support her child.[15]

It would seem, then, that at least in prosperous times illegitimacy was accepted by officialdom as part of the pattern of society, and poor single mothers were not discriminated against in an attempt to change their ways, at least as far as welfare payments were concerned. Signs of harsher treatment appeared during the 1870s when the agricultural depression took hold, but it must be remembered that the national campaign to cut public assistance affected other groups too, in particular the elderly.[16] Such discrimination against unmarried mothers as existed, therefore, would seem to be social rather than economic.

Some evidence of social discrimination by the community as a whole can be found, however, when addressing the question raised earlier as to whether some mothers of illegitimate children formed an underclass which behaved in a fundamentally different way from normal society in Colyton. The life histories of just over a quarter of all the known unmarried mothers in Colyton between 1851 and 1881 show that in all probability the only difference between them and their contemporaries who experienced premarital pregnancies was that their lovers did not fulfil the obligation to marry them once a child was conceived. In the first place, they were all singletons, whose average age at the birth of their illegitimate child was close to the mean age at which Colyton girls married, a fact indicating that they were simply following the common custom of intercourse before marriage and that if the fathers of their children also obeyed the local convention and married them once they were pregnant, they would have been indistinguishable from the majority of women in the community. Second, taken together as a group they were of a rather higher social standing overall than the remaining unmarried mothers. Lastly, they were less likely to marry than the other mothers, which may indicate that illegitimacy was looked on with greater disfavour by the men from among whom they would otherwise have expected to take a husband. They were typified by the daughter of a Colyton businessman of some standing, who sued a young baker for maintenance for her illegitimate son. The court was told that the defendant had seduced the applicant under a promise of marriage, and 'then deserted her and married a young lady of Colyton'.[17] The magistrates found in favour of the woman, and a maintenance order for 2s 6d a week was granted.

These were the 'wronged women' so often appearing in the fiction of the time, but in Colyton, like a number of other Victorian stereotypes, they represented only a minority and in many ways were indistinguishable from their peers. However, the majority of unmarried mothers, numbering almost three-quarters of the whole group and including both singletons and repeaters, did indeed display certain features which set them apart from the rest of society. Many of them were poor, but it was not poverty alone which distinguished them. A survey of poor households, that is to say those where at one time or another the heads had received help from the Poor Law,[18] shows that while one-third of poor families were involved with illegitimacy, two-thirds were not, so that while poverty may have played a part in encouraging illegitimacy in certain families it is by no means possible to equate poverty and promiscuity among the population as a whole.

The principal feature which distinguished this underclass, as they might be termed nowadays, was their network of kin relationships with other individuals connected with illegitimacy, either within their own families or those of the men they married. Although only two unmarried mothers were themselves illegitimate, more than half of them had aunts who had had illegitimate children, or uncles who had married women who had already had a child out of wedlock, while as many as two-thirds of them had sisters or brothers equally closely connected with illegitimacy. Indeed, a number of unmarried mothers experienced more than one of these relationships. It is harder to trace the families of the men these women married, coming as some of them did from outside the parish, but even so, more than half the husbands are known to have had links of a similar nature.

A further indication of this underclass acting as a separate group is that the majority of households connected with illegitimacy were to be found in only one of the five administrative divisions of the parish, known as tythings. This tything occupied the southern half of the town and contained more of these households than the other four tythings put together. Furthermore, the census reveals that even within the southern tything, families of the underclass were to be found living in groups, interrupted by only a few scattered households apparently free from illegitimacy. It cannot be said whether these colonies grew up because their members tried to obtain housing close to each other; because the rest of society did not wish to live near them; because their living accommodation was so poor that no one else wanted it; or because the parish authorities deliberately segregated them. Whatever the case may be, the families in such groupings were separated in their living areas from other townspeople, and were linked through a combination of environment and intermarriage into a sub-society living somewhat apart from the rest of the community. Families could and did leave this sub-society through death, infertility or migration, while some brothers and sisters of the unmarried mothers escaped through marriage into families unconnected with illegitimacy. But as they left, new recruits came in, not only from immigrant families, but from girls born and brought up in the parish with no trace of illegitimacy in the parental generation. Once a girl became a repeater, or a set of sisters produced illegitimate children, thus joining the underclass, social disapproval would make marriage outside it more difficult for all the members of the families concerned, whether they themselves were single mothers or not, and would thus reinforce the cohesion of the group through intermarriage.

Notes

1. In May, 1885, an inquest was held at Colyford on the illegitimate son of Elizabeth Sanson, a young widow of three years standing. The child died a few hours after birth, but the doctor could find no marks of violence and thought the death was due to congestion of the brain. The jury brought in a verdict of death by natural causes. *Devon Weekly Times* (hereafter *D.W.T.*) 29.5.1885.

2. See P. Laslett, K. Oosterveen and R.M. Smith, eds, *Bastardy and its Comparative History*, London, 1980, table 3.8, p. 96, and table 1.1c, p. 17.

3. Illegitimate births were traced not only from the baptismal registers, but from the parish burial book naming the parents of the dead children, the minute books of the Guardians of the Poor which record payments to single women in childbirth or the provision of coffins for their offspring; and the decadal censuses, taken in conjunction with family reconstitution. Twenty-five single mothers whose only known connection with Colyton was that their child was baptized or buried there have been omitted from the sample.

4. Of the 90 mothers of illegitimate children, 62, or 69 per cent, had 1 illegitimate child; 18, or 20 per cent, had 2; 7, or 8 per cent, had 3; 2, or 2 per cent, had 4; 1, or 1 per cent, had 5.

5. Women leaving Colyton unmarried, 19, or 21 per cent; staying in Colyton for at least 10 years unmarried or until death, 19, or 21 per cent. Marrying, 52, or 58 per cent.

6. Devon Record Office Axminster Union Minute Book (hereafter D.R.O. A.U.M.B.), vol. 11, 30.5.1872.

7. See K.D.M. Snell and J. Millar, 'Lone-parent families and the welfare state', *Continuity and Change*, 2 (3), 1987, pp. 387–422.

8. D.R.O. A.U.M.B., vol. 9, 5.6.1864.

9. Ibid., vol. 11, 30.5.1872.

10. D.A. Gunn-Johnson, 'A County Catholic: a study of the emergence of the Oxford Movement in an East Devon Parish'. Unpublished thesis accepted for the Archbishop of Canterbury's MA degree, December 1994, p. 173.

11. Ibid., p. 33.

13. Ibid., pp. 180–83.

14. D.R.O. A.U.M.B., vol. 11, 19.3.1874.

15. Ibid., vol. 12, 20.12.1877.

16. Ibid., vol. 12, 14.10.1875 to 6.7.1876.

17. See D. Thomson, 'Welfare and the historian', in L. Bonfield, R.M. Smith and K. Wrightson, eds, *The world we have gained*, Oxford, 1986, p. 373.

18. *D.W.T.*, 25.10.1867.

19. See J. Robin, 'Illegitimacy in Colyton, 1851–1881', *Continuity and Change*, 2 (2) 1987, pp. 324–35 for a full account of how poor households were assessed, and what evidence was used to connect families with illegitimacy.

Chapter 10

A Shifting Population

'There have always been Starkadders at Cold Comfort' is a recurrent cry in Stella Gibbons's parody of the earthier type of novel set in rural England,[1] and the belief that, at least until the twentieth century, country towns and villages contained largely settled populations with continuity over very long periods of time dies hard among those without a detailed knowledge of local history. Of course, some families did succeed in remaining in their home parish for many generations. In Colyton, for instance, the Sampsons, the Strowbrydges, the Yonges and the Drakes regularly provided men to serve as Feoffees from the sixteenth to the early nineteenth centuries,[2] though by the 1850s only the first two names were still represented in the chamber; while in chapter 5 it was remarked that some of the surnames in the second half of the nineteenth century were derived from Flemish immigrants arriving in the district 300 years earlier. Even so, families which can be traced from father to son through several generations while living in the same parish were in the minority, and for that very reason they stood out in folk memory.

In reality, the movement of rural populations in England is a phenomenon of long standing. It has been shown from lists of inhabitants kept by the rector of the time that in the Nottinghamshire village of Clayworth, not far short of two-thirds of the individuals in the community in 1678 were gone twelve years later, and although just over a third of the absentees had died, the remainder had left the parish to be replaced by outsiders coming in.[3] Two hundred years on, a comparable degree of population movement could be found in rural parishes in different parts of the country. In Elmdon, a village in north-west Essex, the figure over the same period was 48 per cent, and in Compton Chamberlayne in Wiltshire it was 55 per cent.[4] In Colyton itself, 54 per cent of those present in 1851 had disappeared ten years later. The cumulative effect of this kind of movement is shown by the continuing contraction of the group of boys and girls aged up to nine years in 1851 who were the subject of chapter 4. By 1891, when the individuals concerned would have been between forty and forty-nine years of age, only 13 per cent of them remained in Colyton.[5]

However, much of this interchange of population involved young people who left their home parishes before or at marriage. A third of the children present in Colyton in 1851 migrated before the oldest were twenty years of age, and more than half of those still present ten years later left before they were thirty. It might be thought that once the surplus population of young people had been shaken out, those who remained in Colyton, now in their prime of life, would settle down to bring up their families in the parish where they themselves had spent their childhood. Yet a third of those present in 1871 left Colyton before the end of the next decade, and a quarter of the total remaining in 1881 migrated before 1891, leaving only fifty of the original 337 boys and thirty-one of the 296 girls still in the parish.[6]

Closer examination of the histories of the cohort boys who stayed on as men shows that in the majority of cases, they themselves came from families not long established in Colyton, for nearly seven out of ten had either been born outside the parish, coming in with their parents before they were ten years old, or had fathers or paternal grandfathers who had entered from elsewhere.[7] Nevertheless, some long-established families did exist, in which father and son had been baptized in the parish church or chapel for anything from three to eight successive generations. In whatever way such families may have supported themselves in the past, by 1891 none of their descendants within the cohort was either a member of the professional and landowning class, or a farmer, and although the greater number could be described as belonging to the middling class, only three of them were shown on the electoral roll as owners of houses, let alone land. Indeed, George Bull, whose paternal ancestors can be traced back to his five-times great-grandfather John, baptized in 1612, was in 1891 employed as a mason, and in receipt of help from the Feoffees, who instructed their bailiff to ensure that he had 5s a week 'for necessaries' over a four-week period;[8] while Samuel Purse, a farm labourer who was on the Feoffees' list of the poor, came from a family which was established in Colyton by 1703, when his great-great-great-grandfather was baptized. Such deep-rooted families were, however, the exception rather than the rule.

Cohort members of 1851 who stayed on in Colyton into middle age were comparatively few in number, and by definition excluded those who came into the parish after marriage. Moreover, their subsequent life histories cannot be traced with any degree of certainty until the full enumerators' schedules for the 1901 census, naming all individuals, are released by the Registrar General, an event which under the 100-year rule of confidentiality cannot occur until 2001. Another way needs to be found of assessing how important migration after marriage was to the community as a whole. The solution has been to examine the experiences not of the cohort members themselves, but of their fathers, whose presence or absence in Colyton after marriage can be traced from 1841, or even before that date in some cases, through to 1891.[9]

'Life history' is perhaps a rather pretentious term for what in most cases can only be a minimal collection of data gathered from censuses published once every ten years, from the records of the Guardians of the Poor and the Feoffees, from the electoral registers and from the records of births, marriages and deaths. Even so, information from these sources does allow the 239 fathers of cohort children to be divided into two main groups, namely the 55 per cent who were born in Colyton and the 45 per cent who were not, and then to be subdivided into those who certainly experienced some migration after marriage, even if this was short-lived, and those who apparently spent their whole married lives in the parish. Not surprisingly, it was the Colyton-born fathers who were the most likely to stay on throughout their married lives, with two-thirds of them showing no evidence of migration after marriage, compared to only three out of ten of those fathers born outside Colyton.

One of the ways by which migration can be traced is through the knowledge which the censuses provide of the birthplaces of a man's children. For example, in 1841 James Pavey, born in Colyton, was living with his father and mother on their farm in the parish. By 1851 he had married a Colyton girl, fathered six children, and become a farmer himself. He was still farming in Colyton at the time of each census up to his retirement, and even then he did not leave the parish. Here, it would seem, was a typically stable family, with a head who spent his life in the place of his birth. But although James's first child was born in Colyton, his second was born in Northleigh, his third in Musbery, and his fourth, fifth and sixth in Ilminster, Somerset, indicating that in the ten years between 1841 and 1851 he, his wife and his ever-increasing family had moved at least three times before settling back into the parish for good. Without evidence of this kind, much that occurred between the censuses cannot be retrieved. Any family or individual could have left Colyton for one or more periods of work, and yet have been back in the parish when each census was taken.

Differences in migration patterns did not only depend on whether a man was a born Colytonian or someone coming in from outside. The social class of the individual also had a considerable effect on his movements. The fathers of cohort members in the professional and landowning class, though few in number, were the ones who showed the most movement, having with one exception either come into the parish with their families from elsewhere, or left it at some time after they married. This is not surprising, as curates, surgeons and solicitors could go wherever opportunity beckoned, while landed proprietors were able to realise their assets and move on if it suited them to do so.

The next most mobile group comprised the farmers and dairymen. There is a twofold explanation for this. First, the great majority of farmers did not own their farms, but were tenants on leases that were usually renewed for seven, ten or fourteen years, so that it was easy for them to move as the leases expired if they found they could get better terms elsewhere. Second, the dairymen were even less tied down, as they rented their dairy cows and buildings on a yearly basis from the farmers, often with rent-free living accommodation, and could therefore move frequently if they wished. It was quite usual for farmers' sons to start their independent working lives as dairymen, and this may account for James Pavey's moves in the 1840s, between leaving home and returning as a fully-fledged farmer. From the evidence of their children's birthplaces farmers and dairymen alike moved within a fifteen-mile radius of Colyton, strengthening the view that their natural territory extended some distance beyond a single parish. Men in this group were more likely to feel rooted in the district than in Colyton itself.

Third in the degree of migration they experienced were the farm labourers, whose pattern of local movement mirrored that of their employers, occurring as it did almost entirely within fifteen miles of Colyton. Taking the farmers and their workers together, just under six out of ten showed evidence of having moved into or out of the parish after marriage. This position was reversed for the business owners and the self-employed, together with the former's workers. These were the groups which provided the highest proportion of stable families, with 66 per cent of the employers and 56 per cent of their employees appearing to have settled continuously in Colyton once they married. If only those fathers born in Colyton are considered, the proportions remaining in the parish all their married lives were even higher, standing at 75 per cent and 71 per cent respectively.

The key to this stability, as far as the employers were concerned, lay in the nature of their work. A successful buyer and seller of goods, or supplier of services, needed to build up a regular clientele and to establish 'goodwill', which became a valuable part of the business if it were sold. Frequent migration would make this process more difficult. Another stabilizing factor was the ownership of property. The electoral registers show that nearly half of Colyton's business class became owners of freehold property in some form or other as the years went by, thus strengthening their position within the parish, both materially and socially. Indeed, property ownership within Colyton was an essential qualification for becoming a Feoffee or even a Twentyman, positions which gave their holders considerable standing.

Just as the agricultural workers mirrored the migration pattern of the farmers, though to a lesser degree, so did the wage-earners in relation to their employers. On the one hand, a stable employer was likely to provide continuing employment to a satisfactory worker, so enabling him to remain in Colyton for his working life; on the other, with no property ownership to tie him down, a wage-earning craftsman was able to look for work elsewhere if the terms of his employment were unsatisfactory, or if he lost his job, even though a move was complicated by the fact that he would have to look for housing in his new place of employment, unlike the farm worker with his tied cottage. However, evidence from the birthplaces of children born outside Colyton shows that the wage-earning craftsmen, too, moved mainly within the same fifteen-mile radius of Colyton as the farmers and their workers.

Taking all the cohort's fathers together, the effect on Colyton's community of both local and more distant migration stands out clearly, with half the married men and their wives forming a stable core of couples who remained in Colyton for all their married lives,[10] surrounded by a shifting population made up of those coming into the parish with their families, very largely from within a fifteen-mile radius, and those leaving Colyton to live and work elsewhere. Unfortunately, although evidence is available on where fathers who entered

Colyton originated, little is known of where they went if they decided to leave. It seems reasonable to assume that just as families from nearby parishes came into Colyton to work, so married Colytonians would move locally in their search for job opportunities, particularly as the fifteen-mile radius probably represented the maximum distance within which households could conveniently and cheaply move from one place to another.

However, there is definite evidence that some married couples moved much further afield. The Feoffees helped four families, as well as some individuals, to emigrate to America by contributing towards their travelling costs,[11] although in 1855, at the height of the Crimean war, they suspended such grants 'under the present circumstances of the country'.[12] In the same way, they helped James Anning, his wife and five children to travel to Bristol, some fifty-four miles away as the crow flies, after James had found work there. Subsequently two more families were subsidized to go to the same town, while others were assisted to travel to Beaminster in Dorset, Jersey and London. The Feoffees were, however, cautious as usual, specifying in one case that the journey money be handed to the head of the family 'only when he actually leaves the parish'.[13]

Marriage then did not ensure that a couple would remain in Colyton for the rest of their lives. For those who did settle down in the parish, however, the prospect of old age and how to meet it came ever closer as the years went by.

Notes

1. Stella Gibbons, *Cold Comfort Farm*, St Albans, 1973, p. 23 et seq.

2. R.G. White, *The History of the Feoffees of Colyton 1546–1946*, Bridport, 1951, frontispiece. The Pole family, which also provided Feoffees over the period, were from Shute, and not Colyton itself.

3. P. Laslett, 'Clayworth and Cogenhoe', in H.E. Bell and R.L. Ollard, eds, *Historical essays 1680–1750*, London, 1963, pp. 157–84.

4. See J. Robin, 'Elmdon. Continuity and change in a north-west Essex village, 1861–1964', Cambridge, 1980, table 48, p. 190, and unpublished material on Compton Chamberlayne in Wiltshire, held in the Cambridge Group for the History of Population and Social Structure.

5. J. Robin, *From childhood to middle age: cohort analysis in Colyton 1851–1891*, Cambridge Group for the History of Population and Social Structure Working Paper Series no. 1, 1995, table 19.

6. Ibid., table 18.

7. Two men who were born illegitimate and whose fathers cannot be traced have been omitted from the sample. The remaining forty-eight cohort men in 1891 have been divided as follows:

	No.	%	
Those born outside Colyton	8	17	
Those who were born in Colyton but whose fathers were not			69%
(one-generational Colyton families)	10	21	
Those in two-generational Colyton families	15	31	
Those in three-generational Colyton families	6	13	
Those in four-generational Colyton families	4	8	
Those in five-generational Colyton families	2	4	31%
Those in six-generational Colyton families	2	4	
Those in eight-generational Colyton families	1	2	
			100%

8. Devon Record Office (hereafter D.R.O.), F 17/9, 23.1.1891.

9. For a full account of this group, see J. Robin, *From childhood to middle age*, 1995, pp. 24–8 and table 12.

10. Ibid., table 12 shows that 50 per cent of all cohort fathers experienced some post-marital migration, while 50 per cent did not.

11. D.R.O. F 17/7, 18.3.1852, 9.6.1853; F 17/8, 6.3.1862, 14.6.1881.

12. Ibid., Г 17/8, 23.4.1855.

13. Ibid., F 17/8 16.6.1854, 31.1.1856, 6.11.1872, 16.10.1854, 13.8.1855, 10.11 1864.

Chapter 11

Old Age

Even today, people on the verge of old age are concerned to find the answers to two major questions. The first is whether their income will be sufficient to maintain a lifestyle reasonably similar to the one to which they have been accustomed, once they have ceased to work; the second, in some measure connected with the first, relates to who will care for them when they are no longer capable of looking after themselves. These two uncertainties were faced by old people in Colyton 150 years ago, and had an even greater impact in view of the life-long poverty of such a large proportion of the workforce, which for them made saving for old age an almost impossible task.

Before discussing how these questions were answered for Colyton's elderly in the second half of the nineteenth century, a definition of 'old age' must be found. In the absence of a standard retirement age for men and women, the adoption of a figure for the time at which individuals might be considered elderly is necessarily arbitrary. Here, sixty years has been taken for both sexes as marking the onset of old age, even though, as will be seen later, a considerable number of men and a smaller proportion of women continued to work well past their sixtieth birthday.

Financial security in their last years for people of both sexes was obviously influenced by the degree of material prosperity which had been reached before retirement. The over-sixties in Colyton in 1851 have therefore been divided into two groups. On the one hand were the wage-earning craftsmen and tradesmen and the labourers, together with their wives or widows, and the unmarried women of the working class, who owned no real estate and who had been part of a low-wage economy all their lives; and on the other, the men and women of the classes comprising the better-off self-employed, the business owners, the farmers and dairymen, the professionals and the landed gentry. As it was the poor who were in the majority, their financial position in old age will be discussed first.

It was not until 1908 that Lord Asquith's government introduced a non-contributory old age pension, which provided 5s a week for those deserving poor who were seventy years of age or older,[1] and it may be asked how the elderly members of the poorer classes managed to survive when they were past work in the days before this piece of legislation was put into effect. The answer lies in the Poor Law, which, as has been said in an earlier chapter, had by 1851 been providing for the needy for over 300 years, in one way or another.

Contrary to popular belief, recourse to the Guardians of the Poor after the New Poor Law was introduced in 1834 did not necessarily mean that old people had to leave their homes to end their days in the workhouse. The Poor Law Amendment Act of 1836 stated that two Justices of the Peace could direct that any adult person who from old age or infirmity of body was wholly unable to work could be given relief without being required to reside in such an institution.[2] As a result, care in the community could be provided through outdoor relief, in the form of a permanent weekly allowance which was in effect an old-age pension, although the time of life at which it was granted depended on when an individual without private financial resources became incapable of earning a living, rather than on his or her age.

Evidence from the census returns of 1851 shows that in Colyton at least, it was the rule rather than the exception to maintain the old within the parish. There was no Colytonian over sixty years of age of either sex residing in the Axminster workhouse on census day, while just over a quarter of the sixty-five elderly working-class men in the community were on outdoor relief. Nearly two-thirds were still working, two men who had served in the Forces were on army pensions, and only three had neither an occupation, a pension, nor a regular payment from the Guardians of the Poor.

The position of women was rather different, as wives shared the fortunes of their husbands, but if only the thirty-six elderly women in the two poorest classes who in 1851 were either widowed or single are considered, the census shows that they too were supported through the Poor Law when this became necessary. Not surprisingly, the proportion who went on to permanent relief was greater than for men, as their employment opportunities were fewer, but even so, a third were at work in 1851. Over a half were on parish relief, while only four had no occupation and may therefore be assumed either to be living on savings, or more likely, enjoying financial help from their children or kin, since all were living in the households of close family members.[3]

The 1851 census returns, however, simply provide a snapshot of pensioners on one particular day, and so cannot throw a great deal of light on the ages at which individuals had stopped working. Fortunately, there is another way by which men's retirement ages can be assessed, by using the records of the Feoffees of Colyton.

The Feoffees had a rule, which they maintained until 1878, that they would not give monetary help to anyone who had received assistance from the Poor Law during the past three months. At the same time, they provided a Christmas payment each year to the heads of poor families, and to some poor individuals living alone, their treasurer meticulously recording the names of all the recipients until the year 1873, when these detailed records cease. A man may be listed as receiving such annual payments for many years, and when they stop abruptly, even though the individual concerned is known to have continued to live in Colyton for at least one full year or longer, it may be assumed, not that he ceased to be poor, but that regular payments through the

Poor Law made that person ineligible for further Feoffee support.[4]   It is
therefore possible to discover the approximate ages at which poor elderly men
whose names were removed from the Treasurer's list went on to permanent
outdoor relief, and in the case of those who later died in Colyton, how long
their retirement lasted.[5]

Thirty-six men received regular Christmas bonuses and other seasonal help
from the Feoffees between 1851 and 1873, only to have all support withdrawn
when they became pensioners of the Poor Law. People grow old at different
rates, so it can be no surprise that retirement came at a variety of ages, from 61
to 83 years, although the average stood at 70 years and 4 months, a figure
which corresponds closely to the median age of 70 years and 6 months. The
question remains as to how long these elderly men survived to enjoy a more
leisurely life style, once their working days were over.

Nowadays, most people retiring from paid work may expect to live for a
number of years in good health, enjoying what has come to be known as the
Third Age, a period when personal fulfilment can be sought, free from the
demands of the obligatory working day experienced in the Second Age, before
finally entering the Fourth Age, a time of physical and mental decline leading
to dependence on others and finally death.[6] It might be thought that in the more
rigorous days of Victorian England, a working man would continue his labours
until he dropped, so passing directly from his Second to his Fourth Age or to
death itself.   The evidence from Colyton, however, tends to refute this
supposition.   Admittedly just under a quarter of the men who were on the
Feoffees' list in 1851 died while they were still in harness, but for the majority
who survived to draw their pensions from the Poor Law, retirement could last a
considerable time. The average length of the period between ceasing work and
dying for the thirty-six working-class men who ceased to receive help from the
Feoffees and who went on to outdoor relief between 1851 and 1873 stood at
6.4 years, and although two men only survived for a year as pensioners before
they died, two more lived for fifteen years after they had retired, and one for
sixteen years.[7]

Whether the men under discussion had the physical strength to enjoy their
often quite lengthy retirement it is difficult to say. They may have been the
victims of painful but non life-threatening conditions such as rheumatism, or
they may have enjoyed good health for several years. Such evidence as there is
suggests that illness may have been a factor in bringing about the retirement of
at least ten of the pensioners, for each of them had received help for sickness
either from the Poor Law or from the Feoffees at least once in the year before
they ceased work. Nevertheless, these men retired on average only just over
two and a half years earlier than their contemporaries for whom there is no
evidence of ill health, while the average length of their retirement was
fractionally greater than that of the other pensioners.

Still more difficult to assess is how far a poor man in Colyton in the mid-
nineteenth century had opportunities for self-fulfilment in his Third Age, or

indeed what would constitute such fulfilment. It is, however, possible to say that financially he would be required to change his previous life style very little, if at all. It has been estimated that at this time the usual Poor Law pension of 2s 6d or 3s a week was the equivalent of 80 per cent of the spending power available to younger working-class people, compared to the 40 per cent allocated to pensioners today,[8] although it must be admitted that at a time when even those in work were living on the knife-edge of poverty, it would not be possible to maintain an elderly person on a sum considerably below that which it took to support a younger man.

What scanty evidence can be gleaned from the minutes of the Axminster Guardians of the Poor confirms that 2s 6d to 3s was the usual weekly allowance in the Axminster Poor Law district in the 1850s. For example, in 1852 Sir John Kennaway approached the guardians on behalf of Mary Bole, an aged pauper who did not want to go into the workhouse, but preferred to live with her daughter in Exeter. The guardians granted Mrs Bole 2s a week, but raised the allowance to 2s 6d in 1854, and to 3s a week in 1856.[9] Nearly thirty years later, the Honiton Guardians of the Poor granted 3s 6d a week to an old woman when she left their district to live with her son in Colyford.[10]

The working classes of Colyton, then, approached old age knowing that there was an alternative to the workhouse, and that the Poor Law, through which the community looked after its elderly, would support them when they could no longer earn a living. The position of the middling and upper-middle classes was rather different, because means-testing ensured that the resources available through the Poor Law were diverted to those most in need. They therefore had to rely on their own endeavours when it came to financing themselves and their dependants in their last years. Although exactly half the fifty men aged sixty and over in these classes in 1851 owned property of sufficient value to allow them a place on the electoral registers, and a further nine were well enough off to have retired already, for some at the lower end of the scale the need to provide financial security for themselves and their families caused them to continue working even longer than did their contemporaries who relied on the Poor Law. The proportions of better-off and poor men in the sixty to sixty-nine year age group in 1851 who were still working were very similar, standing at 79 per cent and 82 per cent respectively, but by the time the seventy to seventy-nine year age group was reached, the balance had changed, with half of the more prosperous men still in harness, compared to only a third of the working class. A carpenter, thatcher or shoemaker with a small business employing only one or two people, and who had brought up a large family, might well find it difficult to save enough to retire.

As by definition members of the middling class did not appear on the Feoffees' list of the poor and so did not receive the annual Christmas bonus, it is not possible to discover at what ages retirement actually took place. Even so, it is known that increasing age and infirmity caused a few men to approach the Feoffees for financial help. An example is the case of a 67-year-old grocer, the owner of a freehold house and garden in Colyton, who sold up in 1851 and moved elsewhere with his wife. Seven years later, the couple returned to Colyton from Jersey, 'in great distress and very infirm', and were given £5 by the Feoffees eight months before the husband died.[11] Three years after that the 1861 census shows his widow as being on outdoor relief as a pauper. Nor was this couple the only example of middling-class members who could not continue to support themselves unaided in old age. Two small farmers had to relinquish their tenancies and went on to the Feoffees' list of the poor, and although one left Colyton altogether, the other obtained work as an agricultural labourer, and ultimately retired on a Poor Law pension at the age of seventy-three. It appears, then, that a safety net was available through the Poor Law to the formerly better-off when their private resources were exhausted.

This, however, is not the end of the story, because if the children of parents who had needed to seek assistance from the Poor Law were themselves among the better-off, then the Axminster guardians would approach them to contribute towards the cost of their fathers' and mothers' relief, whether that was provided in the workhouse or in the community, or indeed in one case in the Exminster Lunatic Asylum. This policy had been in place at least since 1847, when relieving officers nationally were instructed to investigate 'what relatives the applicant may have who are liable and able to contribute to the relief afforded to him'.[12] In the 30 years between 1851 and 1881 the guardians were forced to threaten court action against only six Colyton-based children unwilling to contribute towards their parents' support, and none of these cases involved working-class offspring, even though in other parts of the country, such as Norfolk, farm labourers were required to maintain their elderly parents, in spite of the low wages they received.[13]

The increasing pressure brought to bear by the agricultural depression, however, resulted in a similar number of cases arising in the ten years from 1881 to 1891 as had occurred during the preceding thirty years. Again it was the middling-class children of Colyton who were asked to pay up. Some of these six cases were settled comparatively quickly, with sons offering partial contributions towards the cost of the total outrelief afforded to their parents, and one case was withdrawn when it was found that the son was illegitimate and that his 'father' therefore had no claim on him. In other examples, reluctance on the part of the children to pay caused the proceedings to become very long drawn out. John Anning, a master mason who in his middle age had been employing three men, was reduced to asking for outdoor relief for himself and his wife in October 1884, when he was sixty-one years old. He was granted 4s a week, and his six sons were asked to contribute. They agreed to pay 1s a week each, and the elderly couple's relief was discontinued. Then began a long saga of the guardians trying to extract money from the sons, and the sons evading payment as long as they could. A month after relief was first granted, the parents were admitted to Axminster workhouse, because the sons had not paid up. They were soon sent back to Colyton, this time with 5s a week outdoor relief, and again the sons were called upon to pay. Their reluctance to do so led to summonses being issued against three of them, but the threat of the law induced them to agree to contribute 10d a week each. However, they soon fell into arrears, and in a further attempt to force a financial contribution from them, the Guardians discontinued relief to the old people altogether, only to have to start it again four weeks later, this time at 6s a week. The Justices of the Peace then made orders for payment on the three sons who still refused to contribute. There is no doubt that times were hard for the sons as well as the parents, for one of them went bankrupt in 1886. Fortunately, after their father's death the sons appeared to find no difficulty in providing for their mother, who was described in the 1891 census as 'supported by her children'.[14]

It may well be that those offspring who had to be forced to contribute to their parents' maintenance were only a small minority, but there is unfortunately no indication of how many children in any class in fact gave direct financial assistance to their parents without being pressured to do so by the Poor Law authorities.

While there is evidence that some men from the more prosperous classes were unable to maintain their position in old age, the fortunes of the thirty-seven elderly widows and single women in the same social group are less clear, because the 1851 census provides no indication of how nearly a third of them managed financially. However, just under half of the group were shown to be of independent means, being described as living on the interest of monies, or as annuitants, landed proprietors, or householders, while around one-fifth were in work, in some cases carrying on the businesses left by their former husbands, and in others acting as assistants to other family members. In one exceptional case, however, a 79-year-old spinster was described as a pauper, even though she was living in the household of a cousin who ran a school with eighteen boarding pupils.[15] It would seem that a closer relationship than that of 'cousin' was required before one relative could be asked wholly to maintain another.

Who will look after me?

The second major question to be answered is how Colyton's elderly, of whatever class, could expect to be cared for when they were no longer able to look after themselves without help. Many people who feel themselves growing old still look to their children as the first line of defence against loneliness, or if they wish to avoid residential care. For this reason, the fate of old people in Colyton will be discussed not only in the light of social class and sex, but also according to whether they had any children who might be of help to them, particularly once their marriage partner had died, or whether this line of support was denied to them through childlessness. A detailed account of the living arrangements of a cohort of men and women aged fifty to fifty-nine in 1851, carried through to 1871, has already been published,[16] but in this chapter an attempt is made to paint with a broader brush, particularly because the comparatively small sample and the large number of variables, coupled with the inevitable lack of evidence as to exactly why any particular residential arrangement came about, mean that purely statistical results must be approached with care.

In 1851, Colyton contained 190 men and women who were sixty years of age and over, and who, whether married, widowed, separated, or in one case single,[17] had had one or more offspring who survived to adulthood. The individuals concerned, together with their unmarried children in the days when the latter where still living at home, had formed 145 separate families, but by the time the census was taken, half of these units had reached the 'empty nest' phase of the lifecycle, when all the sons and daughers had gone to establish themselves elsewhere, whether inside or outside the parish. The other seventy-two families, however, still had at least one single child remaining in the household. In this respect there was very little difference between the social classes, and so no distinction will be made between them here.

Nowadays it would be thought unlikely that such a large proportion of elderly parents would still have unmarried children living at home with them, but this is not such a surprising situation as it might seem, for the parents came from a generation where women were likely to bear children as long as they remained fertile, a period which could extend into the late forties. As a result, it was by no means unusual for parents in their sixties to be providing a home for children still under marriageable age. Then some men had married women considerably younger than themselves, so that they found themselves fathering offspring at a time when others might expect to become grandfathers. Moreover, it has already been shown in chapter 4 that children who remained in Colyton did not usually set up house independently before marriage, and therefore the age at which they left the parental home depended on when, or whether, they found a suitable partner. On the other hand, a stereotype exists of the self-sacrificing Victorian daughter who deliberately rejected her marriage opportunities in order to stay at home and care for her parents in their old age.

To discover how many elderly parents never experienced an empty nest, it is necessary to find out which of the seventy-two family units containing both an elderly parent or parents, and an unmarried offspring in 1851 still retained at least one child up to the death of both father and mother.[18] In fact, there were thirty such families, or just over a fifth of all the sets of elderly parents who are known to have had children and who ended their days in the parish, forming what would nowadays be considered a very sizeable minority.[19] The question arises as to whether the unmarried children who remained at home did so out of duty, or for mutual convenience.

Statistical records alone, while often providing sound evidence as to what happened, cannot necessarily explain why events occurred as they did. Nevertheless, they do in this instance produce some pointers towards possible motivations. In the first place, not all the unmarried children staying at home, whether with married or widowed parents, were daughters. Nine of the thirty families concerned had retained only sons, in another four both a son and a daughter were present, while seventeen contained only daughters. It is not impossible that some of the sons had stayed to look after their parents, or parent, but it is much more likely that they did so because they had not been able, or did not wish, to find a wife. There are also possible reasons, other than the desire to care for the older generation, why more than half of the twenty-one daughers concerned were still at home. One girl was mentally handicapped and it is reasonable to assume that she was receiving care rather than providing it, and four more unmarried daughters had illegitimate children with them, so that their presence was more likely to be due to a failure to marry than to a deliberate decision to care for aged parents. Three daughters were still within the normal marriageable age when their parents died, while another four, together with their widowed mothers, had been taken into the households of other family members, which would imply that they did not hold sole responsibility for their parents' care. For the rest, it is impossible to say whether they remained at home because they had been unable to find a suitable partner, or because they deliberately sacrificed marriage, or a life of independence through work, to look after their fathers and mothers. Two unmarried daughters did return to Colyton in middle age to live with their parents, and in their cases it may be assumed that their purpose was to care for the older generation, although even that cannot be certain. Nevertheless, wherever the balance may have lain between convenience and duty as far as the children's behaviour was concerned, it would be true to say that elderly parents in Colyton in the second half of the nineteenth century could not with any certainty expect that they would have unmarried children free to look after them in their last days.

Single children, however, were only one line of defence in the fight against loneliness and incapacity in old age. Married sons and daughters who remained in Colyton were also available, close to hand, if help were needed.

While both husband and wife remained together, the married children of elderly parents were seldom called on to provide residential care, and indeed, in 1851 only one old couple had been taken into the household of a married child. In a handful of cases, married or widowed children were to be found in their parents' households, but in all save one of these the arrangement was only temporary, and may be regarded as the parents extending hospitality to the younger generation rather than the reverse. The real value of married children to their fathers and mothers only became apparent when the death of one parent left the other facing widowhood.

Altogether, eighty-three of the men and women who were sixty or over in 1851 and who stayed in Colyton until they died[20] were either already widowed in that year, or became so later, and it is through the analysis of their living arrangements revealed in the last census before their deaths that the importance to them of their children, whether married or single, can be shown. Here, however, differences between the social classes begin to be noticeable, even though with such small numbers any pattern may well be more apparent than real. Nevertheless, on the evidence available, it may be said that while two-thirds of the widowed in both the better-off and the working classes were in the same household as an offspring, whether single or married,[21] the more prosperous were slightly more likely to be living with unmarried than with married children. Well-to-do widowers and still active widows who did not wish to cease heading their own households were able to pay for domestic help, whether daily or living-in, and could also afford to maintain those daughters who had not married, for whatever reason. In the working classes, on the other hand, the position was reversed, with more than four out of ten widowers and over half of the widows being taken into the house of a married son or daughter.

There can be little doubt that what made it possible for so many working-class married couples to take in a widowed parent or parent-in-law was the regular weekly pension which the elderly received through the Poor Law. Without this money coming into the household, a farm labourer or a wage-earning artisan would find it very difficult to accept another mouth to feed, but the extra 2s 6d or 3s a week accompanying the elderly parent would be of real benefit to a household where the main wage earner received only 8s a week in cash. On the other hand, the average pension was insufficient to allow an old person with no other resources to live entirely independently in a separate dwelling for which rent had to be paid. Mutual benefit dictated that the widowed parent should give up his or her own home and join the family of a married child.

It remains to be seen what kind of arrangements for extreme old age were made by the elderly people who had children but did not live with them, and whether these dispositions differed to any large degree from the residential patterns of the group who, as far as is known, were childless. Once again, married couples had their partners to rely on, so only the widowed, the separated and the single will be considered here.

Even though a third of widowed or separated parents in all classes lived apart from their children, they were not necessarily cut off from them, and nearly four out of ten had sons or daughters, nearly all married, living within the parish to whom they could turn if need arose. Indeed, some were living in the same street as their married children, or even next door to them. However it was the better-off rather than the working class who were in this position, which would indicate that where a choice was available, as it was to the economically independent, some elderly persons preferred to live near their children rather than in the same household. This choice, however, was not freely available to the poor, and no elderly widower in the working classes who was living apart from his children had either a married son or a married daughter in the parish to whom he could have attached himself.

There was an alternative to living with children, while remaining part of the family, and that was to take in other relatives, or more commonly in old age, to join their households. Again, the working class were much more likely to follow this route than the well-to-do, and although the number of cases involved is far too few to be statistically significant,[22] they do indicate that for the poor, the pooling of resources enabled the elderly to remain in the community. One widower was taken in by a married nephew, and a widow by a kinsman; two widows had illegitimate grandsons of earning age with them and a third was living with a widowed sister.

There remain those widowed or separated people who lived apart from all kin. Some of the better-off met this situation by employing living-in domestic servants, and one man became a boarder in a house owned by himself and occupied by a farmer and his family. Even so, three elderly widowers and one widow in this class were living entirely by themselves, although they may well have employed daily servants to look after them. In the working classes, two widows maintained themselves by working as living-in servants, two widowers each took in a woman separated from her husband, together with her child, raising the possibility that they were living together as a married couple would do, and one widower himself became a lodger. For those elderly poor unable to make any other arrangement, it seems likely that the Poor Law authorities organised small households where at least two unrelated people on outdoor relief lived together, presumably so that they could help each other as required, and in order to make their pension money go further than if they lived independently. In the end, only one working-class widower and one widow from this group were living entirely alone.

The last group to be considered, namely those who as far as can be ascertained had never had children to whom they could turn, numbered fifty-seven individuals in 1851. Thirteen of them were still married at the time of the last census taken before their deaths, but forty-four were either widowed, separated or single. It might be thought that the residential arrangements of these individuals who were without the support of either a marriage partner or a child would closely resemble those of the elderly who had had children, but who were in much the same position because their spouses had died and all their offspring had left the neighbourhood. There were, however, two major differences between the two groups. In the first place, the childless were considerably more likely to leave the parish before they died, and a third of them did so, compared to only one in five of the group which had brought up children. In the second place, a larger proportion of the remaining 29 individuals who ended their lives in Colyton were living with relatives, particularly if they were part of better-off society.[23] This tendency is emphasized if the fifteen elderly people who left Colyton are considered, for all the well-to-do women in this group had been in the households of kinsfolk before they moved on elsewhere.

The range of relatives offering hospitality was considerable, embracing widowed sisters and brothers-in-law, a widowed cousin, and married and unmarried nephews or nieces. There was a degree of reciprocity in some of these arrangements, however, because in return for a home, elderly female relatives were able to carry out domestic duties for their single or widowed male kin, as witnessed by the descriptions of 'housekeeper' or 'assistant' attached to them in the census returns.

In other respects, the residential groupings of the childless and those who were not living with their children were very similar. What can be said of all the elderly, of whatever class, is that they were unlikely to end their days in solitude. While in the second half of the 1990s 21 per cent of men and 40 per cent of women aged sixty-five to seventy-four were in one-person households, and 34 per cent of men and 68 per cent of women of seventy-five and over were in that position,[24] only 5 per cent of the over-sixties in Colyton in 1851 who stayed on in the parish until they died were living entirely alone.[25]

Notes

1.   D. Thomson, 'Provision for the elderly in England', unpublished PhD thesis, University of Cambridge, 1980, p. 356.

2.   W.H. Dumsday, *Haddon's Relieving Officer's Handbook*, London, 1902, p. 36.

3.   The breakdown for working-class men and women of sixty years and over appearing in the 1851 census by ten-year age sets is as follows:

	60–69		70–79		80–89		All	
	No.	%	No.	%	No.	%	No.	%
Men								
Still working	34	82	6	33	2	29	42	65
On outdoor relief	5	15	8	44	5	71	18	28
On army pension	1	3	1	6	-	-	2	3
No occupation	-	-	3	17	-	-	3	4
All	40	100	18	100	7	100	65	100
Women								
Still working	10	59	2	12.5	-	-	12	33
On outdoor relief	5	29	13	81	2	67	20	56
No occupation	2	12	1	6.5	1	33	4	11
All	17	100	16	100	3	100	36	100

4.   J. Robin, 'The relief of poverty in mid-nineteenth century Colyton', *Rural History*, 1 (2), 1990, pp. 195–6.

5.   Not all elderly working-class persons appeared on the treasurer's list of the poor. In 1851, for example, thirty-two of the sixty-five men aged sixty or over were excluded. Of these thirty-two, 56 per cent were already on parish relief and had therefore been struck off the list; 31 per cent were born outside Colyton and may have been omitted under the Feoffee's rule that no-one without legal settlement in Colyton should be assisted. The remaining four men, making up 13 per cent of the total, were all born in Colyton. They were still working, and it may be that they were considered to be sufficiently well provided for from their own earnings.

6.   P. Laslett, *A fresh map of life*, London, 1989, p. 4.

7.   The breakdown by age group of working class men aged sixty years or more who retired between 1851 and 1873, and the mean length of each group's retirement, is as follows:

Retirement at age	No.	%	Average length of retirement in years
60–64	5	14	5.6
65–69	7	19	4.9
70–74	19	53	7.6
75–79	4	11	3.75
80+	1	3	9.0
All	36	100	6.4

8.   D. Thomson, 'Welfare and the historian' in L. Bonfield, R. Smith, and K. Wrightson, eds, *The world we have gained*, Oxford, 1986, pp. 355–87.

9.   Axminster Union Minute Book (hereafter A.U.M.B), vol. 7, 6.2.1852, 9.6.1854 and 28.3.1856.

10.   Ibid., vol. 13, 5.4.1883.

11.   Devon Record Office (hereafter D.R.O.), F 17/8, 12.2.1858.

12.   W.H. Dumsday, *Relieving Officer's Handbook*, 1902, p. 31.

13.   A. Digby, *Pauper Palaces*, London, 1978, p. 227.

14.   D.R.O. A.U.M.B. vol. 14, 16.10.1884 to 18.8.1887.

15.   The exact proportions were as follows: no information, 30 per cent; working, 22 per cent (all but one being aged sixty to sixty-nine); independent, 46 per cent; pauper, 2 per cent.

16.   J. Robin, 'Family care of the elderly in a nineteenth-century Devonshire parish', *Ageing and Society*, 4 (4) 1984, pp. 505–16.

17. The marital status in 1851 of the 190 individuals concerned was as follows:-

	Married to a spouse aged 60+	Married to a spouse under 60	Widowed	Separated	Single parent	All
Males	45	23	22	2	–	92
Females	45	6	45	1	1	98

Note: The total number of married couples containing at least one spouse aged 60 years or over was 74.

18. Evidence for such retention comes not only from the residential arrangements shown in the last census before the death of the parents, but also from the life histories of the children concerned, including whether they remained single until after their parents had died. It is of course impossible to know the exact composition of the households concerned at the date when death occurred.

19. Ten families must be eliminated from the 145 units present in 1851 because the parents themselves left Colyton to live elsewhere, and nothing is know of their final circumstances. The thirty family units which retained unmarried offspring up to the death of both father and mother represent 22 per cent of the 135 units which remained in the parish.

20. Four widows and widowers left Colyton before death.

21. Residential arrangements of elderly widowed persons who had had children at the last census before death by social class and sex:

	With unmarried children		With married children		Other		Total	
	No.	%	No.	%	No.	%	No.	%
Better-off classes								
Widowers	4	33.5	1	8.0	7	58.5	12	100.0
Widows	8	38.0	9	43.0	4	19.0	21	100.0
All	12	36.0	10	30.0	11	33.0	33	100.0
Working classes								
Widowers	5	24.0	9	43.0	7[i]	33.0	21	100.0
Widows	4[ii]	14.0	15	52.0	10	34.0	29	100.0
All	9	18.0	24	48.0	17	34.0	50	100.0

(i) Includes one man separated from his wife.
(ii) Includes one woman separated from her husband, and one single mother.

22. As a matter of record, the residential arrangements of those widowed and separated elderly parents who were not living with a child were as follows:

No.	Classes I–III		Classes IV–V		All	
	%	No.	%	No.	%	
Living with kin	1	9.0	5	29.0	6	21.5
Living with servants	5	45.5	–	–	5	18.0
Living as servants	–	–	2	12.0	2	7.0
Living with lodgers, or as boarder/lodgers	1	9.0	3	18.0	4	14.0
Living as part of a pauper household	–	–	5	29.0	5	18.0
Solitary	4	36.5	2	12.0	6	21.5
Total	11	100.0	17	100.0	28	100.0

23. The residential arrangements of the childless widowed, separated, or single elderly persons who stayed in Colyton until death were as follows:

	Classes I–III		Classes IV–V		All	
	No.	%	No.	%	No.	%
Living with kin	5	41.5	6	35.0	11	38.0
Living with servants	5	41.5	–	–	5	17.0
Living as servants	–	–	1	6.0	1	3.5
Living with lodgers, or as lodgers	–	–	5	29.0	5	17.0
Living as part of a pauper household	–	–	3	18.0	3	10.5
Solitary	2	17.0	2	12.0	4	14.0
Total	12	100.0	17	100.0	29	100.0

24. *Social Trends*, 27, 1997, table 2.7, p. 42.

25. Thirty-five of the 247 people over sixty in Colyton in 1851 left the parish before death, leaving 212 individuals, of whom ten, or 5 per cent, were recorded as living alone in the last census before they died.

Chapter 12

Care in the Community

Hardly a chapter has been written here which has not included a reference to the poor of Colyton, particularly in relation to the wage-earning and labouring classes. Records of the Guardians of the Poor for the Axminster district, and of the Feoffees of Colyton, show that four-fifths of the men in these two groups who headed households in 1861 received help in money or in kind from one or both organisations at some time during their lives. Those who were not so relieved were largely either single or childless; fathers in their middle years whose children had reached the age where they could start earning; or incomers who stayed too short a time in the parish to experience a family crisis which needed support from the Poor Law.[1]

For the great majority of the working classes, and for those farmers and members of the middling class who fell on hard times, there were three main sources to which they could turn for help. The first, and by far the most important, was the publicly funded Poor Law, which bore ultimate responsibility for those incapable of managing unaided, just as Social Services do today. The second was the voluntary service provided by the Feoffees of Colyton within the parish, which supplemented the work of the Poor Law, rather as national voluntary organisations nowadays help special interest groups, though on a much smaller scale. The third source of aid was even more limited, as it concerned sickness only, and was to be found in the self-help organisations of the separate Colyton Mutual and Providential Societies for men and for women, which in return for annual subscriptions provided funding for their members during periods of illness. These societies were the forerunners of the more sophisticated concerns, such as BUPA or the Private Patients Plan, which now provide an alternative to the National Health Service for those with the means to join them. However, it was the Poor Law which underpinned the whole system of relief, and which will therefore be considered first.

The burgeoning expenditure of today's welfare state and the belief that it has created a dependency culture are two of the reasons advanced by the government for its reform. In these respects, history is certainly repeating itself, for nearly 170 years ago the Old Poor Law was facing similar problems. Costs were steadily rising, and the view was held at the time, though its validity has since been disputed,[2] that this was largely because under what was known as the Speenhamland system, inadequate wages were often made up by payments from the rates. As a result, employers could underpay their workers, knowing that funds raised from the whole body of ratepayers would be used in much the same way as family income supplement is nowadays to provide enough means for a family, whatever its size, to live on. Malthusian theory held that the relief of poverty in this way made matters worse by increasing the numbers of the poor, because there were no disadvantages in marrying early and having a large number of children. Reformers therefore worked to ensure that support payments to healthy able-bodied men of working age should cease. Their views gained ground, and the Royal Commission of 1832 to 1834 recommended that, except for medical attendance, 'all relief whatsoever to able-bodied persons or to their families, otherwise than in well-regulated workhouses (that is, places where they may be set to work) should be declared unlawful'. At this stage, the commissioners believed that the wives and children of the able-bodied poor should be treated in the same way as the family head, accompanying him to the workhouse if he had to go there, but that outdoor relief, that is to say, support provided in the community, should continue to be available for young orphans, and for sick, insane, crippled, blind, infirm or aged persons who were not part of the labour market.[3] The recommendations of the commissioners were accepted by the government of the day, and were embodied in the Poor Law Act of 1834.

By 1851, the administration of the New Poor Law had evolved to the point where its bureaucratic hierarchy was headed by the newly created Poor Law Board, which comprised the Lord President of the Council, the Lord Privy Seal, the Home Secretary and the Chancellor of the Exchequer, *ex officio*, together with a president who was a Minister of the Crown, and two secretaries, one of whom was eligible to sit in Parliament. In practice, the board was run by civil servants, headed by the non-political secretary.[4] This was the body to which the Guardians of the Poor, who occupied the next rung down on the ladder, appealed for advice when they were not sure of the correct action to take, and to which members of the public could complain if they felt that they were being unfairly treated, as Mary Russell did in 1870 when she was refused outdoor relief by the Axminster guardians.[5] In 1871, the Poor Law Board was merged in a new ministry, known as the Local Government Board.

The function of the Guardians of the Poor was to administer the New Poor Law in the amalgamations of parishes which were set up nationwide after the 1834 Act was passed. Colyton was placed in the Axminster Union, made up of seventeen nearby parishes. The unpaid guardians, who were required to own or occupy property worth at least £25 a year, were in most cases elected by the ratepayers of the union, who provided the funds for relief,[6] and they could therefore be expected to protect the interests both of themselves and of those who voted for them by ensuring that such relief was given as economically as possible within the regulations. All boards of guardians were circumscribed by the instructions received from the Poor Law Board and its successor in London, but they had freedom of action in smaller matters, and it was at this level that the personalities of the individual guardians became important, resulting in some Unions being easier places to live in for the poor than others. As a small example of this, the Axminster guardians towards the end of 1878 received a request from the master of the workhouse that he should be allowed to provide the usual special Christmas dinner for the inmates, and to give a New Year's treat to the children and the infirm paupers. Permission was granted in principle, but one guardian asked if the treat was to include an issue of tobacco to the old men, and objected strongly when he was told that such was the case. Although his objection might be upheld nowadays on the grounds that tobacco is harmful to health, such was not the understanding at the time and the rest of the board overruled him, the chairman remarking that tobacco was the greatest treat the old men could have, and it should not be withheld from them.[7]

The Axminster Board of Guardians met fortnightly throughout the year, but they were not themselves involved in the day-to-day running of the system within the parishes. For this they relied on their two paid relieving officers, who between them were responsible for the whole union, which contained around 20,000 inhabitants.[8] The duties of these officers, laid down by the Poor Law Board in 1847, were to receive all applications for relief within their districts; to examine the circumstances of every case by visiting the house of the applicant, and by fully investigating his or her state of health, ability to work, means, and family connections; to report accordingly to the guardians at their next meeting; and to visit from time to time all paupers receiving relief. By 1871, the officers were being required to visit the homes of all able-bodied sick persons on relief once a fortnight, and all old and infirm individuals once a quarter, keeping a diary with the dates and results of such visits, presumably to circumvent any attempt at deception. Cases of sudden or urgent necessity had to be dealt with by the officer on his own responsibility between meetings of the guardians.[9]

The relieving officers were also responsible for spending and accounting for all the money they received for relief. The sums involved were considerable, each officer disbursing roughly five times as much each year as the entire income of the Feoffees. In 1883, for example, Mr Halse, who was responsible for the district in which Colyton lay, spent £1216 3s 11d in the first six months,[10] compared to the Feoffees' half-yearly income of around £220. For these responsibilities he received a salary of £85 a year.

The stress involved in such a workload may be imagined, particularly during a period of agricultural depression. By 1885, Mr Halse was beginning to show signs of strain, and in April of that year the guardians first commented on errors creeping into his accounts. Eighteen months later, he was summoned to a meeting of the board to justify his bookkeeping, but he failed to attend, pleading illness, and within a few days he had committed suicide. The auditor's report to the guardians on Mr Halse's books showed that although several bills remained unpaid, there was no evidence of any fraud, only an increasing carelessness, which had resulted in a deficit of £43 5s 9d. This sum was repaid to the guardians by Mr Halse's sureties, that is to say the two friends who at the time of his appointment had guaranteed that they would make good any losses which he incurred, up to a specified sum. It is interesting to note that when a new relieving officer was appointed, some of the guardians voted in favour of his salary being reduced from £85 to £75 a year, although they were outvoted by fifteen to six.[11]

The relieving officers were not entirely unaided in their work, because the ratepayers of each parish elected one or more unpaid overseers to help them locally. The overseers were responsible for collecting the poor rate from parishioners who were liable to pay it, and for handing the money over to the guardians. Efficiency in this matter was demanded, and in 1886 the Axminster board agreed that summonses should be issued against any overseers who failed to pay the amount of their parish's contribution to the treasurer by the next board day.[12] This was almost certainly an indication that the agricultural depression, then at its height, was badly affecting the ratepayers of the district. The overseers were also responsible for giving relief in cases of sudden and urgent necessity if the relieving officer could not be reached, but if they did so they were required to report in writing either to the officer concerned or direct to the Board of Guardians. One of the overseers in Colyton in 1858 was involved in an unsavoury incident, when he refused to grant a coffin for the burial of an elderly pauper, Samuel Mutter, who had been born in an adjoining parish but who had lived in Colyton for a number of years. The body was allowed to remain unburied until it started to decompose, when the overseer of Farway stepped in and buried the old man, even though he was neither a native nor a resident of that parish. The overseer for Colyton was called to explain to the guardians why the coffin was refused in the first place, but unfortunately the minutes do not record the result of the interview.[13]

Finally, at the bottom of the hierarchy came the assistant overseers, who, like the relieving officers, were paid employees. Joseph Edwards's contract as Assistant Overseer of the Poor of Colyton has survived, and shows that he was appointed by the ratepayers of the parish in June 1855, the official document being signed by two Justices of the Peace. His pay amounted to 5s a week, with the refund of reasonable expenses incurred through attending meetings with the magistrates or the Board of Guardians. The list of duties which Mr Edwards agreed to undertake for this far from princely sum is too long to reproduce here, but it included acting as secretary to the Vestry and to all the committees appointed by it, and writing the minutes; keeping the accounts of all charity moneys distributed by the wardens or overseers; looking after the documents kept in the Parish Chest and allowing any person who was entitled to do so to make copies or extracts from them; entering up the rate books and recovering arrears owing, if necessary by arranging for summonses to be issued by a Justice of the Peace; keeping the accounts of the parish officers and presenting them for audit; conducting all correspondence arising from the audit of the overseers' accounts; producing printed lists annually of all persons liable to jury service and all electors eligible to vote at parliamentary elections; and advising the parish officers 'in all the duties of their offices, if needed, and also to perform such other duties and services ... as the Commissioners (Poor Law) from time to time at the request of the Parish Officers shall prescribe or direct to be performed by such Assistant Overseer'.[14] Twenty-five years later, when Mr William Gill was appointed Assistant Overseer for Colyton, his two sureties had to put up a bond for £200. His fate was little happier than that of the relieving officer, Mr Halse, who killed himself. He retired after seven years in the post, and was admitted to the Devon County Lunatic Asylum at Exminster in January 1890, dying there seven months later.[15]

This then was the structure through which the Poor Law was administered. It remains to be seen to what extent it met the needs of those it was intended to help.[16]

Nowadays the National Health Service is one of the most valued components of the welfare state. In the mid-nineteenth century, provision for sickness through the Poor Law was heavily means-tested, as indeed were all its benefits, but a surprisingly wide range of services were provided for those to whom the receiving officer considered treatment should be given.

Colyton had its own medical officer, appointed by the guardians and shared with the neighbouring small parish of Shute. From before 1851 up to 1871, this post was held by Mr John Snook, who was a fully qualified surgeon with the degree of MRCS, as well as being a Licentiate of the Society of Apothecaries. He also had his own private practice, in addition to his work for the Poor Law, and was well acquainted with the parish and its inhabitants, having been born and brought up there.

In order to obtain the services of the doctor, the sick person, or someone on his or her behalf, would normally approach either the parish overseer or the relieving officer for an order for the doctor to attend. Cases were divided into three categories – first midwifery; second fractures and accidents; and third, cases of urgency requiring immediate attention. The official concerned had to satisfy himself of the need of the patient involved, but having done so, he would give an order to the Medical Officer, or to another doctor if the former were not available.[17] This at least was the theory. In practice, in urgent cases the medical officer would attend the patient first and ask for an order later. For example, in June 1871 Mr Snook wrote to the guardians asking them to instruct their relieving officer to give him an order covering the attendance he had given to a woman who gave birth prematurely. The guardians resolved that the order should be made.[18] Usually, orders for attendance at confinements were issued well before the expected date of the delivery. Mr Snook's successor, his son-in-law Frederick O'Meara, was in trouble with the guardians for obtaining orders many weeks, and in some cases months, before confinements were due,[19] although this may have been an attempt to circumvent bureaucracy and avoid the difficulties met by his father-in-law.

Mr Snook himself took his duties in relation to midwifery very seriously and worked hard to make the parish midwives more up-to-date in their methods of delivery. In 1852, he complained to the guardians that the midwives were practising what today might be called 'natural childbirth', that is to say, they were delivering women downstairs in an upright position, a course of action which he considered very dangerous, instead of making them lie down in bed. Two years later, he reported that the midwives were persisting in their old-fashioned practices, and the guardians instructed the relieving officer to tell them that if they continued with this method of delivery, their pay would be stopped.[20]

Where fractures and accidents were concerned, Mr Snook was a one-man accident and emergency service. During a single week in 1868, he treated James Bull, who injured his spine when his ladder broke as he was thatching a rick, resulting in paralysis of the lower half of his body; a young man who lost the first finger of his right hand as a result of a gun explosion; a child who suffered a broken thigh and cuts about the head through being knocked down by a horse; a farmer's son whose arm was broken in the same way; a man who jumped over a hedge, caught his leg in a bramble and fell head over heels breaking his arm above the wrist; and finally a fishmonger-cum-chimney sweep, who became drunk at the Royal George, offered to wrestle a man, and was thrown, which resulted in a fracture of the cup of his shoulder joint.[21] Agricultural accidents were only too common, and in another week Mr Snook had to deal with two cases of injuries sustained by men working chaff-cutters.[22]

Mr Snook's brother William, though not medically qualified, acted as his assistant, and also dealt with accidents on occasion, rather as paramedics do today. William, however, was not paid by the Poor Law authorities, and indeed, after 1858 the medical officer had to be qualified in both medicine and surgery before he could treat pauper patients. His professional standing could therefore be higher than that of a rural practitioner who treated those independent poor whose means were just above the line below which relief was granted.[23] There was an occasion in the nearby parish of Kilmington when several parents were summonsed for refusing to allow their children to be vaccinated, but when it transpired that the vaccination was being carried out by their medical officer's assistant and not by the doctor himself, the magistrates concluded that no offence had been committed, and the parents were discharged with a caution.[24]

When it came to the third category of cases, namely those of urgency requiring immediate attendance, the medical officer was obliged to 'attend duly and punctually upon all poor persons requiring medical attention within the limits of the Union assigned to him'. He was also responsible for seeing that the necessary medicines and invalid foods reached the patient, and if the latter was unable to fetch them, then the doctor would either have to deliver them himself, or ask the relieving officer to do so. The medical officer was bound to supply any necessary medical or surgical appliances, excluding only articles such as bread for poultices or cotton wool and calico for dressings, which he would not provide in his private practice.[25]

Pauper patients who found their treatment unsatisfactory could and did complain to the guardians. Mr Snook himself was called upon to explain why he did not visit John Potter of Colyford until he had been sent for three times, although in the event his statement, unrecorded in the minute book, was accepted as satisfactory.[26] The medical officer of Dalwood was asked why he had supplied a bottle of medicine to a pauper without affixing a proper label with written directions as to the dosage. His reply was that the patient was illiterate, and that he had given verbal instructions, although the patient denied this.[27] The same medical officer was in more serious trouble only just over a year later, when a complaint was lodged that he had neglected a patient who died. His inattention was compounded by the fact that when he did finally visit the patient on the morning of his death, he told the man's wife that there was nothing the matter with her husband. The chairman of the guardians suggested that the medical officer should be more cautious in what he said in future, but there the matter was allowed to drop.[28]

It was not only patients who from time to time complained about the medical officers. They also had to face strictures from the guardians. For example, Mr Snook, who was public vaccinator for Colyton District, fell behind in forwarding certificates of successful vaccinations to the Registrar, as required by the Vaccination Act of 1853,[29] while the medical officer of Chardstock was asked why he had prescribed such a large quantity of brandy all at one time to a pauper patient. His reply that 'the nature of the disease rendered it necessary and the man is now convalescent' was accepted as sufficient explanation,[30] although in another Devon parish outside the Axminster Union a patient who had similarly been prescribed a pint of brandy died the next day.[31]

Reading through the minutes of the guardians covering a period of forty years, it becomes clear that the sickness provisions of the New Poor Law were intended to supply good-quality care for the poorest in society, taking into account the state of medical knowledge at the time, but that inevitably the carrying out of these provisions depended on the competence and goodwill of individual doctors and bureaucrats. However, in terms of what is now known as general practice, it is likely that the poorest members of Colyton's community were at least as well looked after, if not better, than those who were slightly above the poverty line.

Today, maternity benefit for some women, death benefit, sickness benefit, visits by community nurses and treatment by hospital specialists, in addition to health care undertaken by general practitioners, are all taken for granted. The very poor of Colyton, too, received such benefits in the second half of the nineteenth century, though often in a minimal and rudimentary form, and only after severe means-testing. Although no special provision was made for maternity allowances under the Poor Law regulations,[32] it has already been shown in chapter 8 that in addition to the sum of 2s 6d paid to women in childbirth, the Axminster guardians gave relief in kind to family heads whose wives had already borne at least three children.[33]   The medical officer could also order special food for nursing mothers and infants who were on outdoor relief, although he was not bound to do so.[34]   Death benefits were covered by the provision of a coffin, and if necessary the costs of the funeral, once an order had been received from the relieving officer or the overseer, while sickness benefit came in the form of outdoor relief, at least half of which had to be given not as cash, but as food, clothing and other articles of necessity.[35]   There is evidence that in some cases the poor also received nursing care in their own homes. For example Mary Bole, mentioned earlier as being on outdoor relief of 3s a week, was granted an extra 1s a week to obtain the services of a nurse,[36] while in 1875 the overseer for Colyton lodged a complaint with the Local Government Board in London that the guardians had refused an allowance for a nurse to the wife of a man called Fowler.[37]   The 1891 census shows that Timothy Smith, a blind widower in his eighties and on partial parish relief, had a nurse living in his house on census day.

Hospital treatment was also available to the poor of Colyton. The Royal Devon and Exeter Hospital, which was founded as a charity in 1742, received both in- and out-patients, and its annual report for 1805–1806 makes it clear that while anyone whose circumstances entitled them to charitable relief could be admitted, those capable of paying for themselves had to be excluded.[38]   The hospital for rheumatic diseases in Bath was some eighty miles away, but the guardians paid for Caroline Richard's visit there to take the waters.[39]   Robert Littley was sent to an institute for the blind to receive training, and on his discharge in 1878 the guardians provided him with the materials necessary to set up business as a basket-maker.[40]   He was still holding down a job in this occupation when the 1891 census was taken. The severely mentally ill were treated in the Devon County Lunatic Asylum at Exminster, which received twenty-two patients from Colyton between 1851 and 1891, some of them experiencing more than one stay in that institution.[41]   This hospital, too, was intended primarily for poor patients, and certainly none of those admitted from Colyton could have afforded to pay the full 9s which it cost to maintain an in-patient for a week,[42] although in a few cases relatives of the patients were asked by the guardians to contribute towards the charge. The expense of keeping a patient in the Devon County Asylum was nearly three times as much as the weekly cost of supporting a workhouse inmate, so patients who needed to remain in Exminster for long periods were a considerable drain on the resources of the union from which they came. Whatever may have happened in private asylums, the popular belief that female patients were incarcerated for many years simply because they had borne an illegitimate child and that their families, or indeed the community, wished them out of the way cannot be upheld for the bulk of the population, on grounds of cost if no other. The Commissioners in Lunacy inspected both asylums and workhouses, and it is most improbable that they would allow patients who were not severely mentally ill to remain at public expense in an asylum. For example, in the Axminster Union in 1885 the commissioners stated that a number of less afflicted patients could properly be maintained in the cheaper workhouse, while reporting that one inmate of the workhouse was 'quite demented' and should be transferred to the asylum.[43] Incarceration in the workhouse of those capable of living outside it was legally impossible, as relieving officers were informed in a circular issued in 1879, which stated that 'paupers cannot be compelled to enter the workhouse. Cases where they refuse to do so should be carefully watched so that out-relief may be afforded if they become urgent'.[44]

Finally, for those poor individuals who could no longer be treated at home for whatever reason, and who were not sufficiently ill, either physically or mentally, to be received by the county hospital or lunatic asylum, there remained the workhouse infirmary. Such infirmaries were originally intended to be no more than sickrooms where the regular occupants of the workhouse could be looked after if they fell ill, the task of nursing such patients being given to other inmates, but increasingly the poor who had been on outdoor relief but who could not be looked after at home had to be admitted. In 1865, trained nurses began to be appointed to the infirmaries, laying the foundations for the ultimate establishment of municipal hospitals.[45]

The scale of provision for health care in the second half of the nineteenth century can in no way compare with what is available today, free of means-testing, under the National Health Service. Nevertheless, the seeds of the future welfare state had already been sown, not only in relation to medical services, but also as far as pensions were concerned. It has been shown in chapter 11 that the aged poor, whether married men, widowers or widows, who were no longer capable of work were supported on permanent outdoor relief, which could fairly be described as a form of old-age pension. There was, however, another group of people who needed financial help over quite long periods, that is to say widows with dependent children. Here again, the relief given depended on the earning power of the mother and any of her children who were old enough to enter the labour market. As earlier chapters have shown, both boys and girls began to work at very young ages, but even so their earnings were small, and widowed mothers continued to need a measure of support for some years. The case of Mary Driscoll, a policeman's widow living in the Bedminster Union with five children, provides an example. Her legal settlement was in Colyton, not Bedminster, and therefore the Axminster Union was responsible for the cost of any relief afforded to her. When she could not support herself and her family unaided, it was arranged that they should be sent to the workhouse in Axminster, but she asked to be allowed to stay in Bedminster, with some outdoor relief, as her children were 'in a way of earning something there different to what they could get if sent home to the Axminster Union'. Recognising a financial bargain when they saw one, the guardians granted her 3s a week relief to be paid in Bedminster for three months, and at the end of that time the grant was renewed for a further three months.[46]

However, widowhood in itself did not qualify for assistance. That was given only if a widow had dependent children and could not earn enough to support them, or if she was unable to make an adequate living on grounds of old age or ill health. An able-bodied widow without dependent children was treated little differently from a man, except that, if relief was necessary, it could be made in the form of outdoor relief rather than the workhouse for the first six months of widowhood, as relieving officers were instructed in 1844.[47]

There remains a third area of great importance in the welfare state, namely unemployment pay, and here direct comparisons break down, because, as has already been explained, one of the major aims of the New Poor Law was to cease support payments to healthy able-bodied men of working age. The alternative provision offered was accommodation in the workhouse, an institution which will be examined in detail in the next chapter.

Notes

1.   J. Robin, 'The relief of poverty in mid-nineteenth century Colyton', *Rural History*, 1(2), 1990, pp. 195–217, gives a full account of the extent of poverty in the parish.

2.   See A. Digby, 'Recent developments in the study of the English Poor Law', *The Local Historian*, 12 (5), 1977, pp. 200–210.

3.   S. and B. Webb, *English Local Government: English Poor Law History*, part II: *The last hundred years*, vol. I, London, 1929, pp. 1–11, 58, 63–4.

4.   Ibid., pp. 185–9.

5.   Devon Record Office, Axminster Union Minute Book (hereafter D.R.O. A.U.M.B.), 10, 28.7.70 and 11.8.70.

6.   Local Justices of the Peace were *ex officio* members of the Boards of Guardians, but they did not usually play a very active role. See S. and B. Webb, *English Local Government*, 1929, pp. 119–21.

7.   *Honiton and Ottery St Mary Weekly News*, 21.12.1878.

8.   The 1851 census shows that the population of the Axminster Union numbered 20,303 in that year.

9.   W.H. Dumsday, *Haddon's Relieving Officer's Handbook*, London, 1902, pp. 30–33.

10. D.R.O. A.U.M.B., 13, 6.9.1883.

11. Ibid., vol. 14, 4.11.1886, 11.11.1886, 25.11.1886, 9.12.1886.

12. Ibid., 13.5.1886.

13. Ibid., vol. 9, 26.2.1858.

14. D.R.O., 3483A/P.O. 41.

15. Information received from the Exminster Asylum Project, University of Exeter.

16. Naturally, Boards of Guardians were liable to interpret the Poor Law differently in different parts of the country, and the relief of poverty in large towns presented different problems from those met with in rural areas. The purpose here, however, is to observe in detail how the Axminster Union in general, and Colyton in particular, were affected.

17. General Consolidated Order, 24.7.1847. See W.H. Dumsday, *Relieving Officer's Handbook*, 1902, p. 37.

18. D.R.O. A.U.M.B., 11, 15.6.1871.

19. Ibid., 3.4.1873.

20. Ibid., vol. 8, 6.2.1852 and 3.3.1854.

21. *Devon Weekly Times*, 10.7.1868.

22. Ibid., 24.1.1862.

23. A. Digby, *Pauper Palaces*, London, 1978, pp. 166–79.

24. D.R.O. A.U.M.B., 13, 5.5.1881 and 19.5.1881.

25. General Consolidated Order, 1847. See W.H. Dumsday, *Relieving Officer's Handbook*, 1902, pp. 29–41.

26. D.R.O. A.U.M.B., 9, 14.10.1864 and 11.11.1864.

27. Ibid., 13, 19.10.1882 and 2.11.1882.

28. Ibid., 13, 10.1.1884.

29. Ibid., 9, 8.10.1858.

30. Ibid., 12, 6.1.1876.

31. Private communication from Dr Richard Adair, Cambridge Group for the History of Population and Social Structure.

32. S. and B. Webb, *English Local Government*, 1929, p. 301.

33. D.R.O. A.U.M.B., 8, 2.9.1856.

34. S. and B. Webb, *English Local Government*, 1929, p. 301.

35. Instructional Letter of Poor Law Commissioners, 21.12.1844. See W.H. Dumsday, *Relieving Officer's Handbook*, 1902, pp. 64–5.

36. D.R.O. A.U.M.B., 7, 25.4.1856.

37. Ibid., vol. 11, 29.4.1875.

38. C. Vancouver, *General View of the Agriculture of the County of Devon*, 1808, reprinted Newton Abbot, 1969, pp. 477–8.

39. D.R.O. P.O., 14, Colyton, 20.7.1859.

40. D.R.O. A.U.M.B., 12, 28.12.1878.

41. Information received from the Exminster Asylum Project, University of Exeter.

42. D.R.O. A.U.M.B., 11, 26.6.1873.

43. Ibid., vol. 13, 20.8.1885.

44. W.H. Dumsday, *Relieving Officer's Handbook*, 1902, pp. 48–9.

45. M.E. Rose, *The English Poor Law 1780–1930*, Newton Abbot, 1971, pp. 161–2.

46. D.R.O. A.U.M.B., 12, 20.6.1878, 4.7.1878, 18.7.1878, 1.8.1878, 21.11.1878.

47. J. Robin, 'The relief of poverty', *Rural History*, 1990, p. 210.

Chapter 13

Living in the Workhouse

The idea of a workhouse as a means of dealing with unemployment was not new to the residents of Colyton when the big Axminster Union workhouse, or House as it was commonly known, was opened as a result of the Poor Law Act of 1834, for the parish had acquired its own workhouse a long time previously. A building which accommodated sixty-six people was established in 1767, with a men's room, a women's room, and separate quarters for the governor. This institution, like so many others in Colyton over the years, was run by a committee chosen from gentlemen, farmers and tradesmen, and was inspected by two of the members every Thursday morning. At first, it was truly a workhouse, in that it was largely used as a place where paupers on outdoor relief could go daily to work. In 1779, for example, it contained nineteen beds, but only one resident. By 1790, the rules of the institution were changed and its functions were increased. Two apartments were set aside for use as a penitentiary; it was laid down that resident children were to be educated in spelling, reading and the Christian religion; and a doctor was appointed to care for the sick. What began as a simple place of work for the unemployed had evolved into a prison and an orphanage as well.[1]

The new union workhouses which were set up after the 1834 Poor Law Act replaced individual parish institutions, and were multifunctional from the start, even though a major intention was that they should provide the only official means of relief for the able-bodied unemployed and their families. The report which led to the Act had recommended that there should be four separate workhouses in each union, one for the aged and those who were incapable of work, so that 'the old might enjoy their indulgences without torment from the boisterous'; a second for children, where they could be educated; and a third and fourth for able-bodied men and women respectively, the able-bodied to be 'subjected to such courses of labour and discipline as will repel the indolent and vicious'. The Poor Law Commissioners, however, decided that one institution must cater for all four categories, partly on grounds of expense, and partly because of the practical difficulty of splitting up the families of the able-bodied into different workhouses when they arrived, and reassembling them when the head of the family was ready to leave.[2] As a result, harsh conditions of life in the workhouses, which were originally intended to apply only to the able-bodied in order to deter them from entering and to encourage them to find work on their own account, had to be endured by all the inmates, regardless of their age or state of health.

As time went on, and experience in running the new workhouses was gained, the 1834 Act was modified in various ways. Perhaps the most important was the Poor Law Commissioners' instruction in 1844 to the Boards of Guardians that admission of the able-bodied poor to the workhouse could on occasion be replaced by outdoor relief, if it was given on account of sudden and urgent necessity, and for a limited period only.[3] This meant that short-term seasonal unemployment, of the kind often experienced in rural districts during slack periods or in spells of bad weather, could be dealt with in the community, and indeed it is difficult to see how workhouses could have absorbed temporary large influxes of men who were laid off for short periods, together with their whole families. Then the Act passed in 1847 laid down that a married couple of over sixty years of age were entitled to a separate bedroom, if they requested it.[4] This provision may have been less generous than it sounds, for in the Axminster workhouse at least, married couples in the required age group were conspicuous by their absence in the ten-yearly census returns, thus reinforcing the conclusion drawn in chapter 11 that most of the elderly received pensions in the form of outdoor relief in their own parishes.

By 1851, then, the Axminster House constituted the only official means of relief for the long-term able-bodied unemployed and their families within the union, and in common with other workhouses was designed to make life sufficiently uncomfortable for such family heads to make every effort to avoid going there. However, it also combined many of the forms of care which until recently have been provided in separate institutions in the welfare state. It was shown in the last chapter that its infirmary took in elderly patients who could not be nursed at home but whose illnesses were unsuitable for treatment in a major hospital; it accommodated the mentally handicapped; it was used as an old people's home; it provided temporary shelter for tramps and vagrants who nowadays might be found sleeping rough in a shop doorway or under a bridge; and a large proportion of its inmates were children under the age of fifteen, so that for them it acted as a children's home. It remains to be seen how successfully these varied functions were carried out in practice, with special reference to the treatment of inmates from Colyton.

The evidence available would suggest that the policy of deterring able-bodied men from entering the House was largely efficacious. It is known that between 1851 and 1859 three married men from Colyton, together with their families, were taken to the Axminster workhouse,[5] while on census day in 1861 there were two complete families present, though they came from other parishes. At Christmas time in 1863, however, there were no able-bodied men at all in the House, and only seven able-bodied women, all of whom had illegitimate children with them,[6] while married men with families were also absent from the workhouse on census day both in 1871 and 1881. On the other hand, it has been suggested that the disappearance of able-bodied men from workhouses in general may have been due not so much to the official policy of deterrence, as to the Boards of Guardians turning a blind eye to outdoor relief being given to such men to supplement scanty occasional earnings, for periods rather longer than envisaged when the 1844 Instructions allowing temporary outdoor relief were issued. Quite apart from the humanitarian aspect, it was cheaper to keep a whole family in the community than to provide for its members in the workhouse.[7] However, it must be said that no direct evidence has been found to suggest how far the Axminster guardians may have pursued such a policy.

When it came to the Axminster workhouse infirmary, it is clear that this was not only used for the elderly sick who could not be nursed in the community. John Power's 28-year-old wife was taken ill in 1854, and was carried to the Axminster House because she could not be looked after at home, where there were already four children under the age of seven. A month later she was back in Colyton and her husband was receiving sickness relief on her behalf.[8] As many as a fifth of all those dying in the House and being brought back to Colyton for burial between 1851 and 1891 were aged between twenty and forty-nine. A living-in nurse was employed in the infirmary from at least 1861 onwards, though it was difficult to recruit suitable staff. In 1882, the Local Government Board in London, possibly unaware of the extent of illegitimacy common in Devon parishes, wrote to the guardians to say that it had learned that the recently appointed nurse, though single, had a son, and that 'in the Board's opinion, the appointment of such persons under such circumstances in Public establishments was open to considerable objection'. The Guardians replied that it was very difficult to obtain the services of an experienced nurse, and that as her son was now a young man, and as she had retrieved her character by an irreproachable career in the meantime, they hoped the Local Government Board would make an exception in her case and agree to the appointment. Two weeks later, the civil servants in London had acceded to the guardians' request.[9]

As far as the mentally handicapped were concerned, it is known that some Colyton families looked after their disadvantaged children for many years, and that in such cases, outdoor relief was provided on a regular basis. For others, though, the workhouse became their refuge. Elizabeth Purse was born in Colyton, although her family has not been traced, and at the age of seventeen she was in the Axminster House, described as being 'of weak intellect'. Ten years later she was again in the workhouse, but this time with a nine-month-old illegitimate son. In 1881, the House contained eleven inmates other than Elizabeth Purse who, in the language of the day, were variously entered in the census returns as being of weak mind or intellect, imbecile, or idiotic. Surprisingly, all but two of these unfortunates had been employed in some capacity or other earlier in their lives, being described as 'formerly farm labourer', 'formerly lacemaker', and so on. It is possible that they reached the workhouse only when their parents either died, or could no longer give them a home, while their disabilities prevented them from earning a sufficient wage to enable them to live independently.

It has already been shown that care in the community was the norm for Colyton's elderly in the second half of the nineteenth century, and indeed, when the Colyton-born occupants of the Axminster workhouse on all five census days from 1851 to 1891 are added together, it can be seen that only eight of them, or 12 per cent of the total, were over sixty years of age.[10] However, there is evidence that at least four of these old people were long-term residents of the House, rather than temporary occupants of the infirmary, as they died in the workhouse and were brought back to Colyton for burial at anything from one and a half to seven years after they were recorded as inmates in the census returns. There are other examples of the use of the workhouse as an old people's home. For instance, a Mr Smith of Colyford offered to pay the full cost of maintaining his father-in-law in the workhouse, quarterly, in advance, at the rate of 3s 6d a week. Mr Smith may or may not have thought this was a convenient way of disposing of a difficult relative, but, as was seen earlier, no-one could be compelled to stay in the workhouse against their will. Four months later, Mr Smith complained to the guardians that his father-in-law had left the House several weeks before the expiry of the quarter, and claimed a refund for the resulting overpayment, which he was granted.[11]

The problem of homelessness existed in the nineteenth century as it does today, but the unemployed vagrants who tramped round the countryside could at least avail themselves of a night or two's lodging in the workhouses they came across on their travels. In 1873, the number of these homeless people was not considered to cause any great problem as far as the Axminster House was concerned. The Local Government Board in London laid down that casual paupers should be given a bath and a task of work, but the guardians considered that it was unnecessary to provide them with sleeping quarters separate from the other inmates, as their numbers were so small.[12] By the time the depression had taken hold in the 1880's the increase in the number of vagrants was giving cause for concern, and a government inspector told the guardians that in other unions the substitution of hammocks for the ordinary sleeping benches had tended to a decrease in the number of tramps seeking shelter in the workhouse. The Axminster guardians instructed their clerk to make further enquiries, but after postponing a decision for several meetings, they quietly let the matter drop.[13] Later in the same year, it was suggested to them that the large increase in the number of vagrants admitted was caused by their being kept in for only one night, and not for two nights as the Casual Poor Act demanded.[14] It is noteworthy that while there were no casual inmates in the House on census day in 1871, and only two in 1881, by 1891 the number had grown to ten, with some of the men having been born as far away as Scotland, Yorkshire and Staffordshire.

Certainly conditions for the tramps do not seem to have been at all agreeable. In one case a vagrant tore the clothes provided for him to wear while in the House, and explained to the magistrate before whom he was brought that he had done so because they were dirty.[15] In another, an inmate was had up for refusing to work and for hitting the porter in the eye, for which offence he was jailed for twenty-eight days.[16] On the other hand, the local press reported that a man who arrived at the Axminster House after it was closed for the night broke into the porter's lodge, lit a fire, helped himself to some soup, and left again early in the morning,[17] indicating that shelter within a workhouse was preferable to sleeping rough outside in the winter.

Finally, if the proportions of inmates in different age groups are used as the criterion, the most important function of the workhouse was to look after the young, for at the end of 1863, just over half of the 154 inmates in the Axminster House were children.[18]

The workhouse received various types of disadvantaged boys and girls. Some were illegitimate, and might be accompanied by their mothers; some were abandoned by their parents, as in the case of the Hancock children, described in chapter 4, who were sent to the Axminster House from Colyton when their father disappeared; and some were orphans. When a middling-class saddler and harness-maker in Colyton and his wife both died in their forties, after illnesses which probably exhausted their savings as they had to turn to the Feoffees for financial help, their two youngest children were sent to the workhouse to be looked after, and they were recorded as inmates there five months after their father was buried.

Other children went in to the workhouse for short periods to provide what would nowadays be called 'respite care' for overstretched parents, usually widowers who had been left with young families to look after. For example, in 1855 William Purse of Colyton, who had been widowed two and a half years earlier, was struggling to bring up five children under twelve years of age with the help of his eldest daughter, then fifteen years old. His case was taken up by the vicar, who asked the Poor Law Board in London if the nine-year-old and the toddler could be taken into the workhouse, while the eldest daughter continued to look after the others at home. The Poor Law Board after due consideration allowed one child to go to the workhouse for five months, and at the end of this time permission was given for a further stay of six months.[19] Evidently the London board felt that short-term care of this kind was an issue that should remain in its control, for similar cases were also referred to it by the Axminster guardians.

However sad life in the workhouse may have been for the children sent there, the intention was to provide them with training which would be useful to them when they were old enough to leave the institution and earn a living outside. In the days before compulsory education, the Axminster House employed a resident schoolmaster and schoolmistress, so at that time the workhouse children should have received a more complete education that their contemporaries in the parishes who had to rely on Sunday schools if they wished to acquire any skills in literacy and possibly numeracy. However, just as it was difficult to find experienced nurses to work in the House, so it appears to have been hard to attract good quality teachers. In 1876, the workhouse master complained to the guardians that the schoolmistress 'had very unevenly cut the girls' hair and had otherwise acted very indiscreetly'. The girls were paraded before the guardians, who concurred that the cut was bad, while one guardian complained that the schoolmaster 'was but a youth' and was seldom to be found in the school.[20]

Later on, the children were sent to the board school in Axminster, at a cost of 2d a head a week, and the guardians authorized the provision of coats and waterproofs to the boys.[21] The resident schoolmaster and schoolmistress were replaced by a children's industrial trainer, but again the work of the appointee was sub-standard, and in 1887 the schools inspector reported that the children were receiving practically no training. As a result, the Local Government Board discontinued its grant-in-aid towards the trainer's salary,[22] and she was demoted to the post of children's caretaker. Even here, she proved ineffective, and only a year later she was criticized for being absent from the House during the evenings and not seeing the children to bed. The fact that the guardians accepted her apology and she continued in post would seem to confirm that it was difficult to attract staff to the workhouse, even in a time of depression.[23]

When the children were old enough to leave the House, they were helped to find work outside, but if things went wrong the orphans among them had no-one to turn to for assistance but the guardians. One boy who had left the workhouse for employment with an Axminster baker was walking through a field with a basket of bread when a donkey, which was known to have attacked people before, fell upon him and bit him so severely that he was readmitted to the workhouse to recover from his injuries. The guardians demanded that the donkey-owner should pay the boy compensation for his suffering as well as refunding the costs of his maintenance in the House. In the event, the owner of the animal offered the guardians £1 to defray the workhouse costs, any unspent balance going to the injured boy.[24] Another orphan, Joshua Richards of Colyton, was apprenticed for three years to a basket-maker, the guardians paying the necessary premium of £10 and negotiating earnings for Joshua of 2d a week for the first year, 4d a week for the second, and 6d a week for the third.[25] When he fell ill some years later, he returned to the Axminster House to die at thirty-one years of age.

The minute books of the Axminster guardians and occasional press reports give glimpses of life in the workhouse, but it must be remembered that the usual was much less likely than the exceptional to feature in either of these two sources. It is therefore very hard, if not impossible, to reconstruct the daily routine in the Axminster House. Very little is known of how the institution was run in practical terms. The guardians' minutes contain a reference to a resident shoemaker, paid £5 a year and his keep,[26] and another, in 1862, to the appointment of a cook at £10 a year,[27] but there was no resident cook in the House in subsequent census years up to 1891. It has already been stated that in late 1863 the House contained 154 inmates, of whom only seven were able-bodied, the remainder being old, infirm or children, and even if a cook came in by the day, she would need help in feeding such a large number of people. Fortunately for the administration in 1863, the seven able-bodied inmates were all women with illegitimate children and it is likely that they did most of the kitchen work and cleaning. Certainly they, or some other inmates, did the laundry, because in 1883 it was minuted that the master of the workhouse would try to provide 'a little extra tea for the women engaged in washing, when they were at work'.[28] It is perhaps not surprising that the vagrant mentioned earlier objected to the soiled clothes provided for him, or that in 1876 a guardian visiting the House found the children dirty.[29]

The view has been expressed that indoor relief provided better accommodation, food and clothing than a labourer or aged person would be likely to obtain outside,[30] and this would seem to be confirmed by figures for the weekly cost of food and clothing per inmate in the Axminster House. The cost varied from quarter to quarter, but between 1881 and 1891 averaged out at 2s 11d a week, so that a farm labourer with himself, his wife and four children to support would need 17s 6d a week in cash if he were to spend a similar amount on each member of his family, a sum which was larger than his earnings even taking harvest payments and perquisites into account.[31] A glimpse of what inmates received for this outlay came in 1889, when the guardians were told that their expenditure, standing at 3s 2d per inmate per week at that date, was the highest of fifteen unions, while neighbouring Honiton was the lowest, at 2s 4⅝d. The subsequent enquiry showed that at Honiton, inmates received three meat dinners a week, and at Axminster only two. Axminster, however, unlike Honiton, provided cheese, but Honiton gave more soup and oatmeal. Otherwise, inmates in the two institutions fared similarly, except that a rather large proportion of the old and infirm in Axminster were on special diets. The enquiry concluded that the lower costs in Honiton were due to all supplies being weighed and checked on receipt, which could not be done at Axminster for want of a pair of scales; to the Honiton matron making a good deal of the inmates' clothing herself; and to the bread being baked in the Honiton House by a resident who had formerly been a baker. The enquiry concluded that laxity and extravagance had been shown at Axminster, but that there had been no intention to defraud.[32] After this, the guardians kept a closer eye on the supplies coming into the workhouse and caused meat containing an unfair proportion of bone and fat to be returned to the contractor, while four months later they complained about the quality of the bread and told the supplier that he must improve it, or it would not be accepted.[33]

The inmates of the Axminster House did have their occasional treats. The Christmas dinner was an annual feature, and in 1863 residents were provided with roast beef, plum pudding, and good ale for dinner, with tea, cake, strong beer and tobacco in the evening, while the Axminster church choir sang carols and anthems to them until bedtime. There was an annual outing, which in 1881 took the inmates to the seaside at Seaton, while on another occasion the children were entertained to tea and games at the house of Mr and Mrs Rodd, repaying this hospitality by singing glees. Visitors were allowed to come to the House once a week, and evidently inmates were able to go into the town, for in 1885 it was reported that they were visiting Axminster too frequently, and in future would only be allowed out if they had a permit showing why they were leaving and giving the time by which they should be back. Beer was provided regularly up until 1880, when it was replaced by tea, cocoa or coffee, and in 1878 the inmates consumed 57 lbs of tobacco.[34]

Not all offers of help from members of the public were accepted. In 1879, Lady Tulloch suggested that she should come to the workhouse on Sunday afternoons to give six boys and six girls a class in religious subjects. The guardians declined the offer, saying that the children already had scripture lessons at the board school, and attended the chaplain's services, and that was enough.[35]

So far, the emphasis has been placed on the inmates of the Axminster workhouse, but it must not be forgotten that the master, the matron, the porter, the nurse and in the earlier years the schoolmaster and schoolmistress were also residents of the institution, and although they had their separate quarters, their daily lives were bound up with those of the inmates. Just as the relieving officer, Mr Halse, and Colyton's assistant overseer were shown in the last chapter to have had stressful occupations, so the same can be said of the workhouse staff, as exemplified by the matron who was in post in the 1880s. The first hint of trouble came in 1885, when she was sufficiently rude to the chaplain's wife and her friend when they visited the workhouse to cause a complaint to be made to the guardians about her behaviour. On the whole, the guardians supported their employee, because although they instructed the clerk to write to the chaplain expressing the matron's regret at the incident, they told him to add that in their opinion the visit of the ladies to the House was irregular. Six months later, matters had taken a turn for the worse, and the matron was asked not to take intoxicating liquor, 'as the only safe means to ensure the proper conduct of the business of the House, and care for the comfort and happiness of the Officers and Inmates'.

For the next year and a half, there was no comment in the minutes on the matron's behaviour, but then the storm broke. She was accused of being intoxicated again, and of abusing the nurse, and the medical officer was called in to advise on her state of health. He subsequently described her as being 'of an irritable temperament and at times liable to much nervous excitement', a state which might be summed up as 'stressed', and said that of late years she had often suffered from debility. The upshot was that the matron was admitted to Exeter hospital, having resigned her post. There were few statutory employment rights in those days, and she was refused superannuation, although the guardians did ask the Local Government Board if she could be paid a temporary allowance until she was well enough to work again. This request was rejected by the Board, on the grounds that it had no power to grant it.[36] She was therefore left with no pension, no home and a very uncertain future.

An enthusiastic new matron was appointed, who at the interview agreed to take up her duties immediately, not even waiting for her luggage to be sent on. Unfortunately within a week she too had quarrelled with the nurse, and left the House without giving notice, the nurse and the porter handing in their resignations at the same time. The guardians were faced with finding an almost completely new staff, only the master remaining, and when the replacements were appointed, the conditions attached to each post stated specifically that beer would not be included in the rations provided.[37]

The survey of the workings of the New Poor Law in Colyton in the last chapter, and of the Axminster workhouse in this, must lead to the conclusion that a safety net was provided for the very poorest in society in many of the areas now covered by the welfare state, although the scale and quality of the relief given was so much lower in absolute terms then than it is now that direct comparison is unprofitable in that respect. Nevertheless, in the context of the generally much lower standard of living of the times, the level of resources expended on the poor in a rural area such as Devonshire was not a cause for shame. The elderly were usually maintained in their own community, the sick were treated in their own houses by a qualified doctor and surgeon, and the destitute and those without family support were given shelter, food and clothing at a standard which, in terms of cost at least, equalled or surpassed that available to labourers in full-time employment. The funding for these types of relief came from the local ratepayers, many of whom in Colyton were not particularly well off, and who were adversely affected by the agricultural depressions of the 1870s and 1880s just as their employees were. Mismanagement and failures of the system inevitably occurred, but in general the community supported its poor.

Notes

1.   A full account of the Colyton workhouse, from which this summary is drawn, is to be found in P. Sharpe, 'Gender-specific demographic adjustment to changing economic circumstances: Colyton 1538–1837'. Unpublished PhD thesis, University of Cambridge, 1988, pp. 109–11.

2.   S. and B. Webb, *English Local Government: English Poor Law History*, part II, *The last hundred years*, vol. I, London, 1929, p. 122.

3.   Instructional letter of Poor Law Commissioners, 21.12.1844, see W.H. Dumsday, *Haddon's Relieving Officer's Handbook*, London, 1902, p. 64.

4.   S. and B. Webb, *English Local Government*, 1929, p. 186, fn. 1.

5.   Devon Record Office (hereafter D.R.O.), P.O.14, Colyton.

6.   Report from the workhouse published in *Devon Weekly Times* (hereafter *D.W.T.*), 1.1.1864.

7.   M.E. Rose, 'The allowance system under the New Poor Law', *Economic History Review*, XIX, 1966, pp. 612–13.

8.   D.R.O. P.O., 14, Colyton, 9.11.1854, and D.R.O. Axminster Union Minute Book (hereafter A.U.M.B.), vol. 8, 29.9.1854–22.12.1854.

9.   D.R.O. A.U.M.B., vol. 13, 12.1.1882 and 26.1.1882.

10. The total numbers of Colyton-born inmates in the Axminster workhouse on census days were as follows: 1851, 18; 1861, 5; 1871, 30; 1881, 4; 1891, 9. Total, 66.

11. D.R.O. A.U.M.B., vol. 12, 25.4.1879 and vol. 13, 29.1.1880.

12. Ibid., vol. 11, 12.6.1873.

13. Ibid., vol. 14, 19.2.1885 and 30.4.1885.

14. Ibid., vol. 14, 6.8.1885.

15. Ibid., vol. 12, 15.2.1879.

16. *Honiton and Ottery Gazette and East Devon Advertiser*, 29.3.1884.

17. *D.W.T.*, 22.1.1886.

18. Ibid., 1.1.1864. The proportion of Colyton-born children in relation to all Colyton-born inmates was almost identical, standing at exactly 50 per cent.

19. D.R.O. A.U.M.B., vol. 8, 28.9.1855, 23.11.1885, 23.5.1856.

20. Ibid., vol. 12, 30.3.1876.

21. Ibid., vol. 14, 15.4.1886.

22. Ibid., vol. 14, 15.9.1887.

23. Ibid., vol. 14, 2.2.1888 and 16.2.1888.

24. Ibid., vol. 13, 5.5.1881 and 19.5.1881.

25. Ibid., vol. 11, 7.1.1875–1.4.1875.

26. Ibid., vol. 14, 15.4.1886.

27. Ibid., vol. 9, 7.3.1862.

28. Ibid., vol. 13, 15.11.1876.

29. *D.W.T.*, 7.4.1876.

30. A. Digby, *Pauper Palaces*, London, 1978, p. 13.

31. The weekly wage of a Devonshire farm labourer, including all payments in kind, has been estimated at 12s 6d a week from 1867–1870, and 16s 7d in 1898. See E.M. Hunt, 'Industrialization and Regional Inequality: Wages in Britain, 1760–1914', *Journal of Economic History*, XLVI (4) 1986, table 6, p. 965.

32. D.R.O. A.U.M.B., vol. 15, 2.11.1889.

33. Ibid., vol. 2, 1.1890 and 22.5.1890.

34. *D.W.T.*, 1.1.1864, 11.8.1881, 26.8.1881; D.R.O. A.U.M.B., vol. 11, 7.3.1872; ibid., vol. 13, 22.1.1885; ibid., vol. 13, 9.9.1880; ibid., vol. 12, 21.3.1879.

35. Ibid., vol. 11.9.1879.

36. Ibid., vol. 14, 30.4.1885, 29.10.1885, 26.5.1887, 16.8.1887, 15.9.1887 and 13.10.1887.

37. Ibid., vol. 14, 21.7.1887, 28.7.1887 and 18.8.1887.

Chapter 14

The Voluntary Sector

The Poor Law was the bedrock on which relief for the worst-off in society was based, but in nineteenth-century Colyton it was supplemented by two other sources, the charitable chamber of the Feoffees, and the Colyton Mutual and Providential Societies for men and women.

The Feoffees extended a helping hand to those who were in need but who did not qualify for means-tested public assistance, as well as to poor individuals in occasional difficulties who preferred not to become paupers, even if only for a short time, if it was possible to avoid doing so. The importance of the chamber of the Feoffees in the general running of the parish has already been discussed in chapter 2, but little has so far been written in relation to their work for the needy. It has been shown that the chamber's average income was around £450 a year, and that from this they found the costs of running the grammar school, maintaining the properties from which their income derived, and contributing towards projects which were for the good of the whole community, such as the water supply, and street lighting by gas lamps. After expenditure of this kind had been accounted for, they were left with a surplus which between 1851 and 1873[1] averaged out at £159 a year, and this they spent on those in need.

The Feoffees' policy was fundamentally different from that of the Guardians of the Poor, in that they refused to provide permanent relief to anyone, leaving that to the Poor Law. Instead, their policy was 'to prime the pump', as a present-day Feoffee has said. As a result, they made many payments to enable people to remain in business after a disaster, or to set themselves up in an occupation, although as a matter of principle they almost never provided the full cost. For instance, they gave £5 to John Drower junior, to help him to buy a mule and cart, his doctor having stated that 'confinement is injurious to his health and he should therefore give up his present business'. Mrs Shephard received £3 towards the expense of apprenticing her daughter. James Hill was given £3 towards replacing pigs which he had lost, and Edith Richards was loaned £2 10s to help her go as a nurse to Bristol hospital, the money to be repaid within two years. The Feoffees even provided an example of workfare, when Hermon Anning, a mason, applied to them for assistance. They employed him to do repair work at their property at Lovehayne 'as the best means of relieving him' but the decision proved unfortunate. When Hermon's bill was sent in, the Feoffees agreed to pay it 'as a charity, but under protest as a gross imposition' and they resolved that he should not be employed again. As a sting in the tail, they told the bailiff to deduct 4s from the bill, for a grate which had been installed without their permission.[2]

The Feoffees also helped individuals in time of illness. Like the Poor Law authorities, they paid for people to visit hospital, and they took out a £10 annual subscription to Exeter Eye Infirmary, which entitled them to recommend poor patients for free treatment. They also made cash payments to the sick. Perhaps unsurprisingly, the highest average payment per application, amounting to £3 17s 1d, went to members of the middling class, from which many of the Feoffees and Twentymen themselves came, for these were people who, in spite of loss of income through illness, would either be unable to meet the means-testing of the Poor Law authorities or would most resist pauperization. More than half the medical relief given by the Feoffees went to those who were likely to be employed by them, that is to say the wage-earning craftsmen and tradesmen, at an average rate of £2 13s 5d per application, while the biggest class of all, the labourers, received only a quarter of all payments, and at the lowest average rate of £1 14s 5d per application. This, however, was natural, because as the labourers were amongst the poorest, the means test would not exclude them from the more comprehensive medical benefits available under the Poor Law. It must be remembered that those receiving help for sickness from the Feoffees would have to pay doctors' bills.[3]

Other payments were made to individuals for a variety of reasons, ranging from the provision of articles of clothing, such as boots, to grants to recently widowed women, contributions to those wishing to emigrate to America, and occasional, but not regular, support for the elderly in distress.

In addition to payments to individuals who applied for help, the Feoffees from time to time distributed either goods or money to all needy members of the community who were on their list of the poor. A typical instance of the first type of relief came in February, 1855, when the weather was exceptionally severe. The Feoffees laid out £20 on pease, bacon and tan turfs (a by-product of the local tannery which could be used as fuel), distributing these items at the rate of one pint of pease, two ounces of bacon and ten tan turfs for every individual in a family 'amongst such of the poor parishioners as may be in real distress this afternoon'.[4] An example of the distribution of money rather than goods came in 1872, when the Feoffees disbursed £52 3s, minuting that 'in consequence of the wet season great distress is caused in the neighbourhood, the labouring class not being able to work but a few days in the week. Therefore the chamber thought it advisable to assist them'.[5] By relieving this type of seasonal unemployment, the Feoffees were helping not only the poor, but also the Poor Law authorities and the ratepayers. In addition, they demonstrated that it was possible to provide immediate relief of this kind at parish level through a small, non-bureaucratic organisation, as opposed to the more cumbersome administrative structure of the Poor Law, where relief had to be channelled through the hierarchy of the Board of Guardians, relieving officer, overseer and assistant overseer.

Coals and blankets were also distributed on occasion, and the Feoffees cooperated with the Vestry in providing a winter soup kitchen, which was popular even before the agricultural depression set in. In 1866 the local press reported that by the end of the season the kitchen had distributed 2,400 gallons of soup made from 720 lbs of beef, 54 bushels of peas, 6½ bushels of flour, 5 cwt of carrots and 3 cwt of onions. The sale price was 2d a gallon, and on no occasion had any soup remained unsold.[6]

From 1855 onwards, the Feoffees bought quantities of seed potatoes which they distributed each spring for planting by the poor, at the rate of 2 pecks for every man, his wife, and every child under ten years of age. One indication of how deeply the agricultural depression took hold from the mid-1870s came in 1880, when the Feoffees agreed that the usual distribution of potatoes should be made, but that they were 'for planting, and planting only, and that the recipients shall be bound to plant them and not to eat the supply thus provided for seed'.[7]

The Feoffees also supported the family through their annual Christmas present to all the household heads on their list of the poor, because the payments, like those of their emergency handouts, were made on a per capita basis for each dependent member of the household. The difference this made can be seen by looking at two household heads, one childless and the other with dependent children under the age of ten varying in number from one to four throughout the period 1851 to 1873. Neither man received any sickness benefit or special individual payment from the Feoffees during this time. The first man, a carpenter, with only himself and his wife to support, received an average of 2s 11d a year over the period; while the second, a farm labourer, had an average annual payment of 6s 5d. Neither sum was large enough to do more than provide a few comforts at Christmas time, but the farm labourer's 6s 5d did represent 80 per cent of his average weekly cash wage of 8s in 1861, and if the Feoffees' bonus is translated into modern terms, taking £155 as the weekly wage for an unspecialized agricultural worker in 1996, then the man would have received £124, a sum which would surely be welcomed.[8]

The relief provided by the Feoffees must have saved many families from applying to the relieving officer in time of crisis, particularly as, until 1878,[9] it was against the rules of the chamber to help anyone who had received parish pay from the Poor Law during the past three months. A farm worker who was unfortunate enough to need to apply to the relieving officer for outdoor relief between 25 October and 24 December would not, therefore, be eligible for the Feoffees' Christmas box, while relief from the Poor Law at other times of the year might endanger unforeseen benefits from the Feoffees. It was therefore in the interests of the poor who needed occasional help to apply for assistance to the chamber in the first instance, rather than to the relieving officer.

Although other parishes may have possessed their own charitable organisations, there is no doubt that the funds available to the Feoffees were on a larger scale than was usual in the district. It might be thought that the poor from other parishes would try to settle in Colyton in order to take advantage of what the Feoffees offered. Here, the rule of the chamber that legal settlement in the parish was necessary before an applicant for relief could be accepted was of major importance, and a proposal to overturn it in 1876 did not even find a seconder. Although the Poor Removal Act of 1861 ensured that no-one who had lived in a parish without recourse to the Poor Law for three years could be removed from there, irremoveability was not the same as settlement, so that poor people coming in to Colyton to work with the specific aim of getting on to the Feoffees' list were not likely to succeed.[10] For example, in April 1884 the chamber granted Bessey Newton £3 towards the cost of a sewing machine, but nine days later the grant was rescinded, as the Feoffees had discovered that she was not a parishioner, and the gift was therefore illegal.[11]

It was unfortunate that during the 1880s, when Colytonians were most in need as a result of the depression, the resources available to the Feoffees for distribution to the poor declined. The farmers were suffering as well as their labourers, and farm rents, from which the chamber largely derived its income, had to be reduced. The minutes of the chamber's meetings during the decade show increasing signs of financial stress. In 1880, the annual subscription to the Exeter Eye Infirmary was held in abeyance 'for want of funds'. In 1881, the balance at the bank stood at only £13, so for six months no further applications for assistance were considered; in 1884, the annual distribution of seed potatoes was cancelled, and it was decided that no more free boys should be elected to the grammar school; while at the end of 1886 the Feoffees resolved that 'in the present state of the finances no applications for help can be entertained'.[12] In times like these the availability of relief through the Poor Law became increasingly important.

There was one further way in which Colytonians could seek to protect themselves against sickness, and that was by joining the Colyton Mutual and Providential Society for men, which was founded in 1849,[13] or the similar organization for women, established in 1853.[14] These bodies were the forerunners of modern insurance schemes such as BUPA or the Private Patients Plan.

The men's society replaced an earlier version, called the Colyton Friendly Society, which had been set up in 1786 as a working-class association to ease suffering caused by personal illness and accident, and to provide contributors with medical treatment and a small income when they fell ill or grew too old to work. It also ensured that they would be decently buried when they died. In return for a subscription of 9d a month, or 9s a year, a member needing permanent nursing received 7s a week for the first three months of his illness, and 4s 6d a week thereafter. If permanent nursing was not required, he would receive 3s 6d for the first three months, followed by a reduction to 2s 6d if he was by then able to 'walk out'.[15]

It may be that by the mid-nineteenth century these entitlements had become impossible to sustain, because the rules of the new society, founded in 1849, were rather more stringent. The subscription was increased to 10s a year, and benefits were cut to 6s a week for those confined to bed and 3s a week if out of bed but unable to work, both up to a maximum of £5. A medical certificate was required before relief could be obtained, and no-one was allowed to receive help for a recurrence of the same illness until he had spent at least a month restored to his former health.

Membership was open to all males of good repute who were between the ages of twelve and forty at joining, provided they had no bodily infirmities, but no benefits were paid out until two years from the date when membership began. The quarterly payments of 2s 6d had to be met promptly, or a fine of 2d was imposed, and non-payment for two successive quarters meant expulsion from the society and the loss of all contributions already paid in, though readmission could be gained by paying off the arrears and meeting a fine of 2s 6d.

The society took strong measures to ensure that no fraud took place. No member receiving sick benefit was allowed to work, or to be out of doors after sunset, or to go more than two miles from home without permission. Habitual drunkards were not allowed to join the society, provided a majority of members agreed to exclude them, and those whose illnesses resulted from intemperance or immoral behaviour were not given the benefit of sick pay; while men convicted of felony or any infamous crime were expelled, along with those who had been sent to prison twice, for whatever offence.

Unfortunately, although the rules of the society survive, accompanied by one or two other relevant documents,[16] no list of members has been found, but the names of those few signing the papers on behalf of the society show that nearly two-thirds came from the middling class, while just over one-third were wage-earning craftsmen. The three trustees comprised the Vicar of Colyton, a landowning J.P. and a solicitor, and labourers were unrepresented, although this of course does not mean that none were members. Those who were childless would find it easier to keep up the quarterly payments than a poor man whose family expenses increased with the growing number of his children, which might lead him to default on his payments and so lose all he had put in. It is possible that the friendly society of the Ancient Order of Foresters, which opened a branch in the parish called 'Pride of the Coly' in 1879 with six members, a number which seven years later had increased to forty, was better suited to the needs of the poorer inhabitants of Colyton.[17]

For members who kept up their contributions there were other benefits as well as insurance against sickness. The Mutual and Providential Society had an additional function in that it acted as a kind of savings bank. When the rules were written in 1849, it was set out that the society would continue until 1862, when the funds in hand would be distributed as a dividend to each surviving member, proportional to the amount he had paid in, after the deduction of anything he had received as sick pay, on the understanding that every member under fifty years of age would leave two years' subscription in the fund, and every member over fifty, three years' subscription, in order to restart the society. All the societies held annual dinners, which were very festive affairs. Rule 31 of the men's society laid down that every member should appear at the annual general meeting wearing a tri-colour rosette provided by the committee from the general fund.

The Colyton Mutual and Providential Society for men survived until the late 1920s. Much less is known about the women's society, although a press report shows that it was flourishing in 1874, eleven years after its inception, with 135 members and a balance of £222 1s 3½d in its fund.[18]

In spite of the efforts of the publicly-funded Poor Law, the voluntary body of the Feoffees, and the self-help friendly societies, many Colytonians in the second half of the nineteenth century lived under the shadow of poverty. Today, such poverty is considered to be a major cause of crime. It remains to be seen in the next chapter how far this was the case in Colyton.

Notes

1. The treasurer's detailed account book (Devon Record Office, hereafter D.R.O., F/17/3) closed in 1873. D.R.O. F 17/2 gives additional information on receipts and payments.

2. D.R.O., F 17/8, 29.7.1857, 7.10.1861, 8.1.1872, 25.5.1886, 6.2.1880.

3. J. Robin, 'The relief of poverty in mid-nineteenth century Colyton', *Rural History*, 1 (2), 1990, p. 205.

4. D.R.O., F/17/8, 2.2.1855.

5. Ibid., 15.2.1872.

6. *Devon Weekly Times* (hereafter *D.W.T.*), 23.3.1866.

7. D.R.O., F 17/8, 4.3.1880.

8. J. Robin, 'The relief of poverty', 1990, p. 215.

9. On 13.12.1878 the chamber resolved that the Christmas dole should be given to parishioners whether in receipt of parochial relief or not. D.R.O., F 17/8.

10. J. Robin, 'The relief of poverty', 1990, pp. 214–15.

11. D.R.O., F 17/8, 14.4.1884.

12. D.R.O., F 17/8, 2.1.1880, 2.2.1880, 7.3.1884, 4.11.1884, 25.11.1886.

13. Public Record Office (hereafter P.R.O.) FS 15/1177.

14. *D.W.T.*, 5.6.1874.

15. Norman Hoare, 'The Community of Colyton and its Poor, 1800–1850'. Unpublished MA dissertation, 1972–1973, Department of English Local History, University of Leicester, pp. 31, 85.

16. P.R.O., FS 15/1177, 25.6.1849, 13.6.1856, 18.8.1887.

17. *D.W.T.*, 26.11.1886.

18. Ibid., 5.6.1874.

Chapter 15

Crime and Punishment

'Law and order' is a phrase much in vogue with politicians of all parties today, and represents a major concern of the British public. Figures published by the Central Statistical Office strengthen the common belief that crime is becoming more widespread and threatening. They show first, that the number of notifiable offences in England and Wales which were reported to the police rose more than nine times from 1.2 for every 100 of the population in 1951 to a peak of 10.5 in 1992, and second, that almost half of the offences involved wounding and almost a third of domestic burglaries are not reported to the police at all.[1] The true figure for the number of offences committed is therefore even higher than that recorded. In contrast, just over a century ago in 1890, only 0.3 indictable offences were known to the police in England and Wales for every 100 of the population,[2] so on this basis, it would seem incontrovertible that society in the 1990s is at considerably greater risk from crime than it was 100 years ago.

However, as always, statistics must be viewed with caution. The low figure for 1890 represented the indictable offences known to the police, that is to say all those offences serious enough to be tried before a jury in courts of assize or quarter sessions, and it therefore excluded the many summary trials before a magistrate. The high figure for 1994, on the other hand, covered notifiable offences, which included not only most indictable offences, but also certain summary offences, such as taking away a motor vehicle, as well as cases which might either be tried by a magistrate, or brought before a crown court if the magistrate or the defendant requested it. In addition, the definitions of crimes to be classified as indictable or summary have changed over time.

There are other reasons for confusion. Just as crime was under-reported in the 1990s, so it was, though to an unknown degree, in the nineteenth century, more particularly in the earlier years when the severity of the punishments meted out for what now appear very trivial offences deterred the more humane members of the public from cooperating in prosecutions.[3] The treatment of juvenile offenders has also changed substantially, while the scarcity of returns on crime in the second half of the nineteenth century which can be put directly against the statistics produced since the Second World War makes precise comparison impossible. Even so, general trends may be discerned which reveal quite different characteristics within each period.

The second half of the nineteenth century, like the period from the end of the Second World War to the present day, was marked by a general rise in economic prosperity, temporarily interrupted by periods of depression. But while in the nineteenth century rates of crime against property fell throughout the good times, but tended to rise when the economy was depressed, in the twentieth century the reverse has been true, with rates rising considerably while the economy has been prosperous, but falling slightly after the onset of depression.

There are many arguments as to why people's behaviour has differed so much when in both half-centuries the standard of living in general has risen. It has been suggested that in the nineteenth century crime against property fell partly because policing became much more efficient once police forces had been established throughout the country, and partly because the increase in prosperity found its way down to virtually all sections of society, so that fewer people were driven by need to commit offences.[4] If necessity were the driving force behind crime, then it would be natural for rates to fall when the standard of living was rising, and to rise when depression intervened.

This argument fails, however, when applied to the second half of the twentieth century, because the rise in crime after the Second World War coincided with the introduction of the welfare state, which provided a safety net on a scale unknown to the poor of 100 years ago. The complexity of the factors which may have helped to cause the steady increase in the number of offences is such that it must be left to criminologists and other professionals to assess how far the present situation is due to unemployment, a widening gap between rich and poor, family breakdown, social deprivation, alcohol and drug abuse, or a change in society's attitude towards discipline and punishment, to mention only a few possibilities. The purpose of this chapter, after all, is to examine law and order in Colyton between 1851 and 1891, and to see how that community treated theft, violence, drunkenness, family desertion and juvenile delinquency, all problems which remain today.

In June 1851, nine Inspectors of Police were appointed to oversee law and order in Colyton. As might be expected, they were men of substance, either living on private means, holding farm tenancies, or running major businesses in the parish, and four of them were already Feoffees. Fortunately, their minute book has survived, running spasmodically from 1851 to 1857.[5]

The first recorded act of the inspectors was very much in line with the procedures followed by the Feoffees for, having decided to appoint two village watchmen, they set up a subcommittee to frame rules embodying the duties which these men were to perform. Once this had been accomplished, they appointed John and Samuel Richards, cousins in their twenties, one a shoemaker and the other a mason, to fill the vacant posts.

Unfortunately, only a few days passed before the young men went on strike, and refused to work unless their wages were increased and their duties very much diminished. The inspectors would not comply 'with so dictatorial and unreasonable a demand' and the watchmen were summarily dismissed.

In their second attempt, the inspectors chose two considerably older men, probably hoping that they would prove less insubordinate. The choice of Samuel Farrant, a 43-year-old farm labourer with a large number of children to support, appears unexceptionable, but the appointment of James Tucker, even without the benefit of hindsight, was a curious one. In the first place, Tucker was sixty-three, which seems old for such a physically demanding job; and second, he was living apart from his wife, with a lodger called Rose Norris who was also separated from her husband. In any event, the two men were installed as constabulary watchmen at 8s a week each, and began their duties towards the end of August.

Only six weeks had passed before the inspectors were faced with more trouble. The new watchmen were showing as little respect for authority as their predecessors. Tucker and Farrant came before the board complaining about 'their unprotected condition resulting from the incompetence of the Magistrates and from the evil disposition of some of the inhabitants of Colyton'. They therefore petitioned the inspectors for the immediate supply of great-coats, capes, lanterns and arms. Worse, at the same meeting it was reported that Tucker was being sued for assault by two Colytonians.

The inspectors rallied round their watchman and engaged a lawyer to defend him on the assault charge, and it was agreed that as many of the board as possible would turn up in court to show their support. There is no record of the outcome of the case, but it must be assumed that Tucker was found not guilty, because he remained in post. But it took two months for coats to be issued to the two men, and then it was stressed that the garments were only on loan.

Meanwhile, Tucker's unpopularity grew in some quarters in Colyton. His life was threatened, and summonses were taken out against those responsible. Only two months later, the windows of the house in which Rose Norris was then lodging were broken, and when Tucker tried to investigate he was set upon by three women living nearby. When one of the women resisted arrest, the other two, joined by a local man, came to her aid. Tucker again appealed to the inspectors, who asked the magistrates to issue summonses. The chief culprit, Mary Ann Littly, said she was too ill to appear before the justices, even though Tucker reported bitterly that he had seen her at 6 p.m. walking through Umborne Green carrying a penny bag of turnips, and that she had been out on the street between 1 and 2 a.m. on Christmas Eve. In the end, the matter was resolved by Mary Ann receiving a warning from the inspectors, and one of the other women being admonished and promising to behave better in future.

Again, when Tucker was called by a townsman to eject a drunk and disorderly man from his house, he met with resistance, had his coat torn, and was kicked in his private parts. Once more, there seemed to be nothing he could do about this except complain to the inspectors. Clearly, the watchmen lacked the authority, whether legal, moral, or physical, to carry out their duties effectively.

The climax of this unhappy period came in late February in 1852, when Tucker was accused by two respectable townsmen of accepting bribes of liquor to permit public houses and beer shops to remain open after hours. His fellow watchman, Farrant, stated that Tucker had been so drunk that he had had to help him home. The inspectors dismissed Tucker, and Farrant resigned.

This was not quite the end of the affair, because Farrant was told to collect the coat and arms which had been issued to Tucker. The latter, however, refused to give them up until he had been paid all the wages and expenses due to him. This was a matter of real concern, because when the overseer for Colyton was ill, and unable to collect the police rate from which the wages were paid, two of the inspectors had had to advance the watchmen's pay out of their own pockets. Tucker evidently meant what he said, because seven months later it was minuted that he should be allowed to retain his great-coat, lantern and cape on payment of 10 shillings. In a belated happy ending, Tucker and Rose Norris were married six years later, presumably after their respective spouses had died.

After the failure of the watchmen, it is not surprising that the new Board of Inspectors appointed in 1854 decided to employ a member of the Exeter Police Force to keep the peace in Colyton. Police Constable James Holway was appointed, at a salary of 23s a week, nearly three times as much as each watchman had received, though as it was stipulated that this sum included all expenses for clothing, there would be no more claims for great-coats and capes. PC Holway was also to receive the same perquisites as the police constables of Honiton.

The cost of employing such a man had to be of concern to the Inspectors, because, as previously stated, the money came from a separate police rate, levied more widely than the rate devoted to poor relief, and the overseer found great difficulty in collecting it from low-paid wage-earners. The feeling of the magistrates was that 'the bench would hesitate to enforce levying this rate on so poor a class'. As a result, the inspectors agreed to provide the magistrates with a list of exemptions on the grounds of poverty.

Once again the inspectors produced rules for the new police officer to observe. 'He should keep himself as much as possible from the society of low and disorderly characters and avoid spending his time in public houses and beer shops except as duty may require'. He was also to put a stop to vagrancy, to disperse all crowds of boys and others who might be guilty of disorderly conduct, especially after nightfall, and to see that public houses and beer shops kept regular hours. In an early example of 'stop and search', his attention was particularly directed to 'suspicious characters entering the town after nightfall with bundles or packages, the contents of which he should endeavour to ascertain'.

All this may seem a heavy task for a single-handed policeman, but PC Holway came through with flying colours. Early in his term of office, the inspectors received a complaint from a middle-aged lady in Colyford that rude boys had gathered in front of her house, and he was instructed to disperse them in the future, but soon the complaints concerned nothing more serious than smells from the factory making manure, or cattle straying in the streets, and he was congratulated by the inspectors on his work.

This detailed account of law and order in Colyton before and immediately after the advent of a member of the police force supports the view, expressed earlier, that one reason for the decline of crime in the second half of the nineteenth century in England and Wales as a whole was because policing became so much more efficient. Unfortunately, it is not possible to measure such a decline in Colyton, because the records of Axminster petty sessions, where cases concerning Colyton residents were first heard, were destroyed by enemy action in the Second World War. Without such comprehensive evidence, any kind of statistical analysis is impossible. However, sporadic reports in the local press, which are available for most years from 1861 to 1891, do give an impression of the kind of antisocial behaviour which led to an appearance in court, and also of the penalties which were meted out to those who were convicted.

Nowadays, juvenile offenders create a considerable problem for the police, the social services and for society in general. They operate in rural and suburban areas as well as in inner cities. Law-abiding citizens in many areas have become increasingly concerned with the disruption of their daily lives by youths, some of whom are too young to be brought before the courts.[6] But in contrast, only nine children or young people under the age of eighteen from Colyton were reported in the local press over the thirty-year period as having been brought before the magistrates, although of course other cases may have gone unrecorded, and the charges against them were trivial by modern standards. Two boys, aged fourteen and fifteen, were found guilty of damaging mowing grass and were fined 6s 6d each, including costs, a sum not far short of the cash element in the weekly wage of a farm labourer.[7] Four more boys were brought before the bench for bad behaviour in church, and were severely reprimanded;[8] a sixteen-year-old had associated with men in their twenties in an act of public disorder, of which more will be said later; and two children were sent to a reformatory school for five years for stealing apples. The severity of this last sentence is more understandable, at least in the case of one of them, when it is realised that not only was one of her parents waiting outside the orchard to receive the fruit, but that her father had spent time in prison, as evidenced by the payment of outdoor relief to her mother while he was in gaol. It is possible that by sending the child to the reformatory, the authorities thought they were acting in her best interests, by taking her 'into care' in the only way open to them. The second child in the case was not named in the press report, so it has not been possible to investigate his or her family history.[9]

Five months later, the named girl's father was again in court, this time for refusing to contribute 9d a week towards the maintenance of his daughter in the reformatory school, as had been previously agreed.[10] Married men had a legal responsibility for the maintenance of their wives and children, and fathers who tried to escape from their obligations were pursued by the law. When Robert French deserted his wife and two children, leaving them chargeable to the union, PC Chapple tracked him down in Wales and brought him back to stand trial. He was convicted, and sent to Exeter gaol for two months, with hard labour. The police in this case had fulfilled the function of the present day Child Support Agency, and reported cases of Colyton men deserting their families were very rare.[11]

Heavy penalties were also imposed for offences against property. Poaching, which seems to have been looked on at least partly as a sport since representatives of all social classes engaged in it, nevertheless incurred considerable fines, and even prison sentences for persistent offenders. For instance, Henry Pulman, gentleman, was fined £2 for trespassing in pursuit of pheasants, while John Newberry, who actually poached three such birds, was fined £3 with costs, or one month's imprisonment, being described as 'an old hand' by the magistrate. A sixty-year-old carpenter, also a frequent offender, was given the option of a £2 fine or one month's hard labour for spearing a salmon in the river Coly.[12] Other poachers from Colyton included a draper, a blacksmith who employed labour, and the sons of farmers and small business owners. Even so, the majority of poachers whose occupations are known were labourers, and for them the pursuit of game meant food for their families, if they were successful.

It has already been pointed out that the average wage of a Devonshire agricultural labourer in the late 1860s was around 12s 6d a week, after taking payments in kind into account as well as cash. This represented one of the lowest wages for farm work to be found in any English county, and agricultural labourers in low wage areas could afford only a little meat, depending on bread as their major food supply.[13] It is therefore not surprising that in addition to poaching, food figured largely in the thirteen cases of theft involving Colytonians which were reported in the local press between 1861 and 1890. Just over half the offences involved stealing either fowls, eggs, apples or onion seed, and the penalties handed out seem draconian in the light of modern sentencing. Samuel Purse, a farm labourer in his mid-twenties, was sent to prison for one month's hard labour for stealing twenty-two eggs.[14] Thomas Hawker received a similar sentence, although with the option of paying a 25s fine (the equivalent of three weeks' cash wages) for stealing a fowl, which the police constable found boiling in a saucepan over the fire, even though Hawker told the bench in mitigation that he stole the bird through poverty, and that he had been drunk at the time. In the event, he escaped going to prison, because his mother paid 15s into court and promised the balance of the fine by the end of the week.[15] Another offender was sentenced to three weeks' hard labour for stealing apples, and a blacksmith who rented an allotment from the Feoffees and stole onion seed from another allotment holder was handed a similar sentence.[16]

Thefts of other types of property were treated equally harshly. A prison sentence was imposed on a Colytonian for stealing a shovel, while more serious crimes, such as the embezzlement of £14 and the theft of a box of eight silver spoons, a silver jug and silver sugar tongs were referred for trial in a higher court.[17] Only one case resulted in a fine rather than imprisonment, possibly because the purpose of the theft was to maintain a social custom of long standing. As far back as the 1850s, Colyton residents had been accustomed to break the law on Guy Fawkes Day by rolling burning tar barrels through the streets and letting off fireworks, and on 5 November 1882, George Bull took a petroleum barrel from outside the chemist's shop, presumably with the same purpose in mind. In spite of his plea that he had simply found the barrel on the highway, he was fined 27s 6d with costs.[18] It must be admitted that Colyton had suffered from a number of outbreaks of fire over the years, and a burning petroleum barrel would certainly constitute a danger to wooden barns and thatched cottages.

The town had its fair share of traffic offences, some of which would seem very familiar today if motor vehicles were substituted for horse-drawn transport, although the penalties would not. A fish dealer from Colyton was sent to prison for a week for leaving his horse and cart unattended in Trinity Square, Axminster, for twenty minutes, while another fish salesman from Taunton was charged with reckless driving, having been seen by Colyton's police constable in an advanced state of drunkenness, urging his horse along at a rapid rate. This offence, however, which might be considered more serious nowadays, only rated a fine of 1s with costs, and a caution.[19]

More serious were the offences concerning violence. Of course there were a few examples of a minor nature, as when the wife of a bakery owner was sufficiently exasperated by her neighbour, also a baker's wife, to throw a bowl of water over her while she was sweeping dust from her door, but this action resulted in a fine of 1s, and costs, on grounds of provocation. The only reported case of a sexual assault over the whole period involved a married man kissing a Colyford girl against her will, for which he was fined £1, including costs. The more violent crimes were frequently associated with drinking. For example, Lawrence Hill, a sawyer who was known for attacking people when drunk, entered the White Hart in Queen Street in a quarrelsome and abusive mood. He started an argument with another customer, and when the landlady asked him to leave the premises, he struck her twice, although her son was able to come to her defence. Later the same evening, Hill was seen by PC Chapple near the White Hart, drunk and riotous, and surrounded by a crowd of thirty or forty people – an event which it is difficult to imagine occurring in present-day Colyton.[20]

The worst assaults, however, involved members of the Mayne family. In 1864, one of the Maynes, whose Christian name was not given in the newspaper report, was working with another man called Fowler on Horriford farm, but they both became tipsy, and had a fight. When Fowler found himself getting the worst of it, he swung his firkin at Mayne, knocking him down, and then striking him several times, with the result that Mayne's jaw was broken and he was also badly cut about the throat. A year later, John Mayne, John Perry and Joseph Fowler met at the Bear public house, where they quarrelled over a game called 'The devil among the tailors'. This time it was Fowler who suffered injury, for while he was on his way home, Mayne and Perry jumped out on him from behind a hedge, knocking him over and kicking his head and body. Eventually he managed to crawl back to the town, and the doctor found his skull laid bare in two places, with other grave injuries. Three weeks later, Fowler was sufficiently recovered to give evidence against Mayne and Perry, who had been remanded in custody, and they were committed for trial at the forthcoming quarter sessions.[21]

Ten years later, John's brothers, Samuel and Thomas Mayne, together with George Long, were accused of causing grievous bodily harm to a local farmer, when he and his son tried to eject them from their farmyard. George Long used a heavy bludgeon in the attack, and when it was taken from him by the farmer and his son, the Maynes joined in the affray. Long then picked up a large stone and threw it at the farmer, knocking him unconscious, after which Long and Samuel Mayne ran off, though Thomas Mayne stayed to help carry the farmer back to the house. The following year, Thomas was again in court, having been summoned for severely beating and kicking his mother-in-law, with whom he resided in Colyton, while he was drunk. On this occasion, he was sentenced to six months' hard labour, it being stated that he had been previously convicted for assault on several occasions.[22]

The two cases where Colytonians are known to have died as a result of violence, however, were not brought before the magistrates at all. In the first, which occurred in 1871, Albert Wood killed Simon Summers in a fight, but he was not sent for trial because Summers, who had earlier assaulted his own wife, was judged to be the aggressor. It is interesting to note that the marriage register records that Wood married Summers' widow two years later. In the second case, a pregnant woman died of an internal haemorrhage after quarrelling with her lodger, whom she was trying to evict. The coroner's court was told that neighbours had heard her say, 'The old hound shan't stop here any longer', and had seen blows exchanged, but not to the stomach. The jury returned their verdict as directed by the coroner, namely that death had been caused by violence applied in some way or other to the abdomen, but in what manner it was applied there was no evidence for them to record.[23] As a sad postscript, the dead woman's husband was admitted to Exminster Asylum two and a half months later, to be released as 'recovered' after a stay of three weeks.[24] His name was George Long, so he could have been the same man who knocked the farmer unconscious with a stone, but as there were three labourers all bearing this name in Colyton at the time, it is impossible to identify him as such with certainty.

Violence of the type instanced above was directed against the person, but acts of random vandalism against property of the kind so much deplored today were also experienced in Colyton, though only isolated incidents were reported in the press. The 'rude boys' who gathered outside Miss Sampson's house in Colyford and were the subject of her complaint to the Inspectors of Police in 1854 were paralleled in 1887 by three young men in their early twenties who were charged with smashing John Sutcliffe's windows soon after midnight, having been caught in the act by PC Derges. The young men apologised to Mr Sutcliffe in the morning, and he, being pastor of the Unitarian Chapel, with true Christian charity wished the charges to be dropped, putting the mischief down to 'youthful folly and indiscretion'. The police, however, asked the magistrates to hear the case, as there had been so much damage done recently in the neighbourhood of Colyton by youths and young men throwing stones that action needed to be taken. As a result, the three defendants were fined 10s each, including costs, and were told by the chairman of the bench 'not to be up to such larks again'.[25]

All the lawbreakers already described were acting on their own, or with two or three companions at most, but Colyton experienced two acts of public disorder in which larger numbers of parishioners were involved. The first occurred in 1873, and is of interest because it was a case of the community expressing its displeasure at the actions of one of its members, even though these were not of a criminal nature, by organising a 'skimmetting riding'. The *Oxford English Dictionary* defines such a ride as 'a ludicrous procession, formerly common in villages and country districts, usually intended to bring ridicule or odium upon a woman or her husband in cases where the one was unfaithful to, or ill-treated, the other'. A cart, with an effigy on fire, was wheeled four times past the house of a widow, escorted by a crowd among whom a young man called Harry Bamsey caught the eye in his long-tailed coat and box hat. Stones were thrown and windows smashed, and the four ringleaders, including the sixteen-year-old referred to earlier, were fined by the bench.[26]

By this action, the community humiliated an individual of whose behaviour it disapproved, and in so doing, broke the law. The city of Boston in the United States, 123 years later, is using public humiliation as both a punishment and a deterrent to kerb-crawlers, who are made to clean the streets under the gaze of the television cameras, press reporters, and the local populace, in an effort to eradicate, or at least lessen, a problem which up to now has proved intractable.[27]

When public disorder occurred in Colyton for a second time, it was on a larger scale, and showed a local community divided by a national issue. In 1878, the Christian Mission founded by William Booth in the 1860s was renamed the Salvation Army. By this time, mission stations had spread well beyond London, and in 1881 the Salvationists became active in Exeter, the nearest large town to Colyton. Their aim was to reach the most deprived members of society, whom the churches of all denominations had largely ignored. Recognising that drunkenness was the root cause of much hardship and crime, they insisted that their converts should become total abstainers if they wished to join the army.

Brewers and publicans became alarmed at the Salvation Army's success in converting working-class men and women to teetotalism, and seeing their livelihoods threatened they encouraged a rival organisation to grow up, known as the Skeleton Army.

With hindsight, it is remarkable that police, magistrates and judges should not have welcomed the Salvationists' presence, for in general converts ceased to be lawbreakers, drunkards and thieves, and became useful members of society, but such was the case. In March 1881, Captain Trenhail of the Salvation Army was arrested in Exeter and charged by the police 'with being in and aiding a disorderly mob, singing and shouting and refusing to desist' on an occasion when 100 Salvationists were followed by a mob of 5000 or 6000 Skeleton supporters. Three months later, a Salvation Army march in the same town was pelted with potato skins, pea shells, flour, eggs, mud, stones and water, and it was only because the marchers did not retaliate that a serious disturbance was averted. In October of the same year, Exeter magistrates banned the Salvationists from holding processions, in response to their appeal for protection against the Skeletons.[28]

By 1882, disturbances had spread to Honiton, eleven miles from Colyton, and in 1884, Colyton itself experienced clashes between the two camps. The Salvationists marched through the town, and scuffles broke out. The Axminster magistrates later spent several hours hearing cases arising from the confrontation. Two Skeletons took the initiative by accusing four Salvationists of pushing and kicking them, but both cases were dismissed, one because of insufficient evidence. Two weeks later, it was the Salvationists who brought charges against the Skeletons, one Salvationist claiming that a Skeleton had previously warned him of trouble to come, saying: 'Look here, Thomas, I shall break your ... head; and if I can't do it myself, I shall get someone else who can'.

The chairman of the bench made no secret of his antipathy towards the Salvationists, saying that their processions caused violence, assaults and disturbances of the peace; but he added that unfortunately they had a legal right 'to walk and make a row and disturbance in the streets', and that being the case, no-one could legally interfere with them. He therefore found the Skeletons guilty, and ordered them to pay £2 each, with 12s costs, or go to prison. The fines were immediately paid for each defendant, although it was not reported by whom.[29]

Colyton was clearly not a crime-free zone in the second half of the nineteenth century, but it must be remembered that the offences which have been described were spaced out over a thirty-year period.[30] On the other hand, an unknown number of cases must have gone unrecorded, as the local press was not consistent in its reporting of the magistrates' courts. Even so, an attempt must be made to answer some of the questions raised by the limited evidence available.

First, one may ask why men deserting their families received penalties as severe as imprisonment with hard labour. The reason is unlikely to be disapproval of married couples living apart, for as we saw earlier, James Tucker was appointed by the Inspectors of Police as a constabulary watchman, even though he was separated from his wife and almost certainly cohabiting with Rose Norris. But Tucker's wife was not living in Colyton, and was therefore not a charge on the parish. It would seem that in cases where the local community paid directly for the consequences of an individual's actions, the community's interests were generally placed first. Because Colytonian poor-rate payers and those of the sixteen other neighbouring parishes which combined to form the Axminster Union could relate what they paid to what was received by families in their own parish much more easily than is possible today, when relief is funded nationally, it became important to them that as few people as possible should have to be supported from the poor rate. The heavy penalties imposed on men who left their wives and families to be maintained by the parish certainly seem to have had a deterrent effect, regardless of the individual suffering which must have been endured by ill-matched couples who were obliged to continue living together.

Again, the severity of the sentences imposed for what appear to be quite minor offences against property need an explanation. The answer may lie in part in the generally much lower standard of living experienced throughout the community than is enjoyed today. The theft of onion seed may now seem unimportant, but it would not have done so to its owner, an agricultural labourer below the poverty line, with a wife and five children to support, who received regular relief from the Feoffees, as well as occasional help from the Poor Law, and who was having to pay a rent, albeit a small one, for his allotment. The haul of eight silver spoons, a silver jug and sugar tongs was taken not from one of the comparatively few well-to-do middle class households in Colyton, but from a 75-year-old bachelor, who was a tenant farmer of only fourteen acres, while a blacksmith whose steel screw-pin was stolen was also poor enough to be helped by the Feoffees occasionally.

The larger farmers and landowners from whom fowls, eggs and apples were stolen, and whose game was poached, were the major contributors to the poor rate. There is no direct evidence of their views, but they may well have felt that, having paid their dues towards the relief of the poor as well as to the costs of policing the parish, they were entitled to protect their property. In a comparatively small community, where both police and residents knew each other, and where strangers would be instantly recognizable, the chances of being caught for a misdemeanour were high. In such circumstances, heavy sentences were likely to occur.

It is more difficult to explain the comparatively light sentences for violence. When a drunken Lawrence Hill assaulted the landlady of the White Hart, he was punished by a fine which was lower than that imposed on a poacher for taking a salmon from the river, while Thomas Mayne was only imprisoned for six months after a string of violent assaults, culminating in an attack on his mother-in-law which, according to the press report, left her face much blackened and bruised. It is possible that such assaults were felt to be personal, between individuals who knew each other, and did not represent a threat to the community as a whole, in the way that muggings of strangers by strangers do today. In addition, long prison sentences would be expensive for the ratepayers as the families of offenders would most probably be a charge on the parish for the whole period of their breadwinners' incarceration.

Drunkenness was a thread running through all types of male adult crime in Colyton, with the exception of poaching, which needed a clear head to be successful. Magistrates were frequently told that the offender was tipsy when committing a misdemeanour. Women, in contrast, were rarely in court for drunkenness, only two such cases from Colyton being reported over the whole period; only one woman was charged with theft, and none with a serious assault.[31]

The rights of the individual, however, were not wholly ignored, as is shown by the case of a Colytonian who was not the accused, but the accuser. In 1862, John Hoare, a 62-year-old sawyer and carpenter, brought an action against the police, claiming 5 guineas in compensation for assault and battery.

The case was heard in Axminster County Court before a jury. Hoare was represented by counsel, and as he was on the Feoffees' list of the poor of the parish, it must be assumed that in the days before Legal Aid he had received financial backing from some unknown source.[32]

According to Hoare's account, he had been up to the Compass Inn in Cuckoo Street to receive his wages, and he stayed on there for two hours, partly drinking two quarts of ale. He then moved on to the George Inn, where he helped to drink another two quarts, before returning to his house at about a quarter to midnight. He was standing outside talking to his son when P.C. Stone came by, and told him to go inside. Hoare protested that he wasn't drunk, but the constable said: 'Get into your house or I'll put you in the lock-up'. Hoare said: 'What for?' and PC Stone then took up a great walking stick, knocked him down and stunned him. As a result, he was off work, and therefore unpaid, for sixteen days.

A number of neighbours confirmed Hoare's description of the assault and declared that he was perfectly sober, giving as evidence the fact that his wife did not scold him for being drunk that night, and even bathed his head with vinegar after he had been knocked down.

After the police had put their side of the case, incidentally revealing that the part of the town where Hoare lived was known as Tiger's Bay because of the violent nature of its residents, prosecuting counsel addressed the jury in a way that seems familiar over 130 years later. He said that it was well known that the police 'would stretch a point to gain a case', and begged the jury to remember the importance of the principle involved, whether the labouring classes were to be ridden over roughshod and to be bullied by country policemen. If the police were to command the labouring classes to do this, that and the other, they would soon become their masters, rather than their servants.

The judge, in summing up, declared that there was no evidence whatsoever that the police had exceeded their duty, but the jury nevertheless decided that the police used more force than was necessary and therefore found for the plaintiff, to whom they awarded 1s damages, instead of the 5 guineas claimed, each side to pay its own costs. John Hoare therefore gained a moral but not a financial victory. His case shows that even before Legal Aid it was not impossible for a poor man who felt that he had been treated unjustly to bring an action before the court, and win.

Notes

1. *Social Trends*, 1996, pp. 160–62.

2. V.A.C. Gatrell and T.B. Hadden, 'Criminal statistics and their interpretation', in E.A. Wrigley, ed., *Nineteenth-century society: essays in the use of quantitative methods for the study of social data,* Cambridge, 1972, pp. 377.

3. Ibid., p. 352.

4. Ibid., pp. 377–9.

5. Devon Record Office (hereafter D.R.O.), 3483 A/PC 4. Minute book of Inspectors of Police, Colyton, 1851–1857.

6. For example, see the comments of Frank Field, Labour MP for Birkenhead, as reported in *The Times*, 23.7.1996, p. 16.

7. *Honiton and Ottery Gazette and East Devon Advertiser* (hereafter H.O.G.), 28.6.1884.

8. *Devon Weekly Times* (hereafter *D.W.T.*), 15.10.1869.

9. Ibid., 16.10.1863.

10. Ibid., 18.3.1864.

11. Ibid., 4.12.1874.

12. Ibid., 14.10.1864, 28.9.1866, 7.8.1868.

13. E.H. Hunt, 'Industrialization and regional inequality: wages in Britain, 1760–1914', *Journal of Economic History*, XLVI (4), 1986, appendix, p. 963.

14. *D.W.T.*, 5.3.1869.

15. Ibid., 6.5.1887.

16. Ibid., 25.10.1867, 10.1.1861.

17. Ibid., 10.2.1865, 10.1.1862, 13.1.1881.

18. *H.O.G.*, 24.11.1883.

19. *D.W.T.*, 31.10.1868, 28.9.1866.

20. Ibid., 24.7.1868, 5.9.1890, 24.3.1871.

21. Ibid., 12.8.1864, 8.12.1865.

22. Ibid., 17.4.1874, 12.3.1875.

23. Ibid., 7.7.1871, 5.5.1882.

24. Information received from the Exminster Asylum Project, University of Exeter.

25. *D.W.T.*, 18.2.1887.

26. Ibid., 3.10.1873.

27. BBC 1, Television News, 6 p.m., 22.7.1996.

28. *D.W.T*, 24.3.1881, 14.4.1881, 24.6.1881, 21.10.1881, 17.3.1882.

29. *H.O.G.*, 29.9.1884, 4.10.1884.

30. Not all offences reported in the press have been described here. The total number of Colytonians charged in the different categories were as follows:

    Poaching, 22; theft, 16; assaults, 15; drunk and disorderly, 15; public disorder, 1; traffic offences, 9; juveniles, 8; family desertion, 4; miscellaneous, 16.

31. *D.W.T.*, 3.10.1873, 13.6.1879, 5.9.1890.

32. Ibid., 2.5.1862.

Epilogue

The preface defined the purpose of this book as being 'to tell the story, as faithfully as possible, of one English rural parish in the second half of the nineteenth century through the lives of its people, and to show how the community dealt with perennial social problems in the context of its own time'. Strictly speaking, a single parish can be taken as typical only of itself, but in one respect, Colyton resembled many rural communities in mid- and late-Victorian times in that it exhibited a degree of self-sufficiency which has been lost to modern country-dwellers.

Consumers found it unnecessary to leave the parish in order to fulfil most of their needs. In the absence of district and county councils, the day-to-day administration of local affairs was carried out almost entirely by parishioners, on a voluntary basis, in the shape of the elected Vestry, which was common to all parishes, and in Colyton's case the self-selecting Feoffees and Twentymen. In this way, the administrators were aware of the circumstances of those whom their decisions affected, and the parishioners in general knew directly the individuals who were responsible for running the affairs of the parish. The levy of a church rate on all those with the appropriate property qualifications, whatever their religious denomination, led to the feeling that the parish church was central to the community as a whole, rather than simply to members of the Church of England.

Again, when the decline of lacemaking affected the employment of girls, and the agricultural depressions of the 1870s and 1880s caused the reduction of farming jobs available to boys, Colyton looked after its own by giving the young people of the parish work which, in more prosperous times, had gone to incomers. The Feoffees' expenditure on the poor was confined solely to those who held settlement in Colyton, while at the personal level, such relief as was afforded under the Poor Law was augmented by face-to-face family support given, whether willingly or unwillingly, to elderly parents or other relatives, and to illegitimate children and their mothers.

The implementation of decisions which had been made at higher levels still remained mainly in the hands of parishioners. For example, it was national legislation that changed education from being in large measure the privilege of those who could afford it, to becoming compulsory, and available free of charge to all children; but Colyton's school, although funded by the government and subject to outside inspection, was run on a day-to-day basis by a school board elected by parishioners. In the relief of poverty through the Poor Law, the chain of command ran from the Local Government Board in Whitehall to the Board of Guardians in Axminster, representing seventeen parishes of which Colyton was only one; but the parish had its own elected overseers and paid assistant overseer to ensure that the needs of the parishioners were not overlooked. Although in 1857 the Colyton watchmen were replaced by a police constable from the Exeter force, the officer concerned lived and worked within the parish and so knew and was known by its inhabitants.

Just as the parish was central to the everyday lives of the great majority of parishioners, so it appears to have acted as a focus for their emotions. The violence of the clash between Protestant and Anglo-Catholic was of remarkable intensity, spilling over as it did from purely doctrinal disagreement to matters such as the ringing of the church bells, and to the vitriolic school board elections; while the war between the Salvation Army and the Skeleton Army was not confined to the larger cities but was brought onto Colyton's streets, dividing parishioner from parishioner. It would appear that the way we lived then, in rural parishes at least, was marked by an intense parochialism which for better or worse has been replaced today by more distant and impersonal government from the centre.

Appendix

Early Deaths of Lacemakers and Non-lacemakers

In order to assess whether lace girls were more likely than their contemporaries to die from illnesses other than those relating to pregnancy or childbirth before they reached the age of thirty-one years, the following procedure was followed.

The 374 girls aged seven to twenty recorded in the 1851 census for Colyton parish, excluding the eighteen described as visitors or boarding-school pupils who had no Colyton connections, were divided by occupation and by socio-economic class as shown in table I.

Table I. Females aged 7–20 years by occupational type and socio-economic class, Colyton 1851.

Class	Lacemakers No.	Non-lacemakers No.	All No.
I	–	9	9
II	–	45	45
III	4	58	62
IV	52[(i)]	33	85
V	77[(ii)]	50	127
NK	4	42	46[(iii)]
All	137	237	374

(i)   Includes two girls aged seven years who were of no occupation in 1851, but were lacemakers in 1861.

(ii) Includes five girls, two aged seven years, two aged eight years and one aged eleven years who were of no occupation in 1851, but were lacemakers in 1861.

(iii) These were all girls who had entered Colyton without any known family connections in the parish. All but one were at work.

Class I: Daughters of landed proprietors and members of the professions
Class II: Daughters of farmers and dairymen
Class III: Daughters of business owners, the better-off self-employed, and school teachers
Class IV: Daughters of wage-earning craftsmen and tradesmen
Class V: Daughters of agricultural and other labourers

Three major difficulties then had to be met. First, fifty of these 374 girls came from Colyford tything, where the occupations of girls under the age of 21 years were greatly under-recorded by the census enumerator, only thirteen, or 27 per cent, having any occupation attributed to them, including that of 'scholar'. For this reason the fifty girls concerned were eliminated from the sample, leaving a total of 324 girls distributed between the socio-economic classes as shown in table II, column A.

Second, girls who married and then died before the age of thirty-one years were eliminated from the revised sample, as their deaths may have been related to pregnancy or childbirth, rather than caused by an illness induced by their occupation (see table II, column B).

Third, 201 girls, or 62 per cent of the revised sample, migrated before they were known to have reached the age of thirty-one years, and any of these could have died young elsewhere. They too were eliminated (see table II, column C), leaving in the sample only those girls known to have survived to thirty-one years and beyond, and those unmarried girls known to have died before the age of thirty-one years (see table II, column D).

Table II. Revised sample of female lacemakers and non-lacemakers aged 7–20 years, Colyton, 1851, by socio-economic class.

Class	Lacemakers				Non-lacemakers				All			
	A	B	C	D	A	B	C	D	A	B	C	D
I	0	0	0	0	9	0	- 7	2	9	0	- 7	2
II	0	0	0	0	37	0	- 22	15	37	0	- 22	15
III	4	0	- 4	0	52	- 1	- 28	23	56	- 1	- 32	23
IV	51	- 2	- 25	24	27	0	- 18	9	78	- 2	- 43	33
V	77	- 1	- 44	32	25	- 1	- 13	11	102	- 2	- 57	43
NK	4	- 0	- 3	1	38	0	- 37	1	42	0	- 40	2
All	136	- 3	- 76	57	188	- 2	-125	61	324	- 5	- 201	118

A. Revised sample, after the elimination of fifty girls living in Colyford tything.
B. Girls dying after marriage before thirty-one years of age.
C. Girls migrating before they are known to have reached age thirty-one years.
D. Final sample.

Using this final sample, the proportion of those dying under thirty-one years of age was calculated by occupational type and socio-economic class, as in table III below. It has been assumed that the propensity to migrate by age and marry by age is the same for lacemakers and non-lacemakers.

Table III. Proportions of female lacemakers and non-lacemakers aged 7–20 years, in Colyton, 1851, dying before 31 years of age by socio-economic class.

Class	All		Surviving to post-30 years		Dying before 31 years	
	No.	%	No.	%	No.	%
Panel A. Lacemakers						
I	–	–	–	–	–	–
II	–	–	–	–	–	–
III	–	–	–	–	–	–
IV	24	100.0	21	87.5	3	12.5
V	32	100.0	28	87.5	4	12.5
NK	1	100.0	1	100.0	–	–
All	57	100.0	50	87.5	7	12.5
Panel B. Non-lacemakers						
I	2	100.0	1	50.0	1	50.0
II	15	100.0	13	87.0	2	13.0
III	23	100.0	21	91.0	2	9.0
IV	9	100.0	4	44.0	5	56.0
V	11	100.0	7	64.0	4	36.0
NK	1	100.0	1	100.0	–	–
All	61	100.0	47	77.0	14	23.0
Panel C. All						
I	2	100.0	1	50.0	1	50.0
II	15	100.0	13	87.0	2	13.0
III	23	100.0	21	91.0	2	9.0
IV	33	100.0	25	76.0	8	24.0
V	43	100.0	35	81.0	8	19.0
NK	2	100.0	2	100.0	–	–
All	118	100.0	97	82.0	21	18.0

Bibliography

Documentary sources

Parish Registers

Colyton parish registers held in the Devon Record Office (hereafter D.R.O.) 3483 A/PR3, baptisms 1838–1863; 3483 A/PR15, baptisms 1864–1887; 3483 A/PR8, marriages 1837–1872; 3483 A/PR16, marriages, 1872–1919; 3483 A/PR9, burials, 1836–1852; 3483 A/PR18, burials, 1853–1901.

Colyton parish register held by the Team Rector of Colyton. Baptisms, 1888–.

Colyton registers held in the Public Record Office (hereafter P.R.O.). R.G. 4/3559. Independent chapel, baptisms, 1815–1857; R.G. 8/6. George's chapel, baptisms, 1824–1862; burials, 1832–1862.

Colyton Parish Council: register of public graves, 1859–1878; burial book, 1865–1902.

D.R.O. R 7/8/c. Axminster marriage notice book, 1838–1916.

Listings

Census returns for Colyton parish. P.R.O. 1841, H.O. 107/214; 1851, H.O. 107/1862; 1861, R.G. 9/1373; 1871, R.G. 10/2035 and R.G. 10/2036; 1881, R.G. 11/2129; 1891, R.G. 12/1669.

Census returns for Axminster Union House (workhouse). P.R.O. 1851, H.O. 107/1862; 1861, R.G. 9/1371; 1871, R.G. 10/2033; 1881, R.G. 11/2127; 1891, R.G. 12/1667.

Ecclesiastical Census of 1851 for Devon. P.R.O. 129/279 H.O.

Feoffees' Records

D.R.O. F 17/2, receipts and payments; F 17/3, treasurer's book; F 17/7–9, minutes and order book of Feoffees' meetings; F 17/12–13, garden allotments; F 17/14, grammar school.

Miscellaneous

Colyton Board School Log Book for Boys, 1878, held in Colyton Primary School.

Colyton Board School Log Book for Girls, 1880, held in Colyton Primary School.

D.R.O. 3483 A/PC4. Minute book of the Inspectors of Police, Colyton, 1851–1857.

D.R.O. P.O. 14. Receipt and payment book, Poor Law Commission, Colyton parish, 26.3.1851–20.7.1859.

D.R.O. Voters' list A, south division, 1832–1868; east division, 1869–1885; voters' list B, east division, 1869–1885.

P.R.O. FS 15/1177. Colyton Mutual and Providential Society, 1849–1887.

P.R.O. IR 29/9. Colyton land apportionment, 1844.

Axminster Union Minute Books

D.R.O. volumes 7–15.

Printed Sources

Colyton County Primary School, *Walk around Colyton*, Regional Resources Centre, 1976.

Devon Weekly Times, 1861–1890.

Honiton and Ottery Gazette and East Devon Advertiser, 1883–1884.

Honiton and Ottery St Mary Weekly News, 1878.

Honiton and Ottery Weekly News and General Advertiser, 1879.

The Times, 23.7.1996; 20.11.1996.

Official Publications

Parliamentary Papers, 1851, Census of Great Britain, *Population*, vol. 11, HMSO, 1854, reprinted Shannon 1970.

Parliamentary Papers L, HMSO, 1861.

Report of the Commissioners on Children's Employment, 1863, HC vol. XVIII.

Unpublished References

Gunn-Johnson, D.A., 'A Country Catholic: a study of the emergence of the Oxford Movement in an East Devon Parish'. Unpublished thesis accepted for the Archbishop of Canterbury's MA degree, December 1994.

Hoare, N., 'The community of Colyton and its poor, 1800–1850'. Unpublished MA dissertation, 1972–1973, Department of English Local History, University of Leicester.

Seaward, S., 'Old Colyton. What it was like ninety years ago. A stroll through the streets with a Native'. Reminiscences of Mr Samuel Seaward, dictated to his son, Mr Basil Seaward, and kindly made available by the Reverend David Gunn-Johnson, Team Rector of Colyton.

Sharpe, P., 'Gender-specific demographic adjustment to changing economic circumstances: Colyton 1538–1837', unpublished PhD thesis, University of Cambridge, 1988.

Thomson, D., 'Provision for the elderly in England', unpublished PhD thesis, University of Cambridge, 1980.

Unpublished material on Compton Chamberlayne held in the Cambridge Group for the History of Population and Social Structure.

Published References

Journals

Digby, A., 'Recent developments in the study of the English Poor Law', *The Local Historian*, 12 (5), 1977, pp. 200–210.

Hair, P.E.H., 'Bridal pregnancy in rural England in earlier centuries', *Population Studies*, 20, 1966, pp. 233–43.

Haskey, J., 'Step families and stepchildren in Great Britain', *Population Trends*, 76, 1994, pp. 17–28.

Hunt, E.H., 'Industrialization and regional inequality. Wages in Britain 1750–1914', *Journal of Economic History*, XLVI (4), 1986, pp. 935–66.

Monthly Digest of Statistics, 1981–1995.

Population Trends, 1995.

Robin, J., 'Family care of the elderly in a nineteenth-century Devonshire parish', *Ageing and Society*, 4 (4), 1984, pp. 505–16.

Robin, J., 'Illegitimacy in Colyton, 1851–1881', *Continuity and Change*, 2 (2), 1987, pp. 307–42.

Robin, J., 'Prenuptial pregnancy in a rural area of Devonshire in the mid-nineteenth century: Colyton, 1851–1881', *Continuity and Change*, 1 (1), 1986, pp. 113–24.

Robin, J., 'The relief of poverty in mid-nineteenth century Colyton', *Rural History*, 1 (2), 1990, pp. 195–217.

Rose, M.E., 'The allowance system under the New Poor Law', *Economic History Review*, XIX, 1966, pp. 607–20.

Smith, D.S. and Hacker, J.D., 'Cultural demography: New England deaths and the Puritan perception of risk', *Journal of Interdisciplinary History*, XXVI (3), 1995–1996, pp. 367–92.

Snell, K.D.M. and Millar, J., 'Lone-parent families and the welfare state', *Continuity and Change*, 2 (3), 1987, pp. 387–422.

Social Trends, 26, 1996; *Social Trends*, 27, 1997.

Articles and Books

Bateman, J., *The Great Landowners of Great Britain and Ireland*, New York, 1971.

Beeton, I., *Beeton's Book of Household Management*, London, 1861.

Bouquet, M., *Family, Servants and Visitors: the farm household in nineteenth and twentieth century Devon*, Norwich, 1985.

Bovett, R., *Historical notes on Devon schools*, Exeter, 1989.

Case, R.A.M., et al., *The Chester Beatty Research Institute Serial Abridged Life Tables, 1841–1960*, part I, London, 1962.

Cliff, P., *The Rise and Development of the Sunday School Movement in England, 1780–1980*. Redhill, 1986.

Cronjé, G., 'Tuberculosis and mortality decline in England and Wales, 1851–1910', in R. Woods and J. Woodward, eds, *Urban disease and mortality in nineteenth century England*, London, 1984, pp. 79–101.

Digby, A., *Pauper Palaces*, London, 1978.

Dumsday, W.H., *Haddon's Relieving Officer's Handbook*, London, 1902.

Evans, G.E., *Colytonia: a chapter in the history of Devon*, Liverpool, 1898.

Feinstein, C.H., 'A new look at the cost of living, 1870–1914', in J. Foreman-Peck, ed., *Reinterpreting the Victorian economy*, Cambridge, 1990.

Gatrell, V.A.C. and Haddon, T.B., 'Criminal statistics and their interpretation' in E.A. Wrigley, ed., *Nineteenth-century society: essays in the use of quantitative methods for the study of social data*, Cambridge, 1972, pp. 336–96.

Gibbons, Stella, *Cold Comfort Farm*, St Albans, 1973.

Hastings, J., ed., *Encyclopaedia of Religion and Ethics*, vol. IX, Edinburgh, 1917.

Heath, S. and Minet, P., *Living in and out of the parental home in Spain and Great Britain: a comparative approach*, Cambridge Group for the History of Population and Social Structure, Working Paper Series: no. 2, 1996.

Higgs, E., *Making Sense of the Census*, PRO Handbook no. 23, London, 1989.

Hoskins, W.G., 'The farm-labourer through four centuries' in W.G. Hoskins and H.P.R. Finberg, eds, *Devonshire Studies*, London, 1952, pp. 419–41.

Kussmaul, A., *Servants in husbandry in early modern England*, Cambridge, 1981.

Laslett, P., 'Clayworth and Cogenhoe', in H.E. Bell and R.L. Ollard, eds, *Historical Essays 1680–1750*, London, 1963, pp. 157–84.

Laslett, P., *A fresh map of life*, London, 1989.

Laslett, P., ed., *Household and Family in Past Time*, Cambridge, 1972.

Laslett, P., Oosterveen, K. and Smith, R.M., eds, *Bastardy and its comparative history*, London, 1980.

Mingay, G., *The Agricultural Revolution: changes in agriculture, 1650–1880*, London, 1977.

Mitchell, B.R., *British Historical Statistics*, Cambridge, 1988.

O'Leary, J.G., ed., *The Autobiography of Joseph Arch*, London, 1966.

Page, W., ed., *The Victoria County History of Devonshire*, vol. I, London, 1906.

Palliser, F.B., *History of Lace*, eds M. Jourdain and A. Dryden, 1902, reprinted East Ardsley, 1976.

Polwhele, R., *The History of Devonshire*, vol. I, 1793, reprinted Dorking, 1977.

Pulman, G.P.R., *The Book of the Axe*, 1875, reprinted Bath, 1969.

Reay, B., *Microhistories: demography, society and culture in rural England, 1800–1930*, Cambridge, 1996.

Richardson, J., *The Local Historian's Encyclopedia*, New Barnet, 1974.

Robin, J., *Elmdon. Continuity and change in a north-west Essex village, 1861–1964*, Cambridge, 1980.

Robin, J., *From childhood to middle age: cohort analysis in Colyton, 1851–1891*, Cambridge, Group for the History of Population and Social Structure, Working Paper Series: no. 1, 1995.

Rose, M.E., *The English Poor Law 1780–1930*, Newton Abbot, 1971.

Schofield, R.S., 'Age specific mobility in an eighteenth-century rural English parish' in P. Clark and D. Souden, eds, *Migration and Society in Early Modern England*, London, 1987, pp. 256–9.

Schofield, R.S., 'An anatomy of an epidemic: Colyton, November 1645 to November 1646', in *The Plague Reconsidered*, Local Population Studies Supplement, 1977, pp. 95–126.

Thomson, D., 'Welfare and the historian' in L. Bonfield, R.M. Smith, and K. Wrightson, eds, *The world we have gained*, Oxford, 1986, pp. 355–87.

Thornton, A. and Lin, Hui-Sheng, *Social Change and the Family in Taiwan*, Chicago, 1994.

Vancouver, C., *General view of the agriculture of the county of Devon*, 1808, reprinted Newton Abbot, 1969.

Webb, S., and Webb, B., *English Local Government: English Poor Law History*, part II: *The last hundred years*, vol. I, London, 1929.

White, R.G., *The History of the Feoffees of Colyton, 1546–1946*, Bridport, 1951.

Index